The Sephardim in the Holocaust

Jews and Judaism: History and Culture

The Sephardim in the Holocaust

A Forgotten People

ISAAC JACK LÉVY
WITH ROSEMARY LÉVY ZUMWALT

The University of Alabama Press   Tuscaloosa

The University of Alabama Press
Tuscaloosa, Alabama 35487-0380
uapress.ua.edu

Typeface: Minion

Cover image: *The Deportation* by Alberto Sarfati; courtesy of the Sarfati Children
Cover design: David Nees

Cataloging-in-Publication data is available from the Library of Congress.
ISBN: 978-0-8173-2071-3 (cloth)
ISBN: 978-0-8173-5984-3 (paper)
E-ISBN: 978-0-8173-9324-3

To my Sephardic brothers and sisters,
To the innocent tender children,
To those who were martyred in the camps,
And to those who survived to tell the story,
To you I dedicate this book.

Contents

Figures

Acknowledgments

There are no words to express my gratitude to the survivors of the Shoah for sharing their life histories with me. Their oral and written testimonies safeguard for us a shocking piece of twentieth-century history. I have interviewed so many people that I find myself unable to thank each individually, though I am enduringly grateful to all for their generosity in sharing their stories. Unless otherwise stated, I was allowed to use the name of the interviewee. I am deeply grateful to the following individuals whom I interviewed about their experiences during the Holocaust. For each, I give the following information: name, place of interview, date, and place of origin.

Alalouf, Ana. Bat Yam, Israel, May 20, 1996. Janina, Skopje.

Alcalay, Albert. Boston, October 27, 1988. Paris (some claim that his birth city was Belgrade).

Angel, Sam. Atlanta, Georgia, March 15, 1982. Salonika.

Asef, Jack. Rishon LeZion, Israel, April 25, 1990. Kyustendil, Bulgaria.

Avzaradel, Izahar. Ashdod, Israel, in 1989. Rhodes, Italy/now Greece.

Baruh (Baruch), Aliza Sarfati. Tel Aviv/Hod Hasharon, June 16, 1982. Salonika.

Baruh, Sony, and Elvira (wife). Belgrade, February 17, 1990. Belgrade.

Bella, Carmen. Rhodes, May 6, 2016. Rhodes, Greece.

Ben Rubi, Itzhak (Isaac). Tel Aviv, Israel, several interviews in 1968. Salonika.

Benmayor, Leon. Salonika, June 24, 1982, and August 5, 1984. Salonika.

Benn, Yosef (Joseph). Tel Aviv, June 4, 1982. Macedonia and Bulgaria.

Ben-nun, Sami Menahen. Jaffa, Israel, May 13, 1990. Plovdiv (Filibe under the Turkish rule), Bulgaria.

Bivas, Salomon and Rene. Tel Aviv, Israel, June 7, 1982. Salonika.

Braka, Buko (Bohor) Nissim. Rishon LeZion, Israel. April 25, 1990. Kyustendil, Bulgaria.

Bueno de Mesquita, Max (Meier). Amsterdam, 1982, 1984, and 1985. Amsterdam.

Cohen, Elie. Tel Aviv, June 14, 1982. Salonika.

Cohen, Leon Reuven. Givatayim, Israel, June 1982, 1984, and 1985. Salonika.

Cohen (now Franco), Victoria. Belgian Congo, and Brussels, July 24, 1984. Rhodes.

Daduch, Yosef. Holon, Israel, June 6, 1982. Benghazi.

Danon, Clara, Boina (Bueno Cohen), Ester. Belgrade, February 5, 1990. Belgrade.

Elkoubi, Alfred. Paris, July 15, 1984. Tlemcen, Algeria.

Fintz, Violette. Several letters, interview in Brussels on July 23, 1984, by telephone calls to South Africa in 1985, and 1987 by correspondence. Rhodes.

Gabbai, Dario. Telephone call, California, USA, April 6, 2015. Salonika.

Gofen, Ella. Her mother and several Macedonian women were present. Bat Yam, Israel, April 1990. Macedonia.

Hanuka (Chanuka), Shabetai. Tel Aviv, June 28, 1990. Salonika.

Hatsvi, Yehuda. Tel Aviv, Israel, e-mail September 11, 2005, and September 18, 2011. Salonika.

Kabiljo, Isaac. Sarajevo, February 11, 1990. Sarajevo.

Levi, Isaac Moshe. Sarajevo (president of Bosnia and Herzegovina Jewish Community). February 11, 1990. Born eighty miles from Sarajevo.

Levi, Stella. New York, New York. Several e-mails and telephone conversations. Rhodes.

Maestro, Jacko. Bat Yam, Israel. Telephone calls February 25, 2013, and January 20, 2016. Salonika.

Maestro, Leon. Sarajevo, February 11, 1990. Sarajevo.

Mallenbaum, Allan E. Telephone call, March 12, 2015. Plainview, New York.

Matkovski, Alexander. Skopje, Macedonia, February 3, 1990. Skopje.

Menasche, Raoul. Petah Tikva, Israel, June 3, 1982, and Tel Aviv, June 7, 1982. Salonika.

Missistrani, Isaac. Bat Yam, Israel, summer of 1985 and 1991. Turkey.

Mizrahi, Amelie, and several Rhodian women. Ashdod, Israel, at Izahar Avzaradel's home, July 9, 1990. Rhodes.

Modiano, Samuel (Sami). Telephone call to Rome and Rhodes on May 6, 2016. Rhodes.

Morgues-Algrante, Esther. Correspondence and personal interview, June 30, 1982. Izmir, Turkey.
Mosche, Morris. Tel Aviv, Israel, June 14, 1982. Salonika.
Nahmias, Joseph. Salonika, August 5, 1984. Salonika. (He was hiding during the war.)
Nehama, Joseph. Salonika, summer of 1968. Salonika.
Novitch, Miriam. Lohamei HaGetaot, Israel, June 15, 1982. Nahariya, Israel.
Pessah, Moïse. Kavala, Greece, summer 1990. Kavala.
Profeta, Samuel (Sam). Salonika, June 21, 1982. Salonika.
Refael, Esther. Tel Aviv, June 11, 1982. Corfu.
Refael, Haim (Chaim) Yaakov. Tel Aviv, June 7, 1982, and April 18, 1990. Salonika.
Rekah, Viktor. Tel Aviv, June 10, 1983. Tripoli.
Reuven, Shelomo Mordehay. Tel Aviv, Israel. June 4, 1982. Salonika.
Salan, Yaakov. Tel Aviv, June 10, 1982. Bulgaria.
Sarfati, Alberto. Tel Aviv, June 24, 1990. Salonika.
Sephiha, Haim Vidal. Paris, July 18, 1984, and October 19–20, 1994, in Salonika. Also by correspondence. Belgium.
Sevi, Isaac. Oakland, California, October 12, 1912. Salonika.
Shibi, Baruch. Salonika, summer of 1968. Salonika. (Baruch was a high-ranking Jewish member of the Greek resistance.)
Sotto, David. Atlanta, Georgia, February 2017. Atlanta, Georgia.
Sotto (Soto), Eliezer (Eli) and Lucy. Atlanta, Georgia, March 15, 1982. Salonika.
Stern, Ben. Columbia, South Carolina, March 2, 1982. Lodz, Poland.
Stroumza, Jacques. Jerusalem, July 29, 1985. Salonika.
Taraboulos, Jack (Jacques). Jerusalem, May 31, 1982. Cairo, Egypt.
Tarabulus, Jennie. Jerusalem, May 19, 1982. Seattle, Washington.

I have carried out research in several museums, especially at Yad Vashem, the World Holocaust Center in Jerusalem, and the United States Holocaust Memorial Museum in Washington, DC. I am indebted to their archivists for providing me with testimonials of Sephardic survivors from their holdings. I thank the following individuals associated with institutions:

Angel, Marc D. Rabbi Dr. (Emeritus of the historic Spanish and Portuguese Synagogue of New York, Founder and Director of the Institute for Jewish Ideas and Ideals, prolific author and editor). New York, New York.
Badowska-Buczak (Head of the Archives Wojciech Plosa Jadwiga)

and Piotr Setkiewicz (Director of the Centre for Research at the Auschwitz-Birkenau State Museum), Auschwitz, Poland.

Battinou, Zanet I. (Director of the Jewish Museum of Greece). Athens, Greece.

Bortnick, Rachel (Founder of Ladinokomunita). Dallas, Texas.

DioGuardi, Joseph J. (Former Representative, US House of Representatives). (He and Shirley Cloyes cofounded the Albanian American Civic League). New York.

DioGuardi, Shirley Cloyes (Foreign policy analyst. Since the 1990s she served as the Balkan Affairs Advisor to the Albanian American Civic League). New York.

Greif, Gideon (Israeli historian and specialist in the history of the Holocaust). Israel.

Hamburg, Paul Howard (Librarian at the University of California, Berkeley). Berkeley, CA.

Kassorla, Haim (Rabbi of Congregation Or VeShalom. Atlanta, GA; consultant for Hebrew translations and biblical commentaries).

Katz, Jeremy (William Breman Jewish Heritage Museum). Atlanta. GA.

Lampropoulos, Elias (Pastoral Assistant, Greek Orthodox Cathedral of the Annunciation). Atlanta, GA.

Members of the Library and Archives Departments, especially Leah Wolfson. United States Holocaust Museum. Washington, DC.

Meth, Jack (Son of Rose Meth [Born Ruzia Grunapfel], participant in the Auschwitz-Birkenau smuggling of gunpowder for the Sonderkommando uprising of October 7, 1944). New York.

New, Yossi (Rabbi of Chabad Lubavitch of Georgia). Atlanta, GA.

Novitch, Miriam (Kibbutz Beth Lohamei-Ha'ghetaot, Ghetto Fighters' Museum). D.N. Oshrat, Israel.

Panic, Barbara (Curator of the Jewish Historical Museum of Belgrade). Belgrade, Serbia.

Refael, Shmuel (Director of the Salti Institute for Ladino Studies, Bar-Ilan University). Ramat Gan, Israel.

Zemour, Erika Perahia (Director of the Jewish Museum of Thessaloniki). Salonika, Greece.

I acknowledge the help of the following institutions:

Agnes Scott College McCain Library. Decatur, GA.

Club de los reskatados de los campos de konsentrasion (Association of Survivors of Concentration Camps) on Lewinsky Street. Tel Aviv, Israel.

Davidson College, Davidson, NC.
Emory University, Decatur, GA.
Indiana University, Bloomington, IN.
Stroum Jewish Community Center, Seattle, WA.
University of California, Berkeley, CA.
University of Georgia, Athens, GA.
University of North Georgia, Dahlonega, GA.
Yeshiva University, New York, NY.

In particular I would like to recognize my dearest friend and wife, Rosemary Lévy Zumwalt; without her patience, constant advice, and painstaking editing, this publication would not have been possible. In my deepest desperation, in my anger for God's abandonment of His people and my rage over the nations' animosity toward the Jewish nation, Rosemary was there with encouragement for me to continue.

I would like to acknowledge the generous assistance of those at the University of Alabama Press: Editor-in-Chief Daniel Waterman, Editorial Assistant Carol Connell, and Marketing Coordinator Blanche B. Sarratt. I am particularly indebted to the encouragement offered by Mark K. Bauman, one of the series editors of University of Alabama Jews and Judaism: History and Culture. I am grateful to Lisa Williams for her copyediting, and to Lys Ann Weiss for compiling the index.

Sephardim in the Holocaust

Introduction

For forty years I have been researching and writing on the Holocaust, mainly with respect to the Sephardim. I trace this consuming commitment to my experiences of having left my natal island of Rhodes at the age of ten with my mother, maternal grandmother, paternal grandfather, uncle, aunt, and cousins, expelled as we were by the Italian Fascists in 1938. Many of the Jewish inhabitants of Rhodes were not able to leave. They remained on our beautiful island only to be rounded up and sent to the death camps in 1944.

I was fortunate in so many ways. In 1939 I sailed with my mother and grandmother in the comfort of first class, thanks to the generosity of my mother's uncle David Musafir, who had been born in Milas, Turkey, and was a successful businessman in Montgomery, Alabama. Our trip took us from Rhodes to Genova, and then on to the international city of Tangier, Morocco.[1] I recall the hunger that was part of my daily existence as a small boy of ten. Now, from the perspective of an adult, I know that my hunger was not in any way comparable to that of the victims of the Holocaust. I am aware that, as a reader of my manuscript noted, "while there were some shortages, the Spanish Occupation Government made efforts to provide necessary goods even at the expense of mainland Spain. Foodstuffs were brought from the French Zone or smuggled into Tangier." Nonetheless, I personally experienced the constant struggle to find food, a nearly impossible task for refugees, like my family, who depended solely on the kindness of relatives and of the American Jewish Joint Distribution Committee. I recall standing in long lines with my grandmother to wait for a liter of oil, a dozen eggs, or a kilogram of flour. Often we walked a distance, since the stores near our apartment had run out of food. Just as often we waited in vain, returned home emptyhanded, and joined the line another day. I would accompany my grandmother at four o'clock in the morning. Taking our place in the line, we would wait for the store to open, and then often, after our waiting several hours, the owner would close the door just as we moved to the front of the line. And I remember that my grandmother would cry in disappointment and despair. Along with other children, I often went to school hungry and tried to ignore my hunger pains to pursue the rigorous daily schedule.

How sad it was for some parents to spend the Holydays without a bite to offer the children. How proud my mother was to be able to buy food for Rosh Hashanah when I brought home my prize money from school just two hours before the stores closed. I remember her running to the store to buy half a kilo of beef, a few potatoes, and some vegetables. I had won 200 francs as the first prize from the Remington School for typing, shorthand, and bookkeeping. My school, the Alliance Israélite Universelle, had selected ten students for the course, and luckily I had been one of them.

I remember the generosity of our neighbors who gave my mother two loaves of white bread when we departed on our trip to the United States, undertaken from December 1944 to February 1945, still during World War II. Two weeks later, during the voyage, hungry, I asked my mother for some of the dry stale bread that I dunked in a cup of coffee and then devoured. Later, in my research on the experiences of the Sephardim in the Holocaust, I read of the transport from Salonika to the death camp of the north. And I felt an immediate connection with Errikos Sevillias, who wrote that the food supplies had begun to run out and all that they had left was "rock-hard bread and some *threpsini* [raisin syrup], and limp carrots."[2] My experiences during my refuge in Tangier and my travel to the United States could not match the mental and physical agony of my brothers and sisters during their horrible passage in the trains and their horrific life-and-death struggle in the Hitler death camps. Nonetheless, my experiences have impelled me forward in a quest to document the neglected story of the Sephardim in the Holocaust.

Why have the Sephardim been left out of the Holocaust literature? Many Sephardic scholars have posed this question and have provided answers. Yitzchak Kerem, a researcher on Greek Jewry and the editor of *Sefarad, the Sephardic Newsletter*, states, "Most survivors today of Greek Sephardic descent believe that the Ashkenazim, the Jews of Eastern and Central Europe, have marginalized their suffering. They believe that their experiences have been treated as an afterthought by academics and organizations, most notably Yad Vashem, the Holocaust Museum in Jerusalem, Israel, and the New York-based Claims Conference."[3]

In a similar vein, Aron Rodrigue, the Daniel E. Koshland Professor of Jewish culture and history at Stanford University, notes, "Most of the Jewish victims in southeastern Europe were Sephardi," and their accounts have been left out of all but "the most specialized studies." Rodrigue continues, "It has been too widely assumed that few Sephardim were affected by the Holocaust. . . . The study of Jewish victims has mirrored the emphases of established narratives of modern Jewish history, focusing on Western and Eastern European Ashkenazi Jewries."[4] If those Sephardim from southeastern Europe have scarcely been recognized, then those in North Africa and Libya who suffered from the brutality of Vichy France and the Nazis have been almost completely ignored. When I met and talked with Elie Wiesel in Columbia, South Carolina, on three separate occasions, he encouraged me to write about the experiences of the Sephardim in the Holocaust and to document this neglected piece of history.

I perused a considerable number of accounts made available to me by the family members of survivors and those testimonials published in books, articles, and personal letters written in English, French, Greek, Italian, Hebrew, Judeo-Spanish, and Serbian. In this work I have used the original language when I have judged it important. All translations from Judeo-Spanish, French, and Italian are my own. Friends and colleagues have assisted me with translations from Serbian, Greek, and Hebrew. I have also been able to retrieve material that family members, uncaring and unaware of the value, had thrown in the trash.

I interviewed over 170 survivors during my research trips to Belgium, Canada, France, Greece, Israel, Mexico, the Netherlands, the former Yugoslavia, and throughout the United States. Some of these individuals had lived in the Belgian Congo and in South Africa; and some were from North Africa and Libya. I recorded more than 170 cassette tapes from interviews I conducted about the survivors' experiences, from pre-transport to liberation and subsequent years. Frequently I recorded interviewees two or three times in order to gain additional information or to clarify earlier statements. I have read personal accounts meticulously for their historical and social importance.

To augment information on the emotional aspect of the testimonies, I paid close attention to the expression on the face of a survivor, to the tone of voice, and to the lapses into silence in the narration of the excruciating memories. Thus, the evidence collected was based not only on the spoken word but also on what was left unsaid but carefully observed. In "Testimony and History," which is part of the Database of Greek-Jewish Holocaust Survivors' Testimonies, there is discussion of the importance of that which is left unsaid, "the non-verbal aspects of testimony (silence, embodied memory and mute moments in the interview which are filled with emotions expressed through bodily attitudes)." The author of "Testimony and History" continues, "The 'mute witness,' silence as a choice or necessity and not forgetfulness, also claims a part of the 'truth' and the 'complete' testimony of the Shoah. The historical archive of the testimonies contains all the narratives of the survivors and everything that could not be said."[5]

Holocaust literature helps to chronicle the memory of the victims, but as my research shows, it cannot really capture the emotional impact that has haunted those who lived through the unimaginable. Haim Refael, a survivor originally from Salonika, Greece, came to my hotel in Tel Aviv in June 1982, to talk with me. He recounted, "I cannot speak much because this story makes me sick, do you understand? My son was gone today to the army. My memories come back and devastate me. The thought of those who perished in the camp and my still being alive hurts." Another survivor from Salonika, Greece, and living in Israel since the 1970s told me of his dissatisfaction concerning the publication of his own testimony by "a third party." He expanded, "There is more to my book; pages cannot convey what is difficult to be put into words." In Judeo-Spanish, he said, "No ay palavras ke puedan ekspresar lo ke tuvo lugar en los maldichos kampos" (There are no words to express what took place in the cursed camps). And he continued, "There is no way to communicate our suffering at the hands of dehumanized animals. The writers cannot decipher our thoughts, our dreams, and our everlasting memories of those terrible days in the camps, memories that cannot be effaced from our mind. Moreover, some of the interviewers 'no intienden lo ke les diziamos por manko de no konoser muestra lengua' (do not understand what we were telling them for lack of knowledge of our language); they often misquoted us." From the remarks of this survivor, one can surmise that the accuracy, if at all possible, depends on who is telling the story: the survivor, the interviewer, or a third party. This individual queried, "Who better than the victims?" And after some reflection, he said, "We, too, at times have not been totally precise. After so many years we forget some incidents and unintentionally we communicate what other survivors have reported. As in my case, the investigator added ideas that were not part of my own experience."

Some of those I interviewed dealt with their traumatized memories through silence. Their desire was to obliterate from their minds an important yet horrifying, personal experience. Their muteness was the result of suffering for many years after the catastrophe and the lack of a rational way of expressing the horrors they witnessed. In the summer of 1985, I sat in an outdoor café in Paris with Alfred Elkoubi, a survivor and a native of North Africa who had moved to France. Elkoubi at first expressed his fervent desire to be the messenger of those "cherished ones who perished brutally." Eager to immortalize "the memory of the victims of the death camps," Elkoubi invited me to join him at his residence on Sunday morning to continue the conversation. Soon after my first question, Elkoubi lapsed into silence: the terrible and painful drama was too dreadful to recall. Yet even though he could not speak, Elkoubi did not betray the annihilated. His silence told the story of the degradation of his Jewish brothers and sisters and the shame of all humanity for being bystanders to this massacre. Those who perished and those who survived spoke through Elkoubi's eyes.[6]

S. Lillian Kremer in her study on language of the Holocaust writes, "[T]he prevailing view of many writers and critics was that language was unable to convey the Nazi world and that it is, perhaps, immoral to attempt to write about the *Shoah* imaginatively. Some believe that only the eyewitness accounts of the event are valid. . . . In the years immediately following the *Shoah*, with but a few exceptions, professional writers remained largely silent about 'l'univers concentrationnaire.'" Kremer quotes Elie Wiesel, who asserts that literature of the Holocaust is impossible and who claims that Auschwitz negated any form of literature. "A novel about Auschwitz," Wiesel writes, "is not a novel, or else it is not about Auschwitz. The very attempt to write such a novel is a blasphemy."[7] Kremer identifies Primo Levi as "the supreme chronicler in the view of many of the most respected critics." In *Survival in Auschwitz* Primo Levi remarks on "his recognition shortly after his arrival [in the death camp] that 'our language lacks words to express this offense, the demolition of man.' He elaborated the concept of the insufficiency of language in the context of his masterpiece, demonstrating how ordinary linguistic constructs and connotations fail to convey Auschwitz experience."[8]

Chapter 1, "Journey to the Death Camps," follows the Sephardim from Rhodes, Cos, Corfu, Athens, Salonika, Macedonia, the former Yugoslavia, and France to the relentless cruelties of Auschwitz. Here I draw on interviews I have conducted, on my own family history, and on published testimonies. As the Sephardim stepped from the boxcars, they were told that they would become, as in the title of the poem by Avner Peretz, "siniza i fumo," ash and smoke.

In Chapter 2, "Living and Dying in Hell," I focus on the interminable cruelty in the camps. From the initial selections—lines to the left to the crematoria, to the right to forced labor details; to inside the crematoria to the grisly work of the Sonderkommandos; and to the sadism of the SS—I provide details on the challenges of the Sephardim with differences in languages, physical appearance, even pronunciation of Hebrew, all of which set them apart from the Ashkenazim.

In Chapter 3, "The Revolt of October 7, 1944," I document the courageous involvement of the Greek Jews by drawing from interviews I conducted with survivors and from testimonies of others. In order to discuss the unfolding of the revolt, I explain the layout of Auschwitz-Birkenau and the details of the work units to which the inmates were assigned. My intent is to pull together threads of memories as expressed mainly by surviving Sephardim. This revolt involved intricate planning, sequestering of gunpowder, and complex coordination and communication between Ashkenazi and Sephardi inmates—all done in the strictest secrecy.

In Chapter 4, "Medical Experiments," I detail the horrific medical experiments to which the male and female inmates, both Sephardi and Ashkenazi, were subjected. Because so little research has been focused on the Sephardim who endured the sadism of the SS doctors, my focus is to draw out the accounts from the interviews I have conducted. While survivors of the medical experiments were often reluctant to speak, many eventually shared with me the trauma of their suffering.

Chapter 5, "The Death March," focuses on the preparation of the Nazis for evacuation of Auschwitz I and II, Monowitz, and several subcamps. In January 1945, Heinrich Himmler ordered the destruction of the crematoria and gas chambers before the arrival of the Russian troops in order to conceal evidence of the mass murders and brutalities that took place in the camps. Those inmates still alive were forced into the march of death.

Chapter 6, "Albania, the Mufti, and the Ustashas," connects the survival of the Jews who took refuge in Albania proper with the benevolence of Muslims and Christians who opened their doors to give sanctuary to strangers in need. Albanian hospitality is based on the Laws of the Kanun, a fifteenth-century unwritten law that covers all aspects of social life. Jews were amazed by the commitment of the Albanians to endanger their own lives and those of the members of their families in order to protect not only the native Jews—considered Albanians—but also the emigrants. No such ethos of protection was accorded to the Jews by the Grand Mufti of Jerusalem, who embraced Hitler's vision and promised to bring Arabs and Muslims to the support of the Axis powers. Unparalleled in their cruelty, the Ustashas of Croatia adopted both Islam and Catholicism as official religions.

Chapter 7, "Jews from North Africa and Libya, the Invisible Jews," traces the tentacles of the Holocaust that reached approximately 430,000 Jews of Morocco, Algiers, Tunisia, and Libya in 1939. These historically invisible Jews suffered from the imposition of the anti-Jewish laws, some from internment and some from extradition to Auschwitz and Bergen-Belsen.

Chapter 8, "The Place of God in the Holocaust," brings the book to a conclusion with the unanswerable question "Where was God during the Holocaust?" Other questions resound: How could He watch His people die in such agony, millions and millions burned in the furnaces? Marta Wise of Czechoslovakia had a ready response, "People ask me, 'Where was God during the Holocaust?' My answer is, 'Where was man?'"

The Holocaust haunts me. I can never see a tall chimney at a steam plant

Figure I.1. Glass container with ashes from Auschwitz at the base of the memorial for the martyrs of the Holocaust, Salonika cemetery. Photograph by Isaac Jack Lévy.

without viscerally being transported to the death camps. I recall that every time I saw the chimney at the old steam plant at Agnes Scott College, where my wife, Rosemary Lévy Zumwalt, was the vice president for academic affairs, a freezing cold engulfed me. So did the sight of the trains on the railroad tracks as they passed several times a day along College Avenue. Even today, after so many years, I can visualize my brothers and sisters shoved into the miserable wagons, herded into the showers of poison gas, with their souls soaring to heaven from the diabolical chimneys.

I undertook my researches by first having a list of people to interview. I added to this list by picking up names from those interviewed, by visiting a club for survivors, such as the Greek Club de los Reskatados de los Kampos de Konsentrasion in Tel Aviv. Sometimes I met people over the dinner table as a guest and added other people. Since I am Sephardi, I was one of them.

I, too, had lost family members from Rhodes in the death camps. I was able to share my experience of escaping the Holocaust by taking refuge with my family in Tangier, Morocco. By sharing my own experiences and by speaking in Judeo-Spanish, my mother tongue, I was able to establish a close emotional connection with those who had such painful and traumatic memories of their time in the death camps.

My memories of Rhodes are threaded through with happiness and sadness—the happiness of sunlit hours spent with family and friends in the Juderia, the Jewish Quarters, and the sadness of loss of home and loss of friends. Thus, my research on the Sephardim in the Holocaust is intensely personal. It is a tribute to my people, the Jewish people of Rhodes, of the Dodecanese islands, and of Greece and the Balkans; and to the Sephardim of all lands who have been largely left out of the historical accounts of the Holocaust.

1

Journey to the Death Camps

THE SEPHARDIC SURVIVORS I interviewed and those who have published their accounts have hardly been concerned with the causes and justifications of the horrendous tragedy that befell them. A survivor, originally from Salonika, who chose to remain anonymous, remarked, "We did not truly know much about what was going on in Germany, the rest of Europe, and much less in North Africa and the Arab countries; it was later that we found out and experienced the tortures and killings, the brutality *ke mos kayo sovre muestras kavesas* (that fell on our heads). Even then we hardly knew anything about Hitler, *mahshemo vezihro* (may his name be blotted from our memory), and his maniacal ideas. What was of immediate importance to us was survival in a hostile country where we had lived for centuries and to see the people turn against us."

The Jew knew from his own experiences that he had been the eternal scapegoat, ordained to bear the blame for the prejudices and longings of others, a pariah who survived at the whims of rulers and communities. The Sephardim were now locked in place by the law of the Third Reich. Although some—like my paternal aunt Rachel Tuvi and her family who lived in Athens—found refuge in the mountains, in small villages, or with friends, they were always afraid that if caught, they or members of their family would be executed. They were aware that even their host families were in danger. Even if young and agile enough to flee, the majority of the young could not dutifully and emotionally leave the family in such hours of despair. The grim future was set, and the excruciating journey to the death camps was their destiny.

THE DODECANESE ISLANDS OF RHODES AND COS

As was the case with the Ashkenazim, once the racial laws were issued in Sephardic communities, they, too, bore the same hardships. However, in Italy and in most of its territories under the Italian Fascists, existence was not as brutal as in Nazi-controlled nations. One such example is my native island of Rhodes, Italy (now Greece). From my memories as a nine-year-old child, I recall my mother and others talking about the effect on the Jews of the racial laws, announced on Thursday, September 1, 1938, in the *Messaggero di Rodi*. The next day, on Friday morning, my mother and I went to the Mandraki to do the shopping for Shabbat. The leaders of the Sephardic community gathered together, and among them was my great-uncle Ruben Capelouto. Beside him stood my mother; and I remember standing quietly by her side, sensing the somber mood and seeing the gloom on the faces of all those gathered.

The Jewish population of Rhodes considered themselves loyal to the Italian government, and their sons were enthusiastic participants in the *figlio della lupa*, the Fascist Cub Scouts, in which I was also a member. The Italians, in turn, appreciated the loyalty of the Sephardim to Italy. Violette Fintz recalled the sympathetic attitude of the Italians toward the Jews,

> La kestion di lus italianus? [kun] lus italianus nu avia ningun problema asta il 1936 kuandu impesarun mas muncho a komandar los fashistas i nu il puevlo italianu porke lus fashistas tomaron il poder, mizmu il jurnal. . . . La populasion lokal nu era antisemita . . . ma lus fashistas si. . . . [Kun lus italianus] tantus anyus bivimos muy, muy kontentis kun eyus. I sea la populasion lokal di lus gregos di akel tiempu, nu tiniamus nada di reproshar.
>
> (The question of the Italians? There was no problem with the Italians until 1936 when the Fascists began to give orders, not the Italians, because the Fascists, not the Italian people, took over power, even the newspaper. . . . The local population was not anti-Semitic . . . but the Fascists were. . . . With the Italians we lived for many years very, very happy with them. Even at that time we had nothing for which to reproach the local Greek population.)[1]

When control shifted from the kingdom of Italy to Mussolini and the Italian Fascists, the Sephardim of Rhodes felt deeply the vicious anti-Semitic reports in the local newspaper. Indeed, even though Benito Mussolini's racial policies were in accord with Hitler's, he was supported only by the Fascists but highly unpopular with the king and the majority of Italians, who truly had more strength than he thought.

The new laws had been instituted immediately. Jews who served in the military were dismissed, and some officers who felt utterly betrayed committed suicide. Banks were seized, major companies were ordered closed. The old Jewish cemetery dating back to 1593 was expropriated, and a new one, some kilometers from the city, ordered to replace it. How sadly was this order taken! Over a thousand graves were exhumed. My father, whom I hardly knew, since I was two years old when he died, was the fourth one to be transferred. The highly regarded Collegio Rabbinico, the Rabbinical Seminary, was closed; Jewish teachers and directors of state schools were relieved of their positions; Jewish students were forbidden to attend governmental schools.

Jews who had settled in the Italian kingdom after January 1, 1919, were given six months to leave the country.[2] Marriage between Jews and Aryans, which was characterized as a mixture of races, was prohibited. Certain professions were outlawed for Jews, and the use of servants, especially Aryans, was forbidden. Although people were allowed to attend their synagogues, the storekeepers were ordered to open their stores on Saturday, and the kosher slaughter of animals was forbidden.[3] As a way around these restrictions, my own family and some friends purchased a goat and in secret had it ritually slaughtered by a *shoket* (an approved rabbinical slaughterer).

Still, while the political situation had become severe in Rhodes, the Italians always showed kindness and respect for the Jewish people. When we were told to leave Rhodes, my mother went to the office of Governor Mario Lago with the Certificato di Sudditanza (Certificate of Citizenship) issued in Rhodes to my father, Giacomo Levi, on August 1, 1928. This certificate declared him to be an Italian subject in accordance with decree No. 343, passed on January 1924, which became law No. 1588 on July 15, 1926. With this document firmly in her hand, my mother informed the secretary to the governor that we did not have to leave the island, since we were full citizens of Italy. The secretary, who knew my mother, said, "*Signora*, put that paper away! Put that paper away!" My mother insisted, "I do not have to leave! This is the law." She held out the paper again. At that point, he grabbed the document, shoved it in her purse, and said, "Madame Levi, if my superior had been here, I would have had to seize it. Keep it, someday it will be of use to you."[4]

The Italian official was right. We left the island of Rhodes in 1939 and took refuge in the international city of Tangier, Morocco. In 1944 we sought visas to depart for the United States. Informed that we had to have passports, my mother went to the Italian consulate in Tangier to obtain the proper paperwork. The consulate first refused to give us a passport. As a last resort my mother showed the certificate to the representative, who immediately issued the passports. With this Certificato di Sudditanza, we were the first refugees from the Rhodesli community in Tangier to obtain passports.

Although it is little known, the Vatican ordered all Jewish converts to Catholicism to leave the Church. The story of one such case came from a monastery in Rhodes. A young priest who was raised by the brothers was informed that he, too, had to leave because of his Jewish ancestry. Early the next morning, the brothers heard an unusual noise coming from the atrium. Everyone followed the sound. The Father Superior found the young priest standing on

"3519"

CD. 528

GOVERNO DELLE ISOLE EGEE

CERTIFICATO DI SUDDITANZA

Si certifica che il signor L E V I Giacomo, di Isacco e di fu Levi Lea, nato a Adalia (Turchia) il nel 1898, originario di Adalia Turchia, di condizioni commerciante, è suddito italiano in base al R. D. L. 31 gennaio 1924 N° 343 convertito in Legge 15 luglio 1926 - N° 1588.

Rodi, li I Agosto 1928 (Anno VI)

CONNOTATI

Statura media
Fronte alta
Occhi castani
Naso concavo
Bocca media
Capelli castani
Barba rasa
Baffi a spazzola
Colorito roseo
Corporatura regolare
Segni particolari N.N.

FIRMA DEL TITOLARE

MARCA DA BOLLO LIRE TRE

MARCA DA BOLLO Tassa Sudditanza RODI CENTESIMI 50

P. IL GOVERNATORE
Il Segretario Generale
(Crivellari Quirino)

MEMBRI DI FAMIGLIA

Grado di parentela	NOME	Luogo di nascita	Data di nascita
moglie	Caden Musafir	Milas	1903
figlio	Gedal	Rodi	1927

Figure 1.1. Italian Certificate of Citizenship, Giacomo Levi. Collection of Isaac Jack Lévy.

top of a ladder, pretending to chisel the statue of the crucified Christ from the wall. The father demanded to know what the young priest was doing. He replied that he was following the new law: since Christ was a Jew, he had to take him along. This caused a furor; the Vatican was apprised of it, and according to the people who told this story, the law was abolished. In another legend a statue of the Virgin Mary was crying, her eyes wet with tears. One of the priests tried to dry her eyes with cotton. Unsuccessful, he checked to see if the statue was sweating, but it was made of solid marble. People from all over the island came to view the crying Virgin. Since there was no explanation for the tears, it was deemed a miracle: The Virgin was crying for her people, the Jews, who were being treated inhumanely.[5]

The Jews who did not emigrate continued living in their homes up to the point of the continuous American and British bombardment of the port, which was close to the Jewish Quarters. The Jewish section was almost totally destroyed. The Jewish population took refuge in the villages of Kremasti, Trianda [Ialyssos], Villanova, and Kalamari, among others. Violette Fintz and thirty-five persons were accommodated by the milkman in the stable where he housed his horses. Once or twice a week they were allowed to return to their homes in order to take some clean clothes. Those who settled in Kremasti and Villanova went continuously to the city, because they took little when they left. "Naturally this attracted the attention of the Germans," said Violette. An unfortunate incident took place soon after the relocation to the villages. Jewish girls did not pay attention to a posted sign at the beach in Trianda, which read, "It is forbidden to Jews and dogs to swim." The girls, having many Italian friends, intervened with the mayor, who was also friendly with the Jews, to have the sign removed. Unaware of the individuals involved, the Germans acceded. However, when a German official tried to tease the girls, they insulted him. Upon learning that they were Jewish, two days later the German authorities arrested them.

Michael Matsas, a Greek Jew, in *The Illusion of Safety*, testifies to the kindness of the Italians: "The Italian troops were extremely civilized. They did not confiscate anything, and they did not execute any hostages or burn any villages in our area, even when Italian soldiers were killed by the resistance."[6] When I reported this fact to Violette Fintz, she agreed wholeheartedly. Matsas continues, "On January 20, 1944, the Jews of Rhodes and Cos received the good news that King Victor Emmanuel III [who was against Mussolini's decree] gave back to them and to all the Jews of Italy their civil rights."[7] This humanitarian move took place while the Germans were still on the island. The protection of the Italians lasted for a while even after Italy surrendered to the Allies on September 11, 1943, abandoning the Aegean Islands to the Germans. As late as February 1944, the Jews still "persevered in their hope, deceived also by the attitude of the German High Command that in the approach of the Passover it invited them to prepare unleavened bread."[8] Still, the Sephardim could not settle into a sense of normalcy, due to the constant bombardment of the port by the Allies.

The overt actions of the Nazis against the Jewish population of Rhodes began on July 17, 1944. First the Germans ordered all males thirteen years and older to report by 7 A.M. to the Palazzo d'Aviazione and to bring their cards of identity and permission to work, which the Nazis then confiscated. With the males held as hostages, the women and children were ordered to join them within twelve hours and to bring all their money, gold, jewelry, other valuables, and some food. "Any husband whose wife did not present herself would be immediately executed." Esther Fintz Menascé added, "Si può immaginare lo sgomento, l'ansia, il terrore delle ebree di rodi, che ovviamente non poterono che obbedire" (One can imagine the shock, anxiety, and fear of the Jewish women of Rhodes, who obviously could not but obey).[9]

During the confinement of the Jews in Rhodes, there was a change in the attitude of the Greek population: they now insulted the Jews and teased them with bread and water, which they offered for sale at 10,000 lire. A July 20 ordinance declared that anyone who seized any Jewish goods and properties had to hand them over to the authorities. Still, both the corrupt Greeks and Germans ransacked the Jewish homes. For six days, up to the deportation on July 23, 1944, the German authorities kept the Jews imprisoned without food and water. On the twenty-fifth, escorted by military guards, they marched some three hundred meters to the harbor. During the march, a Greek spy for the British told one of the Jewish leaders that the British knew of the situation and were going to save them. As usual, the British did nothing, even though they saw the boats. A Turkish boat was not too far out of the harbor and stayed away.

Violette Fintz, whom I interviewed in Brussels, and ten survivors from Rhodes whom Rosemary and I interviewed in Ashdod, Israel, praised the Italian municipal government and the Catholic mission for trying to safeguard whatever was salvageable from the homes of the Jews; and they lauded Archbishop Acciari for organizing the delivery of bread, fruit, beverages, milk, and thousands of rations of soup to those held in captivity. The intervention came at a price. Mother Sofia, who tried to help the sick and the children, "was bitterly insulted, taken away and thrown on the ground by a German."[10]

The Rhodeslis left on July 23, 1944, and did not reach Auschwitz until August 16, 1944, a total of twenty-five days. Along with the Jews from Corfu, those from Rhodes and Cos endured the longest trips to the hell of Auschwitz-Birkenau. First they were gathered for transport on the ships. The non-Jewish citizens of Rhodes were forbidden by the Germans to congregate outside the medieval walls during the march from the Palazzo d'Aviazione to the harbor. Those who dared to disobey witnessed the long line of Jews, whole families, with their children and elderly, dragging themselves along with the bundles of what they were allowed to bring. Once they were gathered for transport, they boarded the ships for the trip to the Haidari Concentration Camp, which was located on the outskirts of Athens. Here the Jews were gathered for transport by trains to Auschwitz-Birkenau.

The boats that carried the Jews from the Italian islands of Rhodes and Cos (Kos)—both ceded to Greece by the Treaty of Paris in 1947—and those from Greek Corfu to mainland Greece, and the insufferable cattle cars that transported them to their final destinations, were precursors of what was to come. Violette Fintz told me: "On the 23rd of July 1944, 1,600 Jews from Rhodes and Cos were transported to Piraeus, Greece, in three small ships used to carry petrol [or coal]; some died and were buried on a deserted island. Once arrived, the Germans transferred them to a camp in Haidari where they stayed for four days without food and water. The German attitude on the boats, the port of Piraeus, and the camp was pure cruelty—pushing, beating with lashes, breaking teeth, bloody noses, cut faces, starvation, no bedding, and exhaustion due to the long voyage." One event that remained imprinted on Violette's memory all these years proved to be "an indication of what we still had to suffer. Next to me was a mother with a baby a year old. The child was very thirsty; in order to quench his thirst, he licked the sweat of the mother's face." Violette concluded, "When we arrived in Haidari, the first SS prison in Athens, we were greeted with beatings. I can say that in that camp the cruelties were unimaginable. They left us without food. . . . There were cases that some were dying of thirst and they gave them urine to drink." The adults bore the trials and tribulations with a gray gloom on their faces. As bad as this was, the real problems were ahead of them once they were gathered in preparation for the long, treacherous journey to the unknown.

Violette Fintz recalls the experience in the cattle cars:

> The voyage to Auschwitz was long—overstuffed in the wagons with a heap of dry onions in one corner and a few loaves of bread and two barrels of water, one to drink and a second for sanitary purposes, in the other corner. It was the height of summer, and many died of heat and exhaustion. Since 1938 when the racial laws were introduced on the island, we had no information on the other Jewish communities, much less on what was taking place in Europe. I must tell you, once we arrived at the camp, the Jews of Rhodes trembled with fear of not knowing what else would take place; it was all new to us. Once the doors of the train were opened, the sight was incredible, frightening, ruthless, a real lunatic asylum—bright lights, men in strange uni-

Figure 1.2. *Sarcophagus/The Railroad Car*, metal sculpture by Evangelos I. Moustakas of Pallini, Greece. Courtesy of Moustakas. Photograph by Rosemary Lévy Zumwalt.

forms, dogs barking, and officers pushing and yelling in a language we did not understand; it was worse than Haidari, and every day thereafter became unbearable.

In Haidari the Greek Orthodox and some local leaders who saw the packing of the trains under duress also felt the impact for years to come. Evangelos Moustakas recounted the following haunting recollections during our interview in his house near Athens in August 21, 1984.

I am a Greek sculptor. My name is Evangelos Moustakas [born in Piraeus, Greece, in 1930]. I lived in Pallini di Attica in Greece [quite near the German camp of Haidari]. My father was Chief of the Railway; therefore, I lived near the trains and every day the machines [wagons] passed in front of me. I saw Germans and a lot of people jam-packed in the trains. It was a tragedy for me because my soul always cried and remained in me for so many years, twenty-five years. It never let me sleep, never let me in peace. And fortunately for me I became a sculptor, a Greek sculptor. For years I made so many, many drawings in order to express my feelings. Those were terrible years for my youth and not only for me, but for the children who lived these periods

> of the Second World War. After years of trying to express myself about the tragedy, I began to work as a crazy person, and after many months, working day and night, like a crazy person, I produced first a drawing: a small wagon, a wagon that was like a sardine can full of people, of human beings. After another try, I made a much larger one of iron that finally brought out of me all the weight of my heart that I had for twenty-five years. I completed the sculpture, the *Sarcophagus* [The Railroad Car] in 1964, a train packed with human beings that were taken to the north, to what later on we learned was the death camp of Auschwitz.

The young boy who saw the wagons full of Jews on the way to their deaths could not forget the image, the horror of what he had seen as a child of twelve. During the narrative, Moustakas stopped for a minute and said, "I do not want to forget, but I do not want to remember at the same time." He added that through his work he was able "to remove from myself all that I had in my heart and be able to speak to people, to impress upon the new generation that war does no good." Moustakas's intention was to give humanity hope for the future, "a future that mankind must keep high in his soul. [My work] is a cry against war and against the catastrophes of the world."[11]

SALONIKA

The Greek War of Independence (1821–1829) caused havoc to the Jews of Greece. Regarded as allies of the Ottoman Empire, as diplomats, spies, and traitors, the Jews were massacred and their communities throughout the nation devastated. The destruction of the Jewish Quarter due to the Great Fire of 1917 left some fifty thousand Jews homeless and unemployed. Businesses, synagogues, mosques, and churches were lost.

The arrival of hundreds of thousands of Greeks from Asia Minor resulted in the "exchange of population between Greece and Turkey [which] fundamentally altered the city's ethnic structure."[12] The relationship between Muslims and Greeks worsened with massacres executed by both sides. "On June 12–13, 1914, Turkish irregulars attacked the town of Old Phocaea [in western Anatolia] and began a pillage and massacre . . . killing 50 or 100 civilians and causing its population to flee to Greece."[13] I recall my mother, who at approximately ten years old lived in Milas, telling me that her family hired a young Greek to perform odd jobs. One morning as she was going to school, she saw the decapitated head of the young boy impaled on a lance. To the best of her recollection, there was also a sudden departure of Greeks from the city.

Unlike the rest of Greece, Salonika was a cosmopolitan city with different languages spoken, different religious centers, and different customs. In the 1830s, with the rise of Greek nationalism, Christians gained power. Anti-

Semitism held sway. Several changes were imposed: the use of the Greek language was required, Sunday was established as the day of rest, and the traditional religious life of the Jews was considerably reorganized according to the laws of the Greek state.[14] With the weakening of the Ottoman Empire and the increase in competition from Western nations, Salonika lost its economic predominance. Christian businessmen and professionals rivaled the Jews. As the Greek Orthodox resettled in Greece, a number of Salonikan Jews immigrated by necessity to Western Europe, South America, Constantinople, Palestine, and, particularly, Izmir.

Stephen Schwartz writes that according to Devin E. Naar, "[r]elations between the Salonican Jews and Greek authorities were clearly not as favorable as they had been with the Ottomans. For one, Greece promoted Athens and its port, Piraeus, to the detriment of Salonica and its commerce. . . . Nonetheless . . . with the end of Ottoman rule, and the assumption of Greek citizenship by the Salonicans, the Jewish community preserved a considerable degree of autonomy until the Holocaust, at which time, Jewish Salonica was effectively wiped out."[15] However, those who took refuge with Greek friends, or joined the partisans, and the survivors who returned to Salonica "managed to start a new life from the ruins." During the war there had been "cooperation between the Greek resistance and Haganah, the Jewish resistance of Palestine." The Haganah provided the Greek partisans, EAM-ELAS [National People's Liberation Army], with "medicines, uniforms, blankets and gold."[16]

Alfred Arditti in his statement to Yad Vashem on April 2, 1958, related:

> At the time of the Nazi occupation the Jews of Salonika kept almost all their freedoms, but after a certain time, the Germans ordered to post signs in all Jewish stores indicating that they belonged to Jews. Later they . . . imposed new laws against the Jews of the city. Within one year, the Jews had to be identified with a yellow Star of David, and their freedom of communication and of labor were almost annulled. Young Jews were ordered [in 1941–1942] under penalty of death to present themselves to the offices of the German Labor. The youth was used in various forced jobs—building roads, work in mines and in military camps, etc. The work was difficult, hard, and due to the lack of nutrition, clothing, [and] medicine, and disease, a great number of the young died. The rest of the forced-laborers [were] released when the community paid the ransom of 3.5 billion drachmas required by the Germans.
>
> Later, around the end of 1942, the Germans ordered the creation of four large ghettos where the Jews had to move and abandon their homes, stores, and offices. It is from these places that the Germans collected the Jews in order to transport them to Germany and Poland. . . . The process of transportation

> was the following: Each morning the Gestapo would collect some inmates from one of the ghettos and forced them to be ready to move to the Baron Hirsch within half an hour with only the necessary material. . . .
>
> A lot of Jews, terrified that they would also be transported, succeeded in escaping by removing the yellow Star of David. Some 3,000 of rich Jews from Salonika succeeded by paying large sums of money to escape to the old regions of Greece still under the Italian occupation—Athens and other cities. A smaller number of the young, 17 years old and up, escaped to the mountains and then joined the Greek Partisans.[17]

During my visits to Salonika, especially in 1982 and 1984, I asked Leon Benmayor and Alphonse Levi, president and member of the Jewish Community respectively, to comment on the attitude of the Germans before the deportations from Salonika to the death camps. Following are some of the restrictions imposed on the people:

1. Jews were obliged to wear a yellow star and restricted to live in ghettos.

2. Lawyers, doctors, and professors were forbidden to work.

3. The Jews were restricted to certain areas. Once located in a ghetto, they could not leave it.

4. Homes and businesses were confiscated; so was the Baron Hirsch Hospital.

5. Jewish houses and buildings were seized for housing and offices.

6. The old Jewish cemetery was taken, and the gravestones used by the Greeks and Germans to construct their homes.

7. Jews were forbidden to visit coffee houses or movies and to use public transportation.

8. Radios, telephones, pianos, and valuables—gold, money, jewelry, rugs, etc.—were expropriated.

9. The Jewish newspaper *El Messagero* was forbidden.

10. No one could escape; if they did, they and their families would pay with their lives.

During my interviews I asked some survivors, both in Salonika and Israel, if there were some incidents that they were not able to forget. Without exception it was the Shoah. However, a large part of the Salonikan Jews were outraged by the behavior of a few of their coreligionists, among them Hasson, Albala, and Saltiel, who collaborated with the Gestapo. Saltiel even gave the Nazis a list of the Greek Jews. As Alfred Arditti reported, "They were worse than the Germans."

Leon Benmayor added, "The Greeks were friendly. However, once the Germans were in power, many Greek Christians and government officials collaborated with them. Most of them were our friends, business partners, etc. I still remember the attacks of the press and how the Red Cross was not allowed to intervene on our behalf, even worse the lack of compassion by the Allies. They only needed an excuse, an event, such as the Fire of 1917 [when the Jewish Quarters were destroyed], to blame us. In several cases, it cost the lives of several of our people. Indeed, anti-Semitism was alive, and we could not have helped ourselves."

The tortures began even before the transports from Greece, the Balkans, and the Italian Dodecanese islands to the German camps in Poland and to Jasenovac in the Independent State of Croatia, run by the Croatian Ustashas. Leon Reuven Cohen, a Greek Jew from Salonika, told me, "Todo enpeso kon las muevas leyes rasiales en los getos en los kuales mos estefaron, en los lavoros forsados ke mos asignaron sin piedad kuando dainda estavamos en Gretcha. Pedrimos muestra libertad. Esto era muestro avenir, i no lo saviamos" (It all started with the new racial laws in the ghettos in which they crammed us, in the forced labor details that were assigned to us without pity while still in Greece. We lost our freedom. This was our destiny, and we did not even know it).[18]

The May 15, 1943, issue of the Greek underground *Nea Genea* (Νέα Γενεά, New Generation) summarized the conditions under which the Jews from Salonika—and from other communities as well—were evacuated: "We shall not report the innumerable humiliations, the robberies, the brutalities, and the murders perpetrated by the Germans against the Salonika Jews."[19] Before the deportation to Auschwitz, chief rabbi of Salonika Dr. Zevi Koretz encouraged all his unmarried congregants to marry in order to protect the women. Soulema recounted that a few hours after he was married, he and his wife left Salonika on April 4, 1943, "for hell on earth." He continued, "What a ridiculous honeymoon! Our bedroom suite was a freight car shared with 73 others. . . . We could not lie down, and we were lucky if we could rest a little or catch some sleep sitting on our luggage with our knees against our chins. My wife, my life's companion as we had sworn in front of the Rabbi, snuggled up to me crying and asking from time to time, 'How long will this trip take?'"[20] Indeed, this was a very long honeymoon trip for the newlyweds, who had departed from the main ghetto, the Baron Hirsch camp, where the

Jews of Salonica had been forcibly gathered, right next to the railroad tracks for ease of transport.

During the long and traumatic journey, the people suffered miserably. Deprived of all necessities, they could not take care of their crying children or tend to the frail elderly. Many died of hunger, thirst, or asphyxiation. For some the strain was too much, and they lost their minds. When one of the wagons that transported the Jews of Salonika to Auschwitz was opened at the end of the voyage, half of the travelers were found to be dead. Fifteen had gone mad. Only one was able to stand. The train had left Salonika seventeen days earlier. "In a freight car, painted black and barely adequate for 50 persons, the Germans had crammed 68 Jews in the first convoy, among whom were old men of 90 years, pregnant women, women who have been forcibly separated from their husbands, 10- to 12 year-old children, etc. . . . On leaving Salonika, these unfortunates had a small parcel containing food for two days, and some water. The wagon had no toilets and had been sealed before the departure."[21]

The newly married Soulema told of his initial relief in finally arriving at Auschwitz and of being able to step out of the stench of the cattle car: "What a joy! Everybody was next to their luggage, the children were close to their parents, and the newlyweds holding each other tightly." In a split second, reality intruded. Those who had stepped down from the cattle cars were now "being shoved around." Soulema continued: "The fully armed S.S. guards received us brutally. . . . Of the 2700 deportees in our train 835 were chosen for work, while the other ones were asphyxiated soon after. This was the most shocking hour of our Calvary: our dear ones—elderly parents, our children, and my wife—were snatched away from us. We did not have a chance to say good-bye. That was the extent of our marriage."[22]

Daniel Bennahmias, a member of the Sonderkommando, narrates the following story that has been told time and again by those who survived the tragedy:

> We were crammed into boxcars. We were sealed with steel, a thicket of people so densely packed that even as the strands of our life disintegrated, we knit together and formed a tortured human web within which we were virtually locked into place. When we moved, we all moved. . . . We were young and old: men, women, and children. There was no modesty among us. . . . What were we to do now? How were we to behave? How could we behave? . . . We were mothers and daughters, fathers and sons; we had to deal with the pregnant, the infant, the aged, and every manner of natural occurrences—whether it was menses, a heart attack. . . . Now it so happened that the woman who sat next to my mother in the boxcar died positioned across my mother's chest,

> where her body remained rigidly in place for two days. . . . The corpse lay in her lap and putrefied there.[23]

Dr. Albert Menasche recalls that during the excruciating eight-day trip from Salonika, he wished "to arrive at our destination, and to leave this hell on wheels. . . . The more optimistic amongst us still held some hope." But the arrival was simply an intensification of the nightmare. As the sliding doors screeched open, they faced a band of prisoners dressed in striped uniforms ordering them with a word that sounded unlike anything they had heard before, *Schnell* (quickly).[24]

Isaac Bourla recalls seeing "regular soldiers, as well as officers holding whips and yelling and screaming out orders." He continues, "Never before had I seen on human faces so much anger and hate. They kept shouting the word, '*heraus, heraus*' (out, out)." Since most Sephardic Jews did not speak German, they did not know what the words shouted and spat at them meant. From then on hope vanished and hell persisted. According to Bourla, "The officers in charge of us had now gone wild. They were brandishing their whips and shouting at the people to get down from the wagons even more quickly. They lashed out in all directions. Everyone was shocked and terrified by this reception."[25] As the trains were emptied, Bourla watched an act of sadism on the part of an SS guard manhandling the newcomers: "One of the officers laughingly grabbed a baby from its mother's arms. Holding the baby by one foot the officer twirled it a few times in the air and then threw the infant at the edge of the lorry. The mother gave a heart-breaking cry and fainted. All of us stood transfixed from witnessing such an atrocious act."[26] Leon Cohen, also from Salonika, writes that once his younger sister, Margot, who was expecting, reached Auschwitz-Birkenau, "[t]he fetus was torn out of her womb before she could give birth and this led to her death."[27]

CORFU

From April 1941 to September 1943, the Jews of Corfu were deported. They had lived a secure existence under the Italians. Even though they considered themselves true Corfiotes, there were nonetheless some sporadic anti-Semitic attacks and accusations of blood libels, just as in Greece, Rhodes, and other Greek islands. They were integrated in all aspects of commercial life, and their economic contributions to the island were important.

In September 1943, with the surrender of Italy to the Allies, the Germans occupied the island. One of their first acts was to demand a list of Jews and a detail of their assets. "Instead, Metropolitan Chrysostemos Dimitrious bribed the German commander, and the partisans threatened to attack. Bishop Vassily

Stravolmos wired Hitler, asking him not to deport the Jews." In response to the second demand, the Corfu officials only gave two names, the metropolitan's and Lucas Karrer's, the mayor appointed by the Germans.[28] Chrysostemos told the German commandant, "If you harm these people, I will go with them and share their fate."[29] During the roundup of the Jews of Corfu, a tailor by the name of Savvas Israel and his three daughters escaped to the nearby island of Erikousa. The islanders hid the family and then destroyed all the records in the church so that "the Nazis wouldn't be able to determine who was Greek and who was Jewish."[30]

In early June 1944, the Allied Forces bombed Corfu to draw attention away from the landing at Normandy. On June 10 the Germans, assisted by Greek civilians and the police, took advantage of the attack and detained 1,795 Jews—200 already had been sequestered previously by the local population in the mountains.[31] As the Jews were taken away, some civilians and Germans plundered Jewish homes and shops. "The mayor of the island issued a proclamation, thanking the Germans for ridding the island of the Jews so that the economy of the island would revert to its 'rightful owners.'"[32] At first those detained were confined for five days in cramped quarters in the old Venetian citadel, the Palaio Frourio. On the same day, "with the end of the war in sight," the Germans risked their materiel and personnel in a dangerous transfer of the Jews, first directly to Patras or via Igoumenitsa to the island of Lefkada. According to Armando Aaron of Corfu, they were placed on a *zattera* (a raft) made of barrels and planks and towed by a small boat to Patras. At first they were guarded by Germans, then once they reached Patras, by Greeks who belonged to the "Security Battalion." Finally, they were sent to Haidari for transport along with Jews from Athens onto trains for Auschwitz, an eighteen-day journey, second in length to the deportation of the Jews from Rhodes and Kos. During the journey they were denied food and water.[33] When the train arrived, "no one got out, and lined for inspection. Half of them were already dead, and the other half in a coma. The entire convoy, without exception, was sent to number two crematorium."[34] "Those who died," said Armando Aaron, "were later put in another car, in quicklime, and burned in Auschwitz." According to Ikonomopoulos, "Of the 1795 Jews of Corfu who were deported, only 121 would survive."[35]

After the war the Jewish population of Corfu was 125; today fewer than a hundred remain. Ikonomopoulos writes, "Of the once vibrant Jewish community . . . little is left now: the shells of bombed out buildings, their former stores now owned by Greek Christians and only [one] of the three synagogues that [of the Scuola Greca] existed at that time of the Holocaust."[36] After the war there were some marriages in Corfu, but most of the Jews left for Palestine.

CRETE

Not every Sephardic community reached their final destination. Sam Angel of Atlanta, Georgia, commenting on his experience in the camps, stated that many of his compatriots did not reach the camps. "Fueron echados en las aguas komo peshkados muertos. Se aogaron en poko tiempo. No fueron echados bivos en los ornos ni en las fosas, ni pasaron por los olukes. Ken save? Puede ser ke fueron mazalozos i no sufrieron en los maldichos kampos" (They were thrown into the waters like dead fish. They drowned in a short time. They were not thrown alive into the furnaces or ditches; neither did they have to go through the chimneys. Who knows? Perhaps they were the lucky ones and did not suffer in the cursed camps).[37]

On June 9, 1944, the cargo ship *Danai* transported the Jews from Heraklion, Crete, to Piraeus. The Nazi crew members hermetically sealed all the doors and disembarked.[38] The British submarine HMS *Vivid* was near the Greek Cyclades islands not far from Santorini. Mistaking the *Danai* for a German merchant marine boat, the British submarine fired four torpedoes, sinking the boat and its passengers within fifteen minutes. The British blamed the Germans for transporting under such perilous conditions the 350 Jews together with 48 Greeks of the resistance and 112 Italians who supported the Allies.[39] There are several versions of this story reported by Michael Matsas in *The Illusion of Safety*. Thrasyboulos Spandikadis relates that the Allied planes were notified and did not attack.[40] Nikos Sgourakis recalls that the Germans gathered the Jews and put them in the Venetian castle Makasi. A German woman on May 31, 1944, informed Spandikadis's father, Minas, through Petrakogiorgis, the Cretan resistance leader, of the deportation and wanted the British to know. The next day Gianni Toutongaki, a bank employee, saw the boarding of the Jews, and in a few days a German officer who was on board the vessel returned and told that the boat had been sunk by the British submarine. Sgourakis did not believe that the Germans had sunk their own ship.[41] After a long investigation of the incident with Cretans, German officers, and British secret agents, Shlomo Carmiel, from the University of Tel Aviv, stated that on May 30, 1944, the Jews were not deported but shot. "After their execution the corpses were loaded aboard a ship the Germans later sank in order to destroy every evidence of their crime."[42]

On May 19, 1982, I had a conversation in Jerusalem with Jennie Tarabulus, author of the play *I Never Knew Them*, an account of the Jews of Greece during World War II. One of the characters, the islander, a Jew from Rhodes whose uncle lived in Heraklion, learns that the "Jews were taken from there alright, and from Chania. But the ship never reached Piraeus. . . . The Jews and other prisoners on board were drowned with the ship. Probably too much fuel needed to bring them to Athens. They were going to be exterminated anyway. Maybe they were better off to go that way."[43]

Whether the prisoners were killed by the Germans or the British, sunk for lack of fuel, or massacred in Crete before the deportation is of no consequence now. Fleming writes, "On the day after the roundup, a Christian Cretan schoolgirl recorded her sorrow. 'Oh, they were Greeks, they were our brothers, and their children had fought alongside us for freedom.'"[44] The young girl was referring to the participation of the Cretan Jews in the resistance movement, which had begun in 1941 against the German invasion of the island. With the assistance of the British, the local population—men, women, children, and the clergy—joined the fight with whatever arms they could find.

OLD BULGARIA

By July 1940 the Bulgarian National Assembly, with the support of King Boris III, introduced the Law for the Protection of the Nation, allegedly to control the Communists and restrict the actions of the approximately fifty thousand Jews, mainly Sephardim, living in Bulgaria. The restrictions included exclusion from public service, the right to vote, the choice of place of residence, ownership of businesses, practice of certain professions, and attendance at state universities, prohibition of intermarriage, and imposition of new taxes. On March 1, 1941, "Bulgaria joined the Tripartite or Axis Pact . . . in the hope of reclaiming the territories which it had lost to its neighbors Rumania, Greece, and Serbia (later Yugoslavia) as a result of its military defeats in the Second Balkan War (1913) and again in World War I."[45] The southern part of Rumania (Dobrudzha) was returned on that same day to Bulgaria. Two days later the German army entered Bulgaria. In April 1941 Germany and Bulgaria invaded Yugoslavia and Greece, which resulted in Bulgarian occupation of part of Greek-Thrace, Macedonia, and Pirot in Serbia. In accordance with the plans for the Final Solution, as laid down at the Wannsee Conference on January 20, 1942, the Germans "requested the Bulgarian government in the spring of 1942 to release all Jews in Bulgarian-controlled territory into German custody. The Bulgarian government agreed and took the necessary administrative steps to implement deportations, including the establishment of a Commissariat for Jewish Affairs in the Bulgarian Ministry of the Interior." As news spread of the deportations, Bulgarian intellectuals and clergy members protested.[46]

Several cabinet ministers and parliamentary members, among them Dimitar (Dmiter) Peshev, vice-chairman of the Assembly, Dimitar Ikonomov, Metropolitan Kyril, Archbishop Exarch Stefan, bishops, and forty-one deputies led the protest. In the section "The Rescue of Bulgaria's Jews in World War II," Rossen Vassilev writes, "When Archbishop Stefan learned that at least 800 Jews from Sofia were about to be 'evacuated,' he rushed to the royal palace and refused to leave until the king finally agreed to hear him out. Bishop Kyril of Plovdiv (a future head of the Orthodox Church) sent several telegrams to the monarch and, in a defiant act of civil disobedience, allowed local Jews to take refuge in his church and in his own home. He prevented the deportation of between 1,500 and 1,600 Jews from his diocese, who had been ordered to assemble at Plovdiv's train station during the night of March 9, by vowing to lie across the rails in the path of the first train transport taking them out of the country." Tsar Boris III was in a quandary, pulled as he was in two directions, needing to accede to the Nazi demands for the deportation of the Jews and assailed by "a groundswell of public opposition to his unpopular anti-Jewish measures." He resolved the dilemma by sending Jewish men to labor camps, where, as he told the Germans, he needed them to "maintain Bulgaria's roads and railways."[47] Thus, while the authorities, clergy, and members of the professional organizations and of the public were able to save the Jews of Old Bulgaria from deportation, they could not prevent the relocation of some twenty thousand Jews from the cities and towns to rural areas where the men were placed in forced-labor camps to construct and maintain the roads and railways. In spite of the implementation of the racial laws and the internment of Jews in labor camps throughout the country, Bulgaria was commended by several nations and by Yad Vashem, for in the long run, "Not a single Jew was forced to leave Bulgaria. At the end of the war the Jews returned to their homes, which remained intact and waiting for them."[48]

YUGOSLAVIA

In January 1943 the Bulgarian and German governments "agreed that Jews living in Greece and Yugoslavia Macedonia and in Thrace, administered by Bulgaria since the spring of 1941, would also be surrendered to the Germans for deportation. On Feb. 22 [Alexander] Belev and [Theodor] Dannecker signed a formal agreement to deport 20,000 Jews," some 11,000 from the new territories and the rest from Bulgaria proper.[49] Those living in the Bulgarian New Territories of Aegean Thrace, Macedonia, Pirot, and parts of Serbia were subjected to the Nazi racial laws. They were brutally treated, without mercy, their property looted and their cemeteries desecrated. On March 4, 1943, over four thousand Jews were arrested in Thrace-Greece, then were taken first to Dupnitsa (Dupnica) and Gorna-Dzhumaya internment camps, and then to the port of Lom on the Danube. Jews from Pirot were also moved to the port of Lom. All the Jews were turned over to the Germans, and from March 20 to 22, 1943, they were transferred from the trains to four boats. On the way

Figure 1.3. Boat transporting Jews from Macedonia. Courtesy of the Jewish Community of Sarajevo.

to Vienna, one boat sank, either by accident or intentionally. The Jews from the other boats reached Treblinka on March 26 and 28 and were immediately sent to the crematoria.

From March 11, 1943, the Jews from Skopje, Bitola, and Stip were locked up for a couple of days without food or access to latrines in the Monopoly, a tobacco warehouse, in Skopje. Elena Leon Ishakh from Bitola reported that they were given only minuscule amounts of food, some fit to be eaten. She further reported, "Under the pretext of searching us to find hidden money, gold or foreign currency, they sadistically forced us to undress entirely . . . in some cases they even took away baby diapers. If anything was found on somebody, he was beaten."[50] Ishakh continued telling of the transfer of the Jews to the concentration camp of Treblinka: "The Jews from Skopje camp were deported to Treblinka in three successive transports with 2,338 Jews, left on 22 March 1943 and arrived in Treblinka on 29 March. In each of the freight cars there was a small barrel of water and several buckets into which people could relieve themselves. The luggage that people were permitted to take was 40 kilograms per adult and 20 per child. The second transport with 2,402 Jews left on 25 March and arrived in Treblinka on 31 March 1943 in the evening; the third transport with 2,404 Jews left on 29 March, reached Treblinka on the 5 April 1943."[51] During the journey five elderly people died. Yankiel (Jankiel) Wiernik, an inmate who escaped from the camp, described the fate of the Jews arriving in Treblinka:

> The new transports were handled in a simplified manner; the cremation followed directly after the gassing. Transports were now arriving from Bulgaria, comprising well-to-do people who brought with them large supplies of food: white bread, smoked mutton, cheese, etc. They were killed off just like all the others, but we benefited from the supplies they had brought. As a result, our diet improved considerably. The Bulgarian Jews were strong and husky specimens. Looking at them, it was hard to believe that in 20 minutes they would all be dead in the gas chambers. These handsome Jews were not permitted an easy death. Only small quantities of gas were let into the chambers, so that their agony lasted through the night. They also had to endure severe tortures before entering the gas chambers. Envy of their well-fed appearance prompted the hangmen to torment them all the more.[52]

When I was in Tel Aviv in 1982, I spoke with Yosef Benn, born in 1924 and originally from Macedonia and Bulgaria. As he related, at the beginning of the war he worked with the Agence Juive: "My duties were to save the Jews from Bulgaria and Eastern Europe. We were able to save more than 23,500 of them, including 3,500 from Greece." He continued:

> Many went to the mountains and very few in small boats to Izmir. Even though there were no concentration camps in Bulgaria, according to the laws against the Jews which was set on December 1940 by the Parliament, many measures against the Jews were declared. . . . The government mobilized two thousand men and the young, aged from eighteen to forty-five, to build roads along the railroad near Thrace and other parts of Macedonia. The Jews were closed in ghettos and could only go out two hours per day to get provisions. We were thankful to our Christian friends who could enter the ghettos for bringing us supplies, even offering us money. Still, in 1942, '43, until the liberation in September 1944, the Jewish population lived very frightful moments. The Bulgarians confiscated all our properties, we had to declare everything, and had to close our stores. There was no way to work, our parents had to sell things from the house in order to survive.

I asked Yosef Benn, "How is it possible that a king who kept you alive could act that way?" His response was, "What can I say? Looking back, I can see all the machination and all the maneuvers done by the Bulgarian government." Benn recounted that the Germans "insisted on taking us," in accord with the secret agreement that had been signed by Theodor Dannecker, who was sent by Eichmann to Sofia, and Alexander Belev. "Actually, this was our chance to be saved," Benn continued. "It was not like other zones that had to do what the Germans said. This gave the Bulgarian government a chance to treat the country as a free state. They claimed that there were already parliamentarian laws that took care of the matter." The king refused to turn over the Jews to the Germans. By enclosing the Jews in ghettos, by transferring them to other locales, and by setting up camps for construction of roads, the king tricked the Germans into thinking that he had taken care of "the Jewish problem" in his country. As Benn related, "2,000 stayed in Sofia; 23,000 were taken away and were received by all the *keilot* (synagogues/Jewish communities)."

Benn was witness to the transport of his coreligionists: "We saw the trains from the zone of Gorna Dzhumaya and Dupnitsa (Dupnica), near the Greek frontier, pass. There were other transports. They were Greek Jews. Our people who worked in the tobacco fields near Simitli helped them with provisions." With sadness he remarked, "Unfortunately, we could not help them escape, since they were well guarded by the Gestapo, the Bulgarian police, and soldiers. From Simitli they were taken through Sofia to the port of Lom and then Vienna, where they were turned over to the Germans. From Vienna they were taken through Katovi to Treblinka, not Auschwitz. Other Jews came from Kavala, Serres, Komotini, Thrace, Xanthi, all from Greece. The Jews of Thrace went to Treblinka, and none of them returned."

Benn told of the Jews of Yugoslavia, who were from Macedonia and Skopje, who were taken to Lom and then on to Treblinka. "That is, both parts of Bulgaria that was annexed during the war with the assistance of the Germans. Some 2,500 or 3,000 Jews from Varia and other smaller places were gathered in small synagogues and taken to Auschwitz. In March 1943 the Bulgarian police and soldiers rounded up 7,000 Jews from Macedonia (Pirot) and took them to a transit camp in Skopje, and 4,000 from Thrace to Gorna Dzhumaya and Dupnitsa, and turned them over to the Germans. Also, they took 600 Jews from Felipe. On the tenth of March, the Jews were taken to Treblinka: they all died."

In our conversation in Tel Aviv, Israel, in 1990, Sami Menahen Ben-nun, who was born in Felipe (now Plovdiv), Bulgaria, told me about the experiences of the Jews in Bulgaria during the war, and how many of them joined the partisans. Speaking in Judeo-Spanish, he recounted the following:

> From 1941 to '44 no Jew was taken in the army, but we were forced to work on roads, railway tracks, etc. We were forced to work with no pay. Life was difficult, and we ate meager food. We lived in sheds. . . . No one could run away, since we wore the Star of David. Each one of us had only one garment; when the garment tore, one had to sew the star on the new one again.
>
> From Felipe, young men, boys and girls, escaped to the mountains: a great number died. In 1942–43 I was in the fields near the frontier of Serbia, Yugoslavia. . . . Meanwhile, from 1942 to '43, some seven or eight individuals escaped. All of them joined the partisans in the Mountains of Rodopi, Bul-

> garia. However, I was in the Stara Planina mountains until the end of the war in 1944.
>
> In 1943 Yosef Mair Hillel and Haim Moise Chichek escaped. After Albert Alkolumbre, Leon David Behar, Heskia Komerchero, Sabetai Garti, and others escaped. They escaped little by little so that they would not capture us. Of this group only two stayed alive; the rest died fighting against the Bulgarian Fascists. Also, David Ovadia escaped. He is now a poet and lives in Sofia.

Sami Menahen Ben-nun concluded, "As I said above, I escaped at the beginning of 1944. I also was a member of the partisans."[53]

On April 25, 1990, Rosemary and I spoke with Buka (Bohor) Nissim Braka in Bet Avot, in Rishon LeZion, Israel. Braka was born in 1905 in Kyustendil, Bulgaria, near the border with Macedonia, then Yugoslavia. In 1952 he moved to Israel. He was eager to tell us of his life in Bulgaria during World War II.[54]

> In 1940 we were recruited into the army, not as fighting soldiers, but to dig a highway to the village of Rebrovo, Bulgaria. We worked from the end of April to beginning of November. We lived unprotected, exposed to the elements. In 1941 we were still in the army. It was then that they turned against the Jews. New laws were introduced: we had to wear a yellow star, we were forbidden to be outside after seven P.M., in some cities Jews could not walk on certain streets, they prevented us from holding some jobs. In 1942 we were taken to Lovech in the northwest of the country just to dig. The women were not taken. Those in Sofia were taken away, because at the beginning of March 4, 5, and 6, the Bulgarians wanted to deport them to Poland. It was a group of young Bulgarian Fascists who wanted to harm the Jews. One Wednesday, they started to compile a list of the Jews in Kyustendil. On Thursday, twenty-nine wagons were ready to deport them. Friday morning, we are crazy not knowing what would happen. A Christian neighbor was the head of the city. I went to see him. I asked him, "What is new?" He replied, "Buko, they are planning a terrible thing." He did not say anything else.
>
> On Saturday, March 28, bazaar day, the Christians came from the villages to help us, actually to comfort us. That same night we got together in the *midrash*, the sanctuary of the synagogue. The first word was given to those of Sofia, since the message obtained was that the rich would be sent first. Sunday night, again in the *midrash*, we met to decide what we had to do. I said, "I have a friend who is a lawyer, a close friend of the Germans. I will try to send him and other acquaintances to Sofia [the authorities] to speak with a Bulgarian general and through him to the Germans." They all accepted my suggestion. I went to my friend's house, but, being Sunday, he had left to the village. Several of the individuals present spoke about organizing a delega-

tion. Monday morning, I went to the judge, my friend the lawyer, and said to him, "Friend, go to the general and ask him to help us." "Why not," he said. We both went to the *shofet* [here the chambers of a judge, actually a military ruler] in order to speak with General Jekof. We were told that he was not at home and had gone to his villa because he was sick. At the same time, the building was full of Jews trying to speak to the authorities. At eleven o'clock, my friend was able to reach him. "Here our Jewish friends are like crazy," he told him. Dimitra Jekof was not aware of what was taking place. At night we sent by taxi the group of Christians to see him. However, coerced by the Fascists, a lot of those who promised to go changed their mind; so did the taxi driver.

Meanwhile, we hid the important members of the group until they could leave by train Tuesday morning. They met with the Bulgarian vice-president, Dimitra Peshev. At the same time, the Church, lawyers, and academics tried to change the law against the Jews. The law was not changed, but they postponed it, and we returned home.

Not sure that the laws would change, I gathered all of my possessions—jewels, clothing—and sent them to a friend. At six in the afternoon, I learned from the authorities that we would not be taken. But many other Jews from other cities were assembled in a school because the news of the change of orders was difficult to reach them. However, when the news arrived, they were released. In our city we had very few Fascists; still they were ruthless. We were safe, everything ended well, since we had many friends.

In April 1990 Rosemary and I met Ella Gofen and her mother in their apartment in Bat Yam. A few other Macedonian Jewish women were present. Following an afternoon of coffee and sweets, Ella's mother described their experiences during the German and Bulgarian occupation of Macedonia in World War II.

In 1941 Macedonia was occupied by Bulgaria. There were not many doctors and pharmacists in the region. The few found were mobilized to be sent to the villages of Macedonia; my husband also. In 1942 my daughter [Ella] and I went with him to Prechevo, a village near the frontier with Bulgaria. We lived in a small house. On March 11, 1943, we and other Jews from all over Macedonia were sent to a *Lager* in Monastir and from there to the Monopole in Skopje. We stayed there with one suitcase. We were told that they were going to take us to some villages in Bulgaria, not to Poland. My father-in-law and I were there. From the *Lager*, they first took care of those who had Spanish passports. My family—father, mother, brother, and sister—stayed in one building.

On the sixteenth an order was given to release fifty-two doctors and pharmacists due to the epidemic of typhus. The families were not included in the order, but the doctors and pharmacists did not accept unless the families were also released; the Bulgarians accepted. Once again we returned to the villages in Macedonia. We had to carry a black and yellow star, to see from far away that we were Jews.

There were eight thousand Jews, only seventy-two were released—the doctors, pharmacists, and their relatives. The rest stayed there and were later taken to Treblinka.

In 1943 we saw those transported from Greece, yelling for water. When they were passing through the Monopole, before going to Bulgaria on March 11, we were told, "Don't dare try to save anyone. Take care, trying to save the eyebrows you lose the eyes." They were going to take us back, make us suffer like those in the wagons, and deport us to Treblinka.

Around March 22, 1943, the first transport left with our relatives; we believed that they were going to be released, since we already had accepted to live in a village with a friend who had contact with the municipality. When she went to Bulgaria [looking for them], they already had left.

During our stay in the village, we could not travel. One day my husband wanted to go to Skopje for some medicine. I was going with him. When the authorities found out, they put my daughter and me in a train accompanied by a policeman. We were taken from the village to Old Bulgaria because I broke the law. I had a brother-in-law who had connection with the Bulgarians. He gave them some money under the table, and he saved us. At night I returned [home] with my daughter. Of course, they watched our every single move.

From 1943 to 1945, the partisans used to come to the village. The Albanians helped us. These Albanians lived in Macedonia. They brought us different products—cheese, flour, oil—things to eat that were not available.

In 1945 the partisans came and told us that "the enemy" was coming. We ran to Gorubinse [perhaps Gorince], a village near Albania. There they dressed us as Albanians. The Germans came to Gorubinse searching for my husband. They did not find him, because we knew that they were coming. Then we ran to the mountains. When they left we returned. A few days later, the partisans returned and told us that the Germans and Bulgarians had run away. While the Germans were in the region, they gave the orders and the Bulgarians performed as policemen.

> When we were in the *Lager*, our Bulgarian friends from Prechevo came home and took everything, they stole everything. The sad part is that the night before they took us away, we were together until twelve o'clock in the morning. Our so-called friends knew what was to take place and did not say a word.
>
> My father, mother, brother, and sister died in Treblinka. My father-in-law and mother-in-law were saved by my husband; my father-in-law was also a pharmacist.[55]

On August 24, 1945, when the war was finally over, the Commissariat for Jewish Affairs was abolished. On August 29 all anti-Jewish laws were rescinded. The Jews were able to leave the work camps and the countryside. When they came back to their towns, nearly every Jewish family found their house exactly as they had left it. The Orthodox Church had organized its members to tend the houses of Jews while they were away. Bulgaria was the only country whose Jewish population actually increased during the war.

In an interview in Paris on July 15, 1984, Alfred Elkoubi told me about leaving his birthplace of Algeria, going to Marseille at seventeen and one-half years, and being arrested by the Vichy French: "They were militiamen who came where I worked, holding revolvers. I was not surprised; I had the impression that they would come one day or another." He was transferred to Drancy internment camp, just outside of Paris. He continued: "Everyone knows what Drancy was, the screams, and there it was the French who guarded us. It was the French who took the role of the Germans from Marseille. They took us prisoners." The Germans transferred them to "wagons for animals" and convinced them that they "were going to some sort of paradise, where the families were united. . . . where we could work, live with other people a golden life." Then they arrived in Auschwitz: "There we first saw soldiers dressed in black uniforms jump on us with dogs. At the first selection we realized that we fell in a trap. . . . The separation with the older people was, as you can tell, quite painful. Then the transfer into cells for those who would stay alive and the tattoo on the arm made us aware that we were not human beings, but animals who were marked. From that moment, the struggle for life began. Everyone knows what Auschwitz was. You know that a few meters from the camp the chimneys spat smoke, and we knew what had happened to those who were selected before from us."

CONCLUSION

I have aspired to honor the experiences and the memories of individuals, and their memories of their beloved homelands. I recognize that there is an excruciating consistency in the experiences. In all cases, no matter the places, the Jews were ordered under penalty of death to assemble in selected areas not too far from the rail tracks or from the harbors. They were packed for the long journey in hermetically sealed cattle cars with an average of eighty occupants per wagon with no food, no water, and with only a bucket "para muestros menesteres; todus in pies estefados komo bestias salvajes" (for our special needs; all standing up, packed like savage beasts). Once at Auschwitz the experiences of the Jews were a shared horror. The infamous and dreaded Joseph Mengele, one of the Malachim haMavet (Angels of Death), also known as the ha-Mashchit (the Destroyer), proceeded with the most barbarous of deeds. He oversaw the frightening selections, which separated out family members: the young and robust men and women were chosen for forced labor, and the others—the old, the weak, the sick, the disabled, and mothers with infants—were directed to their deaths. Leon Reuven Cohen sarcastically told me: "It was a good day for the Sonderkommando, those unfortunates chosen to serve in the crematoria. It was a great day for the furnaces that incinerated thousands of innocent victims, some still alive, and fed them to the chimney that vomited flames and smoke that darkened the sky."[56] To immortalize the thousands of his Salonikan brothers and sisters who perished in the ovens of Auschwitz, Avner Peretz wrote the following poem in Judeo-Spanish, "Siniza i fumo" (Ash and Smoke), which he dedicated "To the memory of Salonika—My dream and my love":

Siniza i fumo Bolando, kayendo En un esfuenyo malo Sin salvasion	Ash and smoke Flying, falling Into a nightmare Without rescue.
En la guerta kemada Asentada la fija Pasharos pretos Apretan su korason	In the parched garden The girl sits; Black birds Weigh at her heart.
Siniza i fumo Inchen sus ojos No ay ken ke la desperate A darle konsolasion	Ash and smoke Fill her eyes There is no one to wake her, To comfort her.
Por los sielos, ariva Pasa la luna Tapando su kara Kon una nuve—karvon.	In the sky above The moon passes Hiding her face In a cloud of ashes.[57]

Unaware of the purpose of the selection, many of the newcomers, such as René Molho from Salonika, were not disturbed by the forced division of people, to the right or to the left. "I was glad when my father and mother were put on the truck, so they wouldn't have to walk. I thought it was good that they didn't have to go for forced labor. I remembered the big sign that said '*Arbeit Macht Frei*,' which means, 'Work makes you free.'"[58] Soon they saw guards armed with bayonets and machine guns whipping inmates clothed only with rags. The order of the day was *Macht schnell* (Hurry up); those who did not hurry were viciously whipped. Dr. Albert Menasche further recalls, "We were worn out with fatigue. Not a bench available. We were forbidden to sit on the ground."[59] In the agony of the moment, Menasche remembers, "A familiar face appeared; it was that of a certain Leon Yahiel who had left before us." Yahiel had become a translator for the Germans. "Bluntly and without any preamble, here is the speech he made to us. 'Prisoners, you are in the camp of death here. As I speak to you, your wives and your children are already dead.' He raised his fingers and showed us many buildings whose tall chimneys spit out flames, and continued, 'The flames which you see coming out of those immense chimneys are the product of their burning bodies! Those tremendous buildings which appear to be factories are crematory furnaces. From now on, each one of you is alone in the world, and then, who knows how long even that will last.'"[60] Even with the smell of burning flesh, the newcomers were in denial. Menasche continues: "Hope was so rooted in our human hearts that in spite of everything, we attached no attention to his [Leon Yahiel's] statements."[61] Leon Reuven Cohen couldn't believe how they clung to hope: "No veian a la djente arrastrada de los trenos? Eran siegos? No veian las chimeneas en fuego i no golian la karne kemar ke aogava todo el kampo? De ande toparon esta esperansa?" (Didn't they see the people dragged from the trains? Were they blind? Didn't they see the chimneys on fire, and didn't they smell the burned flesh that choked the camp? Where did they find this hope?).[62] Albert Menasche writes, "Hope did not last for long, just until the barrack doors opened wide and they were greeted by prisoners in striped uniforms, the *Schreibers*, the recorders who meticulously stripped them of their possessions—jewelry, watches, identification papers, photographs, everything of value—and recorded it all on large sheaves of papers, which they gave to the SS officers to whom they reported."[63] Albert Menasche was further mortified by the brutal response of the officer upon asking for "permission to keep my diploma of Doctor of Medicine from the University of Toulouse, as well as my first prize as a flute-player from the conservatory in the same city. 'These diplomas are much too good for a dirty Jew,' was the supervising officer's answer. 'Anyway,' he added with a cunning smile, 'he won't be using them anymore.'"[64] Menasche continues: "Finally, on each person's left arm, a serial number was tattooed. My number was 124,454. Doctor Albert Menasche, the free and respected citizen had ceased to be. In his place there was but the *Haftling* (prisoner) 124,454. *Haftling*, over whom any German soldier, or even any other prisoner having some function in the camp, had the right of life or death."[65]

As a prisoner in Auschwitz, Albert Menasche witnessed too many excruciating atrocities. One that he held close to his heart was the news that his sixteen-year-old Lillian, his "flesh of my life," and his two young nieces, along with eight hundred Jewish girls from Salonika, were sent to their deaths while he was playing music in the camp orchestra. In his reflections Menasche observes, "If fire and gas were some of the chief means of destruction used by Hitler, they were not the only ones: tortures, forced labor, starvation, typhus, etc., were also allies of the crematoria. Thousands and thousands of people died everywhere."[66]

Bourla recalls that he never knew "what the destiny would be on the morrow, much less next month." He continues: "I became like the old-timers, [the *Kapos*, the *Blockältester*], in the *lager*. They avoided talking about the past or the future. The past was over; the future was very dim. . . . You saw the *muselmann* [inmates on the verge of death from starvation], and you knew that tomorrow or next week, or the next, there would be a handful of ashes blowing away on the wind."[67]

They knew that the selections were never-ending: the beatings that broke their backs, the chosen that fed the furnaces that swiftly darkened the sky, the open ditches and pits that burned without respite, the sides of roads where the bodies of the murdered and the weak were left for the animals to devour, the noose for those who tried to escape or had broken the law, and the rivers where bludgeoned bodies were dumped and the ashes were scattered. They knew that the healthy and sick, the aged, the grownups, the young, the infants, and the babies were not exempt. There was no question in their minds that sooner or later they, too, would be annihilated in cold blood. They would become ash and smoke.

2
Living and Dying in Hell

From the arrival at the death camps and throughout their time in this hellish land, there was nothing but barking orders. In what the Polish poet and journalist Tadeusz Borowski (1922–51) refers to as "crematorium Esperanto," the first commands upon arrival at the death camp were the marching order: *Vorwärts Marsch! Schneller! Los!* (Forward march! Faster! Come on!); and the morning greetings: *Aufstehen!* (Get up!), *Schnell!* (Hurry up!).[1] Leon Reuven Cohen explained that the morning *Appell* (the roll call), which often lasted for hours, started with the usual shouting, *Schnell! Anziehen!* (Hurry up! Get dressed!), *Steigt schnell aus!* (Get out at once!). If perchance someone would be late for a formation or would stop moving, the commands were *Raus!* (Out!), *Bewegen!* (Move!), *Aufstehen, Du Stück Scheiße!* (Get up, you piece of shit). Those in charge were free with the use of obscenities for the Jews: *Du Drecksack* (you sack of filth, scumbag), *verfluchter Jude* (cursed Jew), *elende Hunde* (miserable dog/Jews), *Schweine* (pigs), *Aufstehen, Du Bastardjude* (Get up, you bastard Jew), and *Raus mit den Toten* (Out with the dead), or *Bewegen Sie die Toten* (Move the dead). Usually most of the curses were followed by torrents of yelling, hard labor in the freezing cold of winter, and, in the heat of summer, violent beatings, selections, and witnessing people die from weakness and starvation. In sum, the result was total dehumanization.

Heinz Salvator Kounio, a Greek Jewish survivor, describes the brutality of the SS. From the moment of their arrival, the Jews heard the harsh voice of an SS officer: "Get out fast! Get down, pigs, you filthy dogs! You have arrived at a German concentration camp and not at a sanitarium to restore your health. This entire concentration camp has only one exit: the tall black chimney over there and the dense black smoke coming out. All of you will pass through there." Seeing the black smoke and smelling the burning flesh, Kounio recalls, "We became old men within minutes."[2] Ben Stern, from Lodz, Poland, reflected on Hitler's solution to "the Jewish problem." The process was at once simple and diabolical: "destroy the brain" and thus "control the individual." In the ghettos and in the camps, this resulted in Jews living in constant fear.[3]

A young Sephardic woman who witnessed an SS officer snatch a child from a mother's arms, twirl him over his head, and hurl him against the train could not comprehend the lack of emotion on the mother's part: "Ni una lagrima, ni un grito de dezesperasion" (Not even a tear, not even a cry of desperation). In her recollection of this horrendous butchery, this woman could not have realized that the mother had been so traumatized by the brutality of the SS officers that she could not even express her grief. Still, preoccupied that the same fate would befall her other child, the mother held his hand tightly and silently walked with him into the chamber of death.

Another tragic account was given to me by Aliza Baruh (Sarfati), originally from Salonika and a survivor, whom I interviewed in Tel Aviv on June 16, 1982. She tells the story of what happened to her husband's family, all of whom were killed in Auschwitz:

ABS: There I met he who is today my husband.
IJL: What is his name?
ABS: His name is Ovadia Baruh. Also, they killed the entire family, six sisters. They killed one sister five days after she gave birth to a son.
IJL: Why?
ABS: They caught her.
IJL: She was pregnant before?
ABS: She gave birth in Salonika, and they caught her five days after giving birth, and they burn the whole family.
IJL: And the baby also?
ABS: They burn him with the entire family. This tragedy can never be forgotten. And a baby! What animals! How inhuman!

Stella Levi, a survivor from Rhodes, recounts her dilemma upon arriving in Auschwitz. She wanted to assist her blind father out of the train while the "Germans shouted commands that sounded more and more like the angry barking of dogs." Her cousin, Leah, the twenty-six-year-old mother of Peppo Hugno, disregarded the warnings of "some strange Greek Jews from Salonika dressed in striped uniforms and caps [urging the young mothers] to give the babies to the old women." Stella mourns the ghastly end of her cousin: "Poor Leah," she writes, "you did not listen to the warnings of the Saloniklis! But I think you made the right choice, for had you survived as I have, you would have lived a tortured life, hearing constantly the cries of little Peppo calling, 'Mummy, Mummy.'"[4]

Indeed, the mothers made a choice, as Karl A. Plank writes of the "Mother as Comforter" and the "Mothers of Mercy": "When facing the inevitability of a child's death and its certain cruelty, a mother's mercy may compel her to consider actions unimaginable in any other context. To save the child from the Nazi murderer, she may use her own gentler hands to place the child at death's safe remove from further harm. Her mercy may take the form of euthanasia, an act that does not rescue the child's life, but saves his or her death from basic violations."[5] Those who did listen to the warnings of the Greeks on the platforms might have saved their lives but could not save the lives of their children or their parents.

Everyone knew that the selections were never-ending, and death was their companion. There were the unending rows of their coreligionists leading to the furnaces. As Albert Menasche writes, "The sinister parade continued throughout the day's twenty-four hours. The crematoria chimneys and ditches burned unceasingly. The sky seemed permanently blackened by the smoke; at night, it took on a reddish color which illuminated the entire camp. The odor of burning flesh choked our throats."[6] They knew that the aged, the grown-ups, the young, the infants, and the babies were not exempt; neither were the strong or the healthy. They knew that sooner or later they would also be annihilated in cold blood. Gideon Greif tells the tragic story of an old Hungarian Jewish woman who spotted her son, a member of the crematorium crew, while he was stocking wood in the compound:

> Happily, she ran towards him. Her son, who had already been looking for his mother among the dead for a long time, was shocked. His mother asked him what would happen to them.
>
> "You are going to rest here," he replied.
>
> "Where is this strange smell from?"
>
> "From burning rags . . ."
>
> "And why did we come here?"
>
> "To take a bath."
> The son handed the towel and the soap to his mother and both went inside. They disappeared into the hell of the chimney.[7]

Violette Fintz told me of another such incident. After the initial selection dividing a mother and daughter, one for the crematorium and the other for labor, the frightened mother turned to her daughter and yelled, "Me espanto, porke no vienes kon mi?" (I am scared, why don't you come with me?). The daughter broke rank and joined her mother. Holding hands they ended in the gas chamber. In my interview in Ashdod with several Rhodian women, I heard of a similar case. A middle-aged man was being dragged by one foot to a truck to take him to the crematorium. In despair, his son, not able to help him, launched himself against the electrified fence and joined his father in death.[8] There were thousands of similar incidents, tragic encounters, and incredible scenes. Greif writes, "Every day, reports of such incidents were transmitted to us through eyewitnesses. . . . Nothing could surprise us anymore."[9] Even those dehumanized by their long torment in the crematoria felt their hearts would break upon seeing such crimes, such evil committed against these innocent souls.

Shlomo Venezia recalled a talk he gave once to schoolchildren. A young girl asked him if anyone emerged alive from the gas chamber. He related an episode of a man who kept hearing a strange noise while removing the bodies from the gas chamber. At first, they thought that it was gas commonly emitted by the dead. The noise persisted: they heard a wailing, and then the crying of a newborn baby. Stepping over the bodies, they found a baby girl still clinging to the mother's breast whose milk had stopped flowing. They tried to hide the baby, but as soon as a guard discovered her, he, without any hesitation, shot her.[10] With this account Venezia negates Wilfried Heink's claim: "In the memory of survivors . . . there were no survivors of gassings. And if someone survived a camp, he did not survive the gas chamber. Only in films, as in 'Schindler's List,' could people survive."[11] Unfortunately, this was not a Hollywood production: the baby girl did not die from gassing but rather from the gunshot of a callous guard. Venezia's account reverberates with that told by Dr. Miklos Nyiszli, a prisoner of Auschwitz, who served voluntarily as Dr. Josef Mengele's pathology expert. Nyiszli recounts that among three thousand bodies piled outside the gas chamber, the Sonderkommandos "found a frail young girl alive at the bottom of a pile of corpses."[12] Nyiszli found her "in the throes of a death rattle, her body seized with convulsions." The doctor did everything possible to revive her. Not sure of the outcome, he approached SS-Oberscharführer (SS-Sergeant) Mussfeld and asked him to let the child live. Erich Mussfeld replied, "'There's no way of getting round it . . . the child will have to die.' . . . Half an hour later the young girl was led, or rather carried, into the furnace room hallway, and there Mussfeld sent another in his place to do the job. A bullet in the back of the neck."[13]

The Sephardim were not confined to Auschwitz-Birkenau but were also assigned to several other camps, among them Bergen-Belsen, Belzec, Buchenwald, Chelmno, Ebensee, Janowska, Lodz, Majdanek, Mauthausen, Sobibor, Treblinka, and Warsaw. The stories of brutality were overwhelming, and many involved August Miete, who along with Dr. Josef Mengele was known as The Angel of Death. He appointed three Greek-speaking Jews as translators who were free to move in the camp and had the opportunity to witness the actions of this "brutal mass murderer" in Treblinka. Miete had no qualms about shooting inmates in the back of the neck and burning them in pits or sending them to the gas chambers, extracting gold from their teeth, and cremating the corpses. The weak, sick, and crippled, or those wounded by the SS, were lined up next to a pit and shot.

The female guards were selected as supervisors because of their brutality. They generally belonged to the lower classes and often belonged to the Waffen-SS. Maria Mandel in Auschwitz-Birkenau was infamous for her viciousness. She was responsible for the deaths of over half a million Romani, Jews, and political prisoners. Her preference was selecting children for execution. Irma Grese—known as the Beautiful Beast or the Hyena of Auschwitz—was the most abhorred guard. Her presence inspired terror. She took great pride in torturing and shooting the prisoners at random. Her ferociousness was second only to the ferocity of her dogs. Ilse Koch—the Beast, the Bitch, or the Witch of Buchenwald—was known for torturing and shooting prisoners. Perversely, she had the tattooed portions of the prisoners' bodies skinned after she had them murdered and had these made into "lampshades or book covers. She reportedly liked watching others getting tortured and raped and often encouraged guards to commit such acts in front of her."[14]

All of the Sephardic survivors with whom I spoke reiterated their most enduring and agonizing memories. The brutal systematized tortures were a constant part of their lives in the camps inflicted on them at any time, as either a sport or punishment, for any minor mistake, or for no reason at all.[15] Even more excruciating than the ever-present tortures were hunger, forced labor in the Sonderkommando, and the dreadful medical experiments. Starvation stood beside the inmates like companion-corpses waiting to claim their bodies. The situation became worse; the daily rations of watered-down soup and the piece of coarse black bread hardly satiated their hunger, especially after a long day at hard labor. Sam Profeta said, "In spite of long hours of work, the brutality of the SS, the threats of death, hunger drove us into a state of extreme weakness. 'Estavamos tan flakos ke no valiamos ni para fazer muestro lavoro ni para nada. No eramos mas ke guesos i pelejo. Bushkavamos komo perros kualker koza para komer. Ke importa si lo ke topavamos era limpio o suzio'" (We were so thin that we were of no use for work or for anything else. We were nothing but bones and skin. We searched like dogs for anything to eat; it did not matter if it was clean or dirty).[16] A third Greek Jew, whose name I cannot divulge, with tears in his eyes told me, "Guesos solo mos kedava, ni godrura en la karne. Imajinate ke no avia en estos kuerpos bastante azete para alimentar las flamas en los ornos" (Only bones were left, not even fat in the flesh. Imagine, there hardly was in these bodies enough oil to feed the flames in the furnaces).

The Jews of the Balkans, Greece, and especially the Italian Dodecanese islands of Rhodes and Cos suffered even more, if that can be imagined, than other prisoners. Coming from a mild climate, they were not accustomed to the severe winters—icy wind, frost, and snow—and to the hot summers. In the camps they were further marginalized, even rejected by their Ashkenazi coreligionists, who from the beginning refused to consider them as members of the Jewish faith because they did not speak Yiddish, Polish, or German. Henry Levy, a survivor from Salonika, recalled that the Eastern Jews in Auschwitz-Birkenau had little in common with him. "Because we were strangers," he recounted. "Up to the very end they refused to accept that we were really Jews."[17]

Hermann Langbein notes that the Jews in the camps "came from a great variety of environments; had different professions, philosophies, and language; they did not have the same religious ties." In similar fashion, Benedict Kautsky, who was interned in Dachau, Buchenwald, and Auschwitz III, writes, "Conditions were complicated by the fact that in wartime Jews of many nationalities met in the camps and instead of displaying solidarity felt enmity toward one another." The camp administration favored German Jews primarily because of their linguistic ability. Jews who knew neither German nor a Slavic language, for example, most of those from Greece and Italy, had the hardest time.[18] Isaac Bourla realized that he suffered from not knowing Yiddish, the predominant language spoken after German in Buna, a subcamp of Auschwitz-Birkenau, which later became Auschwitz III. "The majority of these prisoners," Bourla writes, "had come from Poland, Russia, and Lithuania, those countries where the language used by the Jews among themselves was Yiddish. . . . Therefore, with the weight of numbers on their side, these Jews looked down upon the Jews from Greece, Bulgaria, Turkey, parts of France, and anywhere else where Ladino, an offshoot of old Castilian Spanish, and not Yiddish was spoken."[19]

Additionally, from the Ashkenazi perspective, the Sephardim did not look Jewish: their complexion was olive, their hair was dark, and they spoke Hebrew with a different accent. The Ashkenazim treated them in a derogatory manner: spitting at them and calling them filthy Greeks. They accused them of being strangers, dirty, insatiable, and always craving the miserable portions distributed to their fellow inmates. Leon Reuven Cohen noted that the Polish Jews and other northern Ashkenazi Jews called them "Cholera" and "whores" and avoided them except when they needed something.[20] The Ashkenazi *Kapos* were harder on the Sephardim than were the Germans. They called them *Grecko banditos* (Greek bandits). They claimed that there were no such Jews in the world because they were too strong, all tanned by the Thessaloniki sun.

Moïse Rahmani quotes the following testimony by Stella Levi: "Concerning our relations with other Jewish deportees. Of course we did not speak a word of Yiddish or German. The others, in the barracks, could not believe that we were Jewish." She continues,

> —You do not speak Yiddish? What are you?
> —We speak Italian.
> —Then, you are Italians. You are Christians. You are Italians, not Jewish.
> This was terrible. It seemed that animosity reigned. When the Ashkenazi women lit candles for Shabbat, I said, "I will recite the prayers. Perhaps you will realize that we are truly Jewish."
>
> Our Hebrew did not seem to be correct to them, our pronunciation was different, but they would realize that we were Jews indeed. The camp kapo, a Polish Jew, asked us what we were talking about. We told her French and Italian. She then put us with Belgian and French deportees. This saved us.[21]

Years after the end of World War II, Lea Aini, an Israeli author and poet and daughter of a Salonikan survivor, remarks on the "same derogatory phrase" that her father had heard in Auschwitz from "'the Ashkenazic prisoners, *chayes, shvartze chayes*'" (beasts, black beasts). With her knowledge of the suffering and degradation that her father endured both in the camps and subsequently in Israel, when she hears the insult *shvartze chayes*, she says, "'[I]t drives me mad.'" While this might seem to be a single derogatory expression and therefore not significant, it represented to Lea Aini and to other Sephardim the dismissal that they experienced with respect to their suffering in the Holocaust. This single derogatory term encapsulated the "forgotten, ignored Greek Jews and their experiences in the Holocaust."[22] Indeed, in 1968, during my first trip to Israel, I heard similar statements from Sephardim about negative references to them by Ashkenazim, who did not believe that the Sephardim had been in the camps.

From my interviews I learned that survivors were not believed, or worse, were regarded as insane by their children, friends, and neighbors because of the stories they related. Batya Shimony comments, "[I]n the death camp . . . Greek Jews were equal to Ashkenazic Jews in the eyes of the oppressor, but not in the eyes of their Ashkenazic fellow victims." Leah's father, as well as those from the Sephardic communities in Europe, North Africa, and some Arab countries, suffered from the lack of respect for the Sephardim by the

Ashkenazim in the camps and in Israel after the liberation. He reflected, "In the concentration camps, when we came, the Ashkenazic Jews didn't believe we were Jews. . . . 'Nein, nicht' [No, no], they said, there are no such Jews in the world, because we were too strong, all suntanned from the sun [of] Thessaloniki . . . 'Tfu, the Grecos, those Greeks,' the Yiddish-speaking Polish Jews said about us, and we were scared because we thought they were speaking German. . . . We didn't understand a single word the SS hollered, and for that we got beat up, kicked, first by the Germans, then by the Yid. . . . Goyim (Gentiles), they called us, the Ashkenazi prisoners, *chayes, shvartze chayes* (animals, black animals)."[23]

Langbein quotes Henry Bulawko describing "how three Greek Jews in the satellite camp Jaworzno [a subcamp of Auschwitz] chased a dog and stole some bones from him."[24] Bella Ouziel in Auschwitz-Birkenau, recalls, "I remember one [Greek] girl. A German had a dog. He threw—not meat, a bone—and the girl left the march to pick up the bone. And right away, the German shot her, right there, in front of us."[25] Shabetai Hanuka and several Greek Jews who were assigned in 1943–44 to clean the Warsaw Ghetto told how a young man, twenty-five years old, Daniel Marcos, also called Alberto Marcos, was killed for picking a green tomato from a plant. "While holding it in his hand, they shot him, right there, we all of us present. 'De tanta ambre, lo ke se topava se komia'" (From so much hunger, whatever was found, it was eaten).[26]

Sam Profeta recounts, "Azian lo ke azian, las akuzasiones se echavan a mozotros" (No matter what happened, the accusations were cast upon us). Were the Greek Jews the only ones to throw themselves on the ground and eagerly lick the dirty mixture of mud and spilled hot soup, or lap water or other nourishment? No. The inmates in the Pomiechow death camp, starving from hours of digging mass graves, did not act differently. The harsh work, sadistic beatings, disease, cold weather, and unbearable hunger turned the emaciated inmates into dehumanized robots always rummaging garbage dumps for raw potato peelings, rotted cabbage, bones, and discarded soup. In desperation, they would scavenge for grass, dandelions, and flowers.

Henry Levy recounts the following treatment of the Greek Jews by the Eastern Jews: "The Greek Jews were given soup from the top of the container [where only watery soup with skinned potatoes floated] while the Eastern Jews mixed theirs from the bottom, which had the potatoes and skins. Complaining meant beatings and whippings from the same Eastern European Jews. So we kept silent about this injustice. If there was a little soup left at the bottom when the food distribution ended, the Polish-Jewish helper would call the Eastern Jews for seconds. We, the Greeks, got nothing."[27]

Eliezer Sotto (Soto) from Salonika was assigned as a barber in a German barrack. While shaving the commandant, he nicked his ear. The commandant wrote a note to the guard. Sotto was alarmed, "I did not know what the note meant . . . maybe go finish this man. The guard took me back to the camp. He said, 'You come with me. Follow me.' So I followed him and went to the kitchen and he gave the little note to the cook. They gave me a loaf of bread and a piece of salami, which was my tip. But I was afraid because I cut his ear and it was going to end."[28] Eliezer continues, "For a short time I had this barbering job. [Soon] I was working . . . inside a tunnel. They have trains with coal to fill them." One night as he finished one job, he was assigned to another one. He had eaten nothing. He continued: "So the next day to the normal job. I started eating *coal* [my emphasis]. To have something in the stomach . . . to work in the stomach. [There] was no way to explain how a human being can survive. Even at this moment I don't believe myself . . . it's impossible. It was a miracle. . . . Before I didn't know what a miracle was . . . but it was a miracle, I survived those horrible things."[29]

The inmates bartered constantly with one another for food, cigarettes, and clothing, and with the Germans who were eager to obtain the gold removed from the teeth of the corpses before the bodies were cremated. Robbing the food of their fellow prisoners even under fear of being caught and whipped or being taken directly to the gas chamber did not prevent them from trying. When asked about any possibility of obtaining food, a few interviewees stated that many bartered for food or even stole from friends. One person remarked, "Muncho negro paso en los kampos, ma avia posibilidades de topar komida, aun a la eskondida" (A lot of bad things took place in the camps, but there were some possibilities to find food, even in secret). Another survivor interjected, "Ya avia modos de komer, solo kon atension; guay si lo kojian" (There were ways to eat, only with caution; woe if he was caught). Judith Sternberg-Newman, the author of *In the Hell of Auschwitz*, writes that she "saw how inmates stole bread from their dying comrades and ate it even if it was soiled with excrement."[30] She confessed that she pulled a concealed bread ration from under the body of a man who had just died. Elie A. Cohen expressed the situation in which the inmates found themselves: "The will to survive crowds out any other thoughts. The instinct of self-preservation is very strong."[31]

Albert Menasche relates, "[Unfortunate as it was,] it was said that at Lager Dachau III, there had been a case of cannibalism. Every prisoner secretly wished his comrade would die, so he could benefit from his ration. Any feeling of pity or altruism vanished from their hearts. Our beastly instincts came forth in all their ugliness."[32] There are testimonies that cannibalism also took place in other camps, in Belzec, Bergen-Belsen, Dachau, Maydane, Mauthausen, Sobibor, and Treblinka.[33] Jews, but mainly Soviet prisoners of war, who were often deprived of food and water for days went mad with hunger and to survive resorted to cannibalism. Shlomo Venezia remembers that the dog of a German guard of Crematorium II went too close to the barbed-wire fence and was killed. For the German, the death of a dog was a real tragedy—the life of a dog was worth more than the lives of a thousand Jews. "That day the guard took it out on us. . . . He ordered the Russians to stuff the dog. The dog's flesh didn't end up in the garbage; I know that several prisoners ate it. Even my brother took a taste."[34] In desperation the inmates consumed raw flesh from both animal and human corpses. While temporarily satisfying their hunger, they contracted different physical disorders from the consumption of infected flesh: dysentery, deterioration of the brain, bacterial infections that in themselves may have caused death. This situation lasted until the end of the war in Auschwitz, Buchenwald, Mauthausen, and other camps. General Miles Christopher Dempsey, commander of the British Second Army, reported in April 1945 that most of the thousands of men and especially women in Bergen-Belsen had died of starvation: "So terrible was the situation that the prison doctors told General Dempsey's senior medical officer that cannibalism was going on," right up to the liberation of Bergen-Belsen.[35]

Even or perhaps especially in these dire straits, the religious principle of *Pikkuah nefesh*, to save a life, which deals with matters of life and death, provided the moral fiber to an otherwise grisly untenable reality: one must do whatever is necessary to save a life, even if this means eating ritually unfit food in order to survive. Devarim 4:9 commands, "Take heed to thyself, and care diligently of your soul (of your life)."[36] I recall hearing in Rhodes that even the holiness of the Sabbath or the *tanit* (fast) during the Day of Atonement can be overridden in such circumstances: "Dizen muestros rabinos ke segun muestra ley la vida de uno es muy importante; salvar esta vida es komo salvar todo un mundo" (Our rabbis say that according to our Law the life of one individual is very important; saving this one life is like saving the world).

Water was as precious and as scarce as food. There was no water to drink, much less to wash with. As one person told me, "Bivian agua del toilet para amahar la sekia. Munchos bivian sus propria pishada" (They drank water from the toilet in order to quench their thirst. Many drank their own urine). Several Sephardic survivors conveyed the same message: "Sin agua, no mos limpiavamos por semanas i semanas. Goliamos mas negro ke los animales, mas negro ke eyos" (Without water, we did not wash ourselves for weeks and weeks. We smelled worse than the animals, worse than them).[37] Sam Angel, who worked in the munitions factories of Mauthausen and Katowice, states, "Guayi si los guardias mos topavan suzios en los *appell* de la manyana o al salir del lavoro, koza ke no era fasil estar limpio en muestra seksion. Entonses era gritos, haftunas, i nada de komer por akel dia" (Woe if the guards caught us dirty during the morning roll calls or when we left work, which it was not easy to be clean in our section. Then it was screams, beatings, and nothing to eat for the day).[38] In the chapter "The Lagerältester of Buma," Isaac Bourla writes: "Cleanliness was a must in order to avoid having lice. Besides, from time to time there was a cleanliness inspection in the block, usually after we had gone to bed. Either the *blockältester* or the *stubendienst* . . . checked each person's feet and ears. Those inmates who were found to be unclean received several blows from a rubber whip and were ordered to get up and go out into the night and wash."[39]

In supreme irony, the Nazis insisted on cleanliness but did not supply water to the inmates to clean their clothes or wash themselves. When the newcomers entered the underground dressing rooms, they were faced with signs in several languages posted on the pillars declaring:

> Clean is good!
> Lice can kill!
> Wash yourself!

Admittedly, the signs were posted with the intent of tricking the prisoners into undressing with the belief that they would be taking a shower.

The Kanada Kommando (Canada Command) was regarded as a privileged group, the assignment to which was especially sought after by prisoners. Their tasks were to meet the trains, and to collect, sort, and store the valuables stripped from the new arrivals before repacking and sending these on to Germany. Even though it was forbidden under penalty of torture or death to sequester valuables, the members of the Kanada Kommando were able to smuggle some of the food and other valuables—cigarettes, gold, jewelry, currency, and clothing—for themselves or to barter with other inmates and Nazis for bread and some personal items. The SS and German guards did not hesitate to take advantage of the spoils. Laurence Rees in his chapter on corruption in the camps writes, "The temptations of '*Canada*' were irresistible—both for the prisoners working there and for the SS. As a result, stealing from '*Canada*' was commonplace."[40] A Sephardic member of "Canada" told me that stealing from the incoming deportees and those who were already dead was not only for his own survival and for bartering but also to help his fellow inmates. "Esto no se puede konsiderar rovar, es bivir en una situasion desgrasiada. Era bivir o morir" (This cannot be considered stealing; it is living in a miserable situation. It was to live or die). Rees comments, "Not surprisingly, however, it was individual members of the SS who personally benefited far more from 'Canada.'" Linda [Libusha] Breder, a member of "Canada," said, "'The Germans kept accumulating wealth. . . . Death was the only thing that was left for us. . . . All of them [the SS men] used to steal. They came there because there was no other place like that, where they got everything.'"[41]

Heinrich Himmler in his October 1943 speech to approximately fifty senior SS figures declared that the riches taken from the Jews were delivered "to the Reich, to the State," and that they did not keep anything for themselves. His SS members, he affirmed, were both hard and "incorruptible." SS-Untersturmführer Fritz Berman boasted, "We are taking from the Jewish pigs about one [billion] Reichsmarks, which I myself carried to Berlin."[42] Grabbing the possessions was not only for nationalistic purposes.

When I asked Leon Reuven Cohen if there was any time that the Germans tried to treat them more humanely, he replied, "Kuando les davamos metalis presiozos komo oro, plata, i de todo lo bueno ke tomavamos de los muertos. Si no se lo davamos era haftunas. Los mazalbashos eran ladrones, i ansi se yenavan las aldikeras" (When we gave them precious metals such as gold, silver [meaning platinum], and all the valuables that we used to take from the dead. If we did not give it to them, it was the whip. The cursed ones were thieves, and this way they stuffed their pockets).[43]

SS-Obersturmbannführer Rudolf Höss reported that what the Germans took from Jews who came from the West was of great value, "precious stones worth thousands of dollars, priceless gold and platinum watches set with diamonds, rings, necklaces of pure rarity. Currency from all countries amounted to thousands of pounds. . . . Eichmann told me on one occasion, that the jewelry and currency [were] sold in Switzerland."[44] Höss also admitted "that 'the treasures brought in by the Jews gave rise to unavoidable difficulties for the camp itself because the SS men who worked for him 'were not always strong enough to resist the temptation provided by these valuables which lay within such easy reach.'"[45] Stealing from the confiscated goods extended to Höss and his subordinate Oskar Gröning, who worked in the Economic Agency, as well as to all ranks of the German staff. "According to the estimate of Paul Bendel, a French prisoner, 'the SS plundered 17 tons of gold from the time the crematoria were erected until November 1944.'"[46] Miklos Nyiszli also confirms that in the area where the prisoners undressed, "the goods were there waiting to be taken [and that] the SS officials received jewelry, leather goods, fur coats, silks and fine shoes. Not a week went by without their sending some packages home. In the packages that had been sent, one found, besides the luxury items already mentioned, tea, coffee, chocolate, and canned goods by the hundreds."[47]

Of course, the stealing of Jewish property was not limited to the camps. For example, on December 23, 1943, the SS declared a *Judenaktion* (Jewish action) in Salonika, which resulted in the confiscation of thousands of Greek drachmas, US dollars, and Swiss francs from the Jewish Community. One wonders whether all these funds were turned over to Nazi Germany. Also in question was the disposition of "Devisenzählung [currency counting] of foreign currency, gold and jewelry belonging to Jewish Spanish Nationals being deported to Bergen-Belsen confiscated by the German Authorities one day before the departure of the 19th Convoy." Did Dieter Wisliceny, responsible for collecting all the valuables, keep some for himself? According to Hagouel, "David Gattegno was allowed to take out a total of 5000 Swiss Francs with him." Wisliceny reported only thirty. Was Gattegno or Wisliceny able to conceal the rest of the money? Hagouel reports, "Wisliceny along with the rest of his detachment, profited from the loot and reported altered tallies to the Reich Finance Authorities." Thus, Wisliceny and the rest of the perpetrators were murderers and thieves.[48]

The most dreaded assignment was that of the Sonderkommandos, inmates assigned to special work units, variously responsible for meeting the newly arrived; escorting them to the supposed showers and helping them to get undressed as quickly as possible; removing the dead bodies from the gas chambers after the SS killed them; combing through the corpses for valuables, including gold teeth and even prostheses; cutting the women's hair; grinding the bones to dust after the cremation, disposing the ashes of the corpses in ditches or throwing them into the Vistula River, or collecting them for asphalt. Their final duty was to clean the gas chamber for the next shipment of people to be exterminated. Leon Reuven Cohen explained to me in an interview that the Nazis killed the members of Sonderkommando every three or four months so that by their deaths the world would not be made aware of the atrocities that were perpetrated in the killing machines. Those Sonderkommandos who miraculously escaped the "maldichos ornos" (cursed ovens) were witnesses to the massacre of babies shoved into the scorching ovens or thrown into the ditches while still alive. How many times they helplessly watched the officers take great pleasure "in saving a bullet" by grabbing a child by a foot and bashing his or her head against the wall.

Some inmates envied the Sonderkommandos. Through their ghoulish tasks of preparing the new arrivals for death, the Sonderkommandos had access to their property. Albert Menasche, who was not part of the Sonderkommandos, described their tormented situation as follows: "They were generally chosen from among the newcomers or selected from the ranks at random. What could they have done?" As "the most feared Commando in the camp,"[49] the Sonder had certain advantages, such as access to decent food, clean clothing, straw mattresses, water, soap and towels.[50] There were disadvantages as well: they were housed in the very interior of the camp without any communication with the outside. Menasche expands on this: "For if in the other Com-

Figure 2.1. *Life in Auschwitz*, oil on canvas by Alberto Sarfati. Courtesy of the Safarti family. Photograph by Rosemary Lévy Zumwalt.

mandos there was one chance in a thousand to escape, in the *Sonder* there was no hope whatsoever. . . . In short, being assigned to the *Sonder* was the equivalent of being cut off from the living world by imprisonment; of working unceasingly at a horrible task, and finally of being gassed and burned. . . . Evidently, if any *Sonder* prisoner by chance had been able to escape his cruel fate, he would have had much to say regarding the shocking, shocking sadism and atrocities committed on pregnant women and dying old men by these insane monsters of the S.S."[51] Hardly aware of the situation in the crematoria, a good number of inmates would have accepted an offer to join the Sonderkommandos. Not part of them, the prisoners-at-large resented the status of the Sonderkommandos and accused them of collaborating in the brutal killings of the Jewish people and of being worse murderers than the Nazis.

Several people have puzzled over the actions and attitudes of the Sonderkommandos. Were they dehumanized, ruthless, arrogant, and rude? Or were they possessed of an understanding, and were they caring? In Hermann Langbein's *People in Auschwitz*, Lucie Adelsberger remarks, "These were no longer human countenances but distorted, demented faces." After their escape, Rudolph Vrba and Alfred Wetzler wrote, "The other inmates have little contact with them, if only because of the terrible smell that emanates from them. They are always filthy, totally unkempt and seedy, and exceedingly brutal and ruthless. It is not unusual for one man simply to beat another to death." Seweryna Szmaglewska notes, "Sonderkommando—drunken Jews who treat their Jewish brethren who are destined to die just as the SS men do. A sad example of human aberration in the blazing jungle that is Birkenau." Yet she adds, "Even so, members of the same Sonderkommando venture to get close to the electric wire and bring the Jewish men and women in the camp last greetings from their relatives before they entered the crematorium. Sometimes they bring along some mementos, photos, or letters as a last sign of life."[52]

A survivor from occupied Bulgaria, who requested to remain anonymous, categorically stated that it was not enough for the Sonderkommandos to make known how difficult it was for them to go through day after day "sufriendo en los maldichos templos de la muerte" (suffering in the cursed temples of death). He queried, if the Sonderkommandos truly suffered from nervous disorders and could not stand the horror of seeing the murder of their families and friends and the destruction of complete Jewish communities, "Why didn't they follow the example of so many of their fellow prisoners, the true heroes, who chose to throw themselves against the electrified fence, into the open pits, and into the ovens?" And he continues, "Para mi suisidarse uviera sido mas desente ke matar tantos desdichados" (For me suicide would have been more decent than killing so many wretched people). As a matter of fact, many Jewish prisoners—Ashkenazi and Sephardi—no longer capable of working or tolerating the viciousness in the camps, chose death to escape a miserable future.

In her works on political theory, Hannah Arendt focused almost exclusively on the themes of conscience, morality, and evil. With respect to the Holocaust, she placed blame on the Jewish Councils, the prisoners, and the Sonderkommandos. Arendt accused the Sonderkommandos of participating in the extermination process and of being traitors to their own people. Greif states that Arendt "condemned them for having committed these crimes in order to escape death."[53] David Joroff quotes her as saying, "Each individual is co-responsible for every wrong, every injustice and every crime committed in his presence or with his knowledge . . . if he fails to do whatever he can to prevent it, he too is guilty."[54]

Jacob Robinson criticizes Hannah Arendt's claims that the Greek Jews in the Sonderkommando "operated the gas chambers and crematoria." Robinson emphasizes, "In no case did any member of the Sonderkmmando operate the gas chambers. The killing centers were under the exclusive supervision of the SS."[55] Gershon Scholem, other scholars, and major Jewish public figures posit that Arendt was in no position to be the moral voice of the camps.

Those of us who were exiled from our countries in the late 1930s, and who lost all of our belongings and lived a precarious existence in a foreign country, did not suffer the consequences of disobeying the diabolic commands of sadistic Nazis. The evil done in the camps, with few exceptions, should be blamed on the perpetrators; they are the ones to be judged, not those who were the victims. Some, including Arendt, have accused the inmates of being immoral, but on what basis? How can one attribute evil to the victims of Nazi Germany? Who will dare be the judge, and on what will the decisions be based—on religious beliefs, on political ideas, on the will of the people, or on personal biases?

Shlomo Venezia states that the mistreatment of children by the vicious SS officers was an act that traumatized especially the members of the Sonderkommando who were responsible under penalty of death to dispose of the corpses.[56] Shaul Chazan, a Greek Jew and member of the Sonderkommando, related how a young SS tore a little baby from his mother's arms and in cold blood killed him and then killed the mother also. These ghastly acts were, Chazan emphasized, never-ending. He witnessed the infamous SS-Hauptscharführer (officer in charge) Otto Moll, supervisor of the gas chambers, take a baby from his mother before the mother was to be gassed, give him candy, hug him, and then throw him into the fire (pit) alive.[57] According to Chazan, Otto Moll regularly pushed people alive into the open pits. In one case, he ordered a naked woman who was sitting on a body to jump into the pit and sing. To extract information, he would interrogate the suspected individual first by torturing—flogging, suspended by the arms, sitting for hours in a squatting position—and then "pour gasoline to the waist, set him on fire, order him to run to the wires, and then shoot him." For Moll and his henchmen, it was a sadistic game. Chazan also saw the excruciating slaughter of large numbers of newcomers. When asked if he had seen any group in particular, he replied, "Yes, once two hundred children aged eight to ten came. They knew they were about to be killed. Someone had told them. They brought them in. It was especially terrifying and ghastly."[58] Again he saw a truckload "of old, sick and disabled people" that were dumped "straight into the pit—while the people were still alive!" He continued: "I saw this twice—once on my first day of work with the Sonderkommando and again, when other transports came. The people were thrown into the 'bunker' and burned alive. I also remember a Greek Jew from the Sonderkommando who jumped into the fire. He saw what was going on and leaped into the pit. That was that."[59]

He, as well as several of his friends, wanted "to live until the day they die." They wanted to live no matter what, yet at times it was impossible to bear the constant tragedies they witnessed. Still, realizing that death was a better alternative, they thought to inhale the gas when the door of the gas chamber opened. They believed that this was the ultimate sight, but it was not.

Those among the surviving Sephardic Sonderkommandos offered quite a different view of their actions. Indeed, even those supposedly dehumanized by their long torment in the crematoria expressed their reaction to such horrible situations: "A eyos se les rompian el korason de ver tal krimen, tal maldad kometida kontra estas almas inosentes, estas almas sin pekado" (For them their heart would break upon seeing such crime, such evil committed against these innocent souls, against these souls without any sin). But there was mundane callousness as well. I recall an interview with Leon Reuven Cohen, who spoke about his memory of taking a short break: "A friend of mine from Salonika and I would rest our heads on the heap of dead bodies [piled] in a hangar waiting to be disposed of and thus ate our lunch." Amazed, I asked, "How could you have done this?" Sadly, with tears in his eyes, he replied, "These were the lucky ones. They would not suffer any longer. It was the children, the babies, the innocent who were killed without a bullet, without even being gassed, just a broken head. What did they do wrong? Why did they deserve such an inhuman end? Who could have committed such a barbaric act? These children were the ones to be pitied, to cry over. The corpses were at rest. We ourselves were the living and waiting and praying to be put in the ovens. Maybe, maybe then we could have found some rest. God help us." At that moment both of us ceased speaking and fell into long silence, and the interview had to be postponed.

I found similar sentiments expressed in the "Trial of Eichmann," in the *Nizkor Project*. Leon Wells, a member of the Death Brigade—Sonderkommando 1005—located at the Janowska concentration camp in Poland. He testified, "After [they collected] the bodies, they put the bones into a bone-grinding machine, and then they would make the ashes disappear by tossing them into the air." The following questioning ensued.

> Q. Were you fed while you were working? Did you get any food?
> A. We got a lot of food.
> Q. Where did you eat? Among the corpses?
> A. On the corpses.
> Q. On the corpses themselves?
> A. Yes, on the corpses.[60]

As heartbreaking as these testimonies are, I don't think that one can take the coarse remarks as a reflection of how Wells felt. Isaac Bourla explained that there was no room for the Sephardi Sonderkommandos to loathe the inmates in the camp; on the contrary, they all felt an ever-lasting fear of the unknown.[61]

Save for a few, such as Nyiszli, the members of the Sonderkommando deserve our understanding and empathy. They had little choice but to accept the miserable position, other than to forfeit their lives. Without exception, those with whom I spoke told of the first experience in the crematoria, how they had turned into horrified spectators at seeing their loved ones—mothers, fathers, siblings, friends, *los inosentes krios* (the innocent children)—forced into the antechambers to undress, herded into the gas chambers to be gassed, pulled from the gas chambers to be piled one on top of the other, soiled with their own blood and vomit, and shoved into the furnaces as hunks of raw meat to be burned into ashes, even as some were still alive. "No eramos siegos; nos moriamos kon eyos . . . sin poder salvarlos" (We were not blind; we died along with them . . . unable to save them). They were torn between throwing themselves into the ovens and onto the electrified wires, which many did, and choosing to live to tell the world the story of the camps. They were aware!

Salmen Lewental, a member of the Sonderkommando who participated in the revolt in the crematoria on October 7, 1944, wrote in his diary, which was "literally unearthed from the ashes" of Auschwitz-Birkenau in 1962, "Why do you do such ignoble work?" He answered the unanswerable: "And here is the crux . . . of our Kommando, which I have no intention to defend as a whole. I must speak the truth here, that some of that group have in the course of time so entirely lost themselves that we ourselves were simply ashamed. They simply forgot what they were doing . . . and with time . . . they got so used to it that it was even strange to weep and to complain; that . . . such normal, average . . . simple and unassuming men . . . of necessity got used to everything so that these happenings make no more impression on them. Day after day they stand and look on how tens of thousands of people are perishing and [do] nothing."[62]

While it has been said time and again that the inmates locked in the crematoria behaved as robots in a monstrous setting, and that they were totally unsympathetic to the suffering of their coreligionists, my investigation proved the contrary. In many instances, they provided support to the newly arrived by helping the old and young undress prior to their entering the gas chambers. They tried to calm and comfort them. They walked to the doors holding their hands. On October 13, 1944, Ya'akov Gabai saw two of his cousins among the four hundred being processed to die. To make their deaths as quick and painless as possible, he recounts, "I told them the truth, and told them where to be [near the ceiling] in the gas chamber, so they would die immediately without suffering."[63] How often, with tear-filled eyes, the stokers recited the Kaddish (mourner's prayer) as they placed the cold and twisted bodies into the furnaces.

When I asked some Sonderkommandos to comment on the accusations of their own people, they responded emotionally:

> Kualo estan avlando? No eramos kompletamente dezaumanizados, insensivles. Izimos todo lo posivle para ayudarlos, i no lo meresiamos. Ken savia la dolor ke sentiamos por kada uno de eyos? (What are they talking about? We were not completely dehumanized, insensitive. We did everything possible to assist them, and we did not deserve it [the accusations]. Who knew the pain that we felt for each one of them?)
>
> Ken tenia la mas chika idea de las lagrimas de sangre ke vertiamos sin ke los maldichos lo supieran? (Who had the least idea of the bitter—bloody—tears we shed without the knowledge of the cursed ones?)
>
> No eramos siegos. Veiamos la dolor en los ojos de los malogrados. (We were not blind. We saw the pain in the eyes of the ill-fated.)
>
> Era mas negro kuando venia de los ninyos sin pekado. (It was worse when it came to the innocent children.)

Indeed, recollections of the children caused the most pain to the survivors. One such example is the heart-rending episode that took place in the antechamber when a Sonderkommando was prevented from helping a young boy. The little boy's eight-year-old sister cried out in an angry voice, "Go away, you Jewish murderer! Don't put your hand covered in Jewish blood on my sweet brother. I am his good mother now, and he will die in my arms."[64]

For their own survival the Sephardim stuck together, protected one another, and risked their lives to save one of their own. Leon Reuven Cohen, who participated in the revolt, felt shame upon seeing women naked, especially one, Clara, whom he knew from Salonika. When he tried to help by giving her a piece of cloth to cover herself, two German soldiers each administered 250 lashes on his buttocks: "Mi trazero era preto. No se komo pude bivir" (My bottom was black: I do not know how I survived).[65] Aharon Rosa, known as the Father of the Greeks, was the only Jew working in the SS infirmary at Auschwitz. "He risked his own life assisting his countrymen by smuggling out medical supplies." During the infamous and murderous "Marcha a la muerte" (Death March), Shlomo Venezia, who died on September 30, 2012, saved Jacko Maestro's brother. "The boy who was weak and vomiting blood surely would have been left on the spot to die and be eaten by animals or been shot by the SS." Venezia and a friend carried him while he recovered.[66] There were others who also sacrificed their lives for their fellow inmates.

Leon Reuven Cohen told me of their compassion for their brethren. He reminded me of a previous conversation we'd had on the subject: "En jeneral no eramos completamente animales, deskorasonados, ya saviamos de muestra terrivle pozision, pero teniamos ke ayudar" (In general we were not completely animals, heartless; we knew of our unbearable situation, but we had to help). Comparing the Sonderkommando to the other sections, he said:

> Esta seksion no se puede komparar ni kon *geinam*. Lo ke tuvimos ke sufrir ayi no puede uno imajinar. Es verdad, mos davan bueno de komer, mos davan de bever. Si, teniamos otros privilejos, ma para kualo? Los ijos de Malach Hamavet mos destruyeron el espiritu. Eramos esklavos en una faktoria de matansa: matansa para los muestros. No era fasil para mozotros ver i bivir las trajedias de kada dia, trajedias ke oy dia, anyos despues ke okurieron no podemos olvidar. Lo ke izimos ayi rompio el alma i el korason aun oy dia.
>
> (This section cannot be compared even to hell. No one can imagine what we had to endure. It is true, they fed us well and they gave us drinks [alcoholic beverages]. Indeed, we had also other privileges, but what for? The children of the Angel of Death destroyed our spirit. We were slaves in a factory for murder: the slaying of our own. It was not easy for us to see and live the tragedies that took place every day, tragedies that even today, years after they occurred, we cannot forget. What we did there broke the spirit and the heart, even today).

As was customary for me, I revisited a crucial point in my second interview with Leon Reuven Cohen. In 1984, once again in his barbershop in Givatayim, Israel, I asked if he could comment further on the continuous criticism of the internees regarding the members of the Sonderkommandos. Leon still maintained that the inmates, too, suffered equally, if not more, the atrocities of the Germans: "In some bizarre way we were better treated, but our agony was unbearable." He still insisted that the prisoners throughout the camp suffered to a greater extent under the leadership of the *Obercapos* and their sadistic subordinates who, either for sport or for cruelty, abused them at will. As Albert Menasche declared and Leon confirmed, the SS, the guards, and anyone in command had the power of life and death over the inmates.

> Lavoravan duro dodje oras al dia, kon kaftonas, matansas, kon poka komida. No les era fasil karear grandes pezos en sus flakos ombros. Guay si kedavan un minuto sin lavorar o si se kaivan de kanserio, ayi estavan los desgrasidados guardias kon sus palos gritando *schnell*, suzios djudios. I los *Kapos* ke no mos konsideravan djudios eran mas krueles. Mas difisil era para los muestros ke no entendian las ordenes en aleman. A estos se les davan mas en la kavesa, en el kuerpo, se les rompian los guesos, i al fin de la tortura o los mandavan al ospital o a kemar. No savian de un minuto al otro, de una ora a la otra, de un dia al otro sus proprio destino. Munchos no sovrebivieron los dolientes palos i el duro lavoro.

> (They worked hard twelve hours a day, with beatings, killings, with little food. It was not easy for them to carry heavy weights [rocks] on their weak shoulders. Woe if they stopped working for a minute or if they dropped with fatigue, there were the dreadful guards with their whips yelling, "Hurry up, you dirty Jews." And the *Kapos* [Ashkenazi Polish] who did not consider us Jews were harsher. It was more difficult for our own [the Sephardim] who did not understand the orders given in German. They were beaten more on the head, all over the body, they would break their bones, and at the end of the torture they either sent them to the hospital or to be burned. They did not know from one minute to another, from one hour to another, from one day to the other what their future would be. Many did not survive the harsh beatings and grueling work.)[67]

When asked if there was any difference between him, as a survivor of the Sonderkommando, and the other survivors from Auschwitz, Shlomo Venezia gave a more balanced answer. Both groups suffered. "Yes, I think so, even if I know that saying so hurts some people's feelings. The other survivors certainly suffered from cold and hunger more than I did, but they weren't constantly in contact with the dead. This vision, day after day, of all those victims who had been gassed. . . . The fact of seeing all those groups arriving at the crematoria and entering without hope was truly terrible to see. If I say that the experience of being in the Sonderkommando weighed much more heavily, this was because I had occasion, in Melk and Ebensee, to share the common experience of other deportees."[68]

Some survivors maintain that the Sonderkommandos should have followed the example of the Greek Jews who gave their own lives by refusing to serve in the "Chambers of Death." This act of supreme courage was listed in the *Kalendarium* compiled by the Auschwitz-Birkenau State Museum and, as Langbein notes, serves as a reminder of the heroism that "all too often remained unnoticed."[69] In various accounts, the Greek Jews are listed as having come from Corfu and Athens. In *The Illusion of Safety*, Michael Matsas states that those heroic men, who chose death rather than serve in the Sonderkommando, were "four hundred young Jews, former stevedores of Salonika's port."[70] Steven Bowman recounts the Germans needed extra personnel to handle the arrival of Hungarian Jews, all of whom were destined for the crematorium, and they selected the Greek Jews for the task. "At least four hundred Greeks [Jews] from the Corfu and Athens transport [of June 20] were ordered [for work] in the Sondercommando. Now something truly unusual happened. These four hundred demonstrated that in spite of the barbed wire and the lash they were not slaves but human beings. With rare dignity, the Greeks refused to kill the Hungarians! They declared that they preferred to die themselves first. Sadly enough, they did. The Germans saw to that. But what a demonstration of courage and character these Greek peasants had given. A pity the world does not know more about them."[71] Michael Molho also records this act of heroism: "In May 1944 several transports from Greece arrived in the camp; from one of the first transports, 320 men were chosen to serve in the crematoria. They followed the *Kapo*. They, as well as one hundred young men from Athens who were also chosen to work in the crematoria, suddenly realizing the true nature of the place where they found themselves and of their role, refused to cooperate. The Nazi discipline did not tolerate the rebellion: promptly the SS surrounded and shot them on the spot. Some were simply wounded. Dead or alive, they were all thrown into the mouth of the crematorium."[72]

Even after the liberation, the allegations against the Sonderkommandos continued. Shlomo Venezia writes, "I heard some absurd rumors about what was supposed to have happened in the Sonderkommando with dead women. But these are just lies, sick rumors initiated by people trying to undermine and discredit the men working in the Sonderkommando. I never heard anything like that during the eight months I spent there."[73]

I inquired about this allegation of the sexual desecration of female corpses by men in the Sonderkommando. One survivor with whom I spoke, and who requested anonymity, categorically denied it: "There were too many rumors all around us; these were never proven. The accusations persisted. We who saw so much tragedy could not have performed in such a despicable manner. Furthermore, this would have been the last preoccupation of the Sonderkommandos; it would have been degrading to the memory of those just exterminated." I then asked him if any sexual affairs took place among the inmates in the larger camp. He replied, "No. Not among us." He then referred me to Daniel Bennahmias's recollection of a rumor that it was the practice of the Germans to have the tureens of soup heavily laced with bromide in order to suppress the "sexual appetite" of the inmates. Ben Stern also related to me, "The Germans added antistimulants in soups in order to abate the desire for sex. I later heard that the women did not want sex for four years."[74] "How about men?" I asked. Ben was not aware of any men who desired sex.

During our interview in Brussels on July 23, 1984, I asked Violette Fintz if she knew of any such incidents. She shook her head, "No." She continued, "Not among our people [from Rhodes]." Violette then recalled, "In the morning there was a barrel with green water in which the Germans added [a substance]; some of the people who drank the water had blisters on the mouth, felt feverish and weak. They used to say that it was used to sterilize us." I then asked her if they lost sexual desire. Her one-word response was "Yes." Then she added, "Ambiertos, lavorandu komu aznus, abuzadus noche i dia, no saviendu el futuro, ken pensava en esto" (Hungry, working like jackasses, abused night and day, not knowing what the future held in store for us, who thought about this).

As usual, I persisted. "Violette, were there not any improper incidents between individuals?" Again she denied it. However, some minutes later, she looked at me and said, "Isaac, I recall a case that took place in my barrack. . . . We had a certain gorgeous young lady from an upstanding family who sang and danced the bolero. [She was] from Rhodes. She lived in our barrack. The *Kapo* Rahela, a Polish Jew, fell in love with her. She made Luna dance the bolero naked with veils, which made her more sexually tantalizing. Some time later, they took her away and we never saw her again. There were many claims. I heard that Luna's sister who lives here in Brussels say, 'She did not feel well, asked to be taken to the infirmary, and was never seen again.'" Violette continued, "We never knew what truly took place. Ma nada entre ombres kon mujeres" (But nothing between men and women).

During my second interview with Leon Cohen, the question dealing with the attitude of the Sonderkommandos in the camp came up. Leon gave the following response: "Eyos fueron forsados a kometer terivles aksiones o perder sus vidas. No lo kerian, ma ke podian azer?" (They were forced to commit terrible actions or lose their lives. They did not want to do it but what could they have done?). After a pause, Leon, in deep thought, added,

> I mozoros, no fuimos ovligados? Kual era la diferensia? Dainda oy mizmo no podemos kitar de los ojos lo ke pasava en estos krueles krematorios. Bivimos, sin bivir. Pertenesiamos al mundo de los muertos. Kuantos de mozotros se echaron bivos en la boka de los fuegos. I a kuantos de mozotros mos kemaron en poko tiempo.
>
> (How about us, weren't we forced? What was the difference? Even today we cannot erase from our eyes what took place in these cruel crematoria. We lived, without living. We belonged to the world of the dead. How many of us threw ourselves alive in the mouth of the fire [crematoria]. And how many of us they burned in a short time.)

Survivors of the Sonderkommando defended themselves against accusations and rumors by countering that others were also guilty: Didn't they steal food and clothing from other inmates, especially from those who were dead? Didn't they behave inhumanely toward others for their own benefit? Didn't some of the women fraternize with the *Kapos*, even with the SS, in order to survive? Didn't some build roads to help the army in its futile war? Didn't some work for I. G. Farben Industries, providing synthetic rubber and fuel for the German army? Didn't they work in the munitions factories that supported the German war machine? Didn't some Jewish doctors, such as Miklos Nyiszli, volunteer to assist the infamous Josef Mengele in his merciless experiments? Well, didn't they?

Langbein quotes Krystina Zywulaska, an Ashkenazi, who addressed similar questions to a member of the Sonderkommando. Zywulaska was drawn to his intelligent demeanor. How, she queried, was he "able to do such work day after day"? Just as her Sephardi counterpart had responded, she also replied with irritation: "Do you people think that I volunteered for this work? What was I to do? . . . Do you think that those who work in a munitions factory had a much nobler occupation? Or the girls who sort the things in Canada so they can be taken to Germany? . . . Do you think that the members of the Sonderkommando are monsters? I tell you, they are like the others, only much unhappier."[75] They shared together the reality of living and dying in hell.

3

The Revolt of October 7, 1944

The contributions of the Sephardim in the planning and execution of the Revolt of October 7, 1944, in Auschwitz-Birkenau have been scarcely mentioned in the accounts of the Ashkenazim, or in the diaries left buried in the grounds of Auschwitz, except the one written by the Sephardi Marcel Nadjari. This revolt involved intricate planning, sequestering of gunpowder, and complex coordination and communication between Ashkenazi and Sephardi inmates—all done in the strictest of secrecy. Yet Ashkenazi survivors and scholars who have written about this aspect of the Holocaust have given credit almost exclusively to Eastern European Jews. Were it not for the published memoirs and oral interviews of Sephardic survivors and the work of Georges Didi-Huberman's *Images in Spite of All*, recognition of their participation in the revolt would have been lost. The revolt instigated by the prisoners in the camp at large and those working in the crematoria was set off by the courageous actions of the Greek Jews who in their fight against a powerful enemy were mainly abandoned by the non-Jewish Polish partisans and the Ashkenazi leaders in the camp and in the crematoria.

NUMBERING SYSTEM AND TERMINOLOGY FOR BUILDINGS

In order to understand the Revolt of October 7, 1944, one must know the numbering systems of the crematoria and the terminology for buildings and job assignments. Only after reading the "Sonderkommando Revolt—Auschwitz—Birkenau, 7 October 1944" was I able to clarify the German numbering style. In the German (old) system, Crematorium I was located inside the main camp of Auschwitz, which was built prior to the construction of Birkenau. When Crematorium I was immobilized in 1943, the Germans continued with the numbering system for the crematoria in Birkenau. Thus, following the German system, there were five crematoria, the first [I] in Auschwitz with II–V located in Birkenau. The majority of the Sephardic survivors, who arrived after the construction of Birkenau and who therefore did not have any knowledge of the crematorium in the main camp, designated the crematoria in Birkenau as 1–4. For historical accuracy, I will designate the crematorium with the Sephardic in Arabic numerals, and the German/old system in Roman numerals, i.e., 1 [II] to 4 [V].[1]

Additional matters add to the confusion. Some people refer to a crematorium without indicating which numbering system they have used. In their comments on certain groups of individuals (Ashkenazi, Sephardi, Polish) or events (labor, escape, uprising), scholars and survivors sometimes give no specifics about the people involved or about the location or time of the action. In other instances, the scholars and survivors place people in different locations and designate events as occurring at different times. Legitimate confusion arises from the fact that specific individuals were, in fact, assigned to multiple locales. For instance, Leon Reuven Cohen was placed for a few days in A-II, quarantine for men; then assigned to Bunker 2, known as the White House; in Crematorium 4; and finally, in Crematorium 2. Shlomo Venezia was placed in A-II, quarantine for men; in Crematorium 3 as a *knochen* (bone collector, responsible for removing bodies from the gas chambers); and in Bunker 2, the White House. Marcel Nadjari also was transferred to several locales. From A-II, quarantine for men, he and 150 Greek Jews were sent to Block 13, from which reputedly no one save Nadjari emerged alive; and then he and eighty Greek Jews moved for a short time to Crematorium 1. Later, Nadjari was assigned to the *auskleideraum* (disrobing room) of Crematorium 2. The rest of Nadjari's Greek inmates—among them Moise, Aaron, Vico, Brudo, and Isaac Baruch—were sent to Crematorium 4.

According to Nadjari's account, the Greek Jews were present in all crematoria. Originally they were separated into four groups: 100 went to Crematorium 1; 100 to Crematorium 2; some 400 went to Crematoria 3 and 4; approximately 600 to the Bunkers; and 11 to the trenches, where they dug ditches—one of the worst jobs of all. "One day, an order came for all the Greeks to work at Bunker 2 by the trenches. In charge were Moll [not a man, not an animal, but a monster] and the *Kapo*. . . . That evening they brought approximately 4,000 Hungarian Jews to the bunker. After poisoning them, group after group, they threw them through the back door into the trenches."[2] Nadjari, who was assigned to Crematorium 2, described the haunting terror of their experiences and how heartbreaking it was watching the Nazis savor the excruciating spectacle.

During my interviews with survivors, I tried to ascertain the tasks they were forced to perform and the locales to which they were assigned. Often they took their time to recall where they were at a certain time. One of them said,

> No saviamos donde estavamos, mos miniavan de un lugar a otro en dias, en oras. Un momento estavamos en el bloko 1 i en poko tiempo en el kuarten. Una vez lavoravamos en un echo, i otra vez, ken save?
>
> (We did not know where we were; they moved us from one place to another in days, in hours. One moment we were in Block I and in a short time in the fourth. At one time we worked on a certain job, and at another, who knows?)

As further complication, several authors and survivors used different terminology for job classifications and different numbering systems for physical units. One of the first to write about the details of the camp, Albert Menasche, attempted to clarify the location of the different *Unterkunf* [*t*] (quarters) by drawing his own diagrams. While the two diagrams are important, the terminology he used to refer to the structures is inconsistent with that used by others.[3]

Camp or Lager

In an attempt to clarify, and thus to lessen the confusion arising from the use of different terminology for buildings and sites in the camps, I suggest that the following designations be used: *camp* or *Lager* for the larger division, followed by *block*, and then *barrack*. Thus, *Konzentrationlager*, *camp*, or *Lager* is used when referring to the concentration camp as a unit, a complex—Auschwitz I (*Stammlager*, main camp), Auschwitz II (Birkenau), and Auschwitz III (Monowitz-Buna, which housed inmates assigned to work in various industrial companies).

Block

Albert Menasche applies designations for places in various ways. On page 42, he uses the term *Lager* incorrectly for *block*. "I lived in this lager [D-II] for approximately seventeen months." On page 40, he incorrectly designates the plan as "General Plan of the Lagers (Birkenau)," when more accurately it should be named "General Plan of the Blocks (Birkenau)." For instance, Menasche uses the following terminology, "Lager A-I (Women's Lager and Hospital Lager for Women) . . . Lager A-II (Quarantine) . . . Lager B-II (Czech Lager) . . . Lager D-II (Workers Lagers)."[4] They all should be designated as blocks. On page 44, Menasche gives a plan of Lager D, which should have been named Block D, formed by rows of barracks, i.e., Administration, Kanada, Kitchen, Tailors, Zonder, W.C., all surrounded by an electric fence. Outside the block was correctly designated as "SS. Barracks."

In *Hitler's Death Camps*, Konnilyn G. Feig designates the barracks as *Camps*. Abraham Dragon refers to them as "Special camps," and Greif as "sectors of

Birkenau."[5] Marcello Pezzetti refers to the blocks as zones, which in turn were subdivided into several sectors (also called "camps").[6]

Barracks

Several barracks formed a block; for example, Block F-IIe, the hospital, was composed of about twenty barracks.[7] However, several inmates denoted barracks as blocks; for example, Block IX and Block XI (*Sonder*) should be Barracks IX and Barracks XI.[8]

"The Construction of the Camp," as detailed in 2018 on the website of the Auschwitz-Birkenau State Museum, clarifies the foregoing with respect to blocks. It explains the division of blocks, for instance of B-Ia and B-IIb, into "62 residential barracks (30 brick and 32 wooden), along with 10 barracks containing washrooms and toilets, 2 kitchens, 2 bathhouses, and 2 storage barracks."[9]

Bunkers

A few miles from Auschwitz I were two cottages, converted into gas chambers, the "Little red house" (Bunker 1) and the "Little white house" (Bunker 2). The Jewish prisoners gassed in these cottages were buried in mass graves.[10]

Kommando

In the words of the Sephardi Sonderkommandos, *Kommando* was used as synonymous for *group, work gang, work team, duty*, or *squad*, but definitely not for *Lager*. Thus, Berry Nahmia wrote, "Today, tomorrow, they will divide you into groups. The *groups* are called *Kommandos* and each of you will be assigned to work in a *Kommando*." Nahmia defines the term as follows: "Here in the camp, it's no laughing matter. You must obey and above all, for your own sake, you must join a *Kommando*, a work gang, otherwise, God help you."[11] Moreover, when referring to a particular group of people with a common task, the inmates and authors used such designations as 57-B to 60-B, without providing an explanation.

Squad 57-B was in Crematorium Number II (1).
Squad 58-B was in Crematorium III (2).
Squad 59-B was in Crematorium IV (3).
Squad 60-B was in Crematorium V (4).

CONTRIBUTIONS OF THE ASHKENAZIM TO THE REVOLT

Particular attention should be given to the Jews from Ciechanow, Poland, who are credited for initiating and organizing the resistance movement in Auschwitz. Historically, they had settled in Poland in the late sixteenth century and generally lived a peaceful existence. Ciechanow was known for its great Torah scholars, respected spiritual judges, religious and educational institutions, and, in the beginning of the twentieth century, the establishment of secular and social organizations. With the capture of Ciechanow by the Germans on September 3–4, 1939, the Jews suffered from racial laws and were sent to hard labor camps. On November 2, 1942, they were ordered to leave the *shtetl* with no belongings and little food; they had no place to go. "The situation got worse and worse," wrote Binyamin Apel. "On November 6th, 1942 the Jewish community of Ciechanow was wiped out. On this bitter day the Germans killed the elders on the spot, some were put into closed sealed train cars, and the stronger placed in ghettos, until they too were sent to concentration camps where many died of hunger, exhaustion, and hard work; thus Ciechanow was 'purified' of Jews."[12] On their arrival at Auschwitz, most of them were immediately liquidated. Those spared were assigned to the Sonderkommando. They realized that once the Germans were defeated, everyone in the camp would be murdered so "that there shouldn't remain anyone to tell the world what crimes they had committed against mankind. We therefore started to talk about an uprising of the lager prisoners."[13]

According to Greif, the Ciechanow Jews "established the core of the resistance movement organization. . . . Its best-known members were Motek Bielowicz (Mordechaj Halelli), the head of the group; Arie (Lejbek) Braun; Israel Gutman [1923–2016]; Jehuda Laufer; Godel Silber; Noah Zabludowicz; and Moshe Kulka (Kolko)."[14] They, however, needed to be part of a well-organized underground movement. "With the assistance of Shimon, a Polish Jew who had lived in France, they located another group of prisoners of various nations: German, French, Poles, etc."[15] Kolko also advised them to get in touch with Bruno Baum, one of the leaders of the resistance in the underground movement. Kolko told a narrow circle of his conversation with Bruno, "Noah Zabludowicz, Mordecai Bilovich (Aaron Gelbart's son-in-law), Laibl Laufer, a Slovakian Jew, Yisroel (Israel) Gutman from Warsaw and Laibek Braun from Ripin."[16]

The group decided that they needed someone who could provide them with gunpowder. As an electrician, Noah Zabludowicz—Roza (Rosa) Robota's fellow Ciechanow Jew—"was able to move around the lager and have contact between the various lager sections, with Poles (who came from the city) and with the Polish underground party."[17] He was instructed by the group "to make contact with trustworthy people working in the ammunition factory, 'Union,' who can help us to acquire arms and ammunition for the underground."[18] Zabludowicz established contact with Robota and asked her for assistance.

While not the sole actors, as many have claimed, Roza Robota and a group of Ashkenazi women played a crucial role in collecting the gunpowder for the Revolt of October 7, 1944. In "Resistance Type: Rebellion in an Extermination Camp," Robota's age was erroneously noted: "The youngest of them was 12 years old and the oldest (Rovota) [*sic*] was 16." Robota was born in 1921, and in 1942 was twenty-one years old. Assigned to the clothes depot, she obtained the assistance of approximately twenty women from the Union Werke Munition Factory.[19] The munition factory manufactured parts for the V-2 rockets, and in one "room of the plant, the Pulverraum," the women "had access to gunpowder. There, nine young women worked, handling the explosive material for the manufacture of trigger caps."[20] However, more than nine women worked in the Pulverraum; and several workers in the building of roads also had access to gunpowder.

Anna Heilman (née Hana Wajcblum) was born in 1928 and died at the age of eighty-two on May 1, 2011. According to the "External Links" section of the Auschwitz Concentration Camp website, "Anna Heilman is the last living survivor of the plot to blow up Crematorium IV at Auschwitz-Birkenau."[21] Perhaps this is true among the Ashkenazi Jews, but some Sephardi Sonderkommandos who participated in the revolt survived her, that is, Shlomo Venezia, who died in 2012, and Dario Gabbai from California, with whom I spoke by telephone in 2013 and 2015. Likely there are others as well.

A truly heroic figure, Anna Heilman was a survivor of the Warsaw Ghetto. When she arrived at Auschwitz, she was placed for some weeks in Lager A (Camp A), quarantine, then, when she volunteered to work in a special Kommando—the Union munitions factory—she was transferred to Lager B. She claims it was her own idea to smuggle the powder to the Sonderkommando.[22] Anna Heilman and a small group of young women from different backgrounds and countries "evolved the ideas of resistance. . . . The idea was what could we do, each one of us, to resist? I [Heilman] thought, 'You are working in the Pulverraum. How about taking gunpowder?' . . . The gunpowder was within our reach. We thought. 'We can use it!'"[23] In March 1943 her sister Eustasia [Esther] Wajcblum, informed her that Adam Krzyzanowski was organizing a resistance group and that "they were in a position to help."[24] Anna Heilman, her sister, Ruzia Meth, and Alla Gärtner, all of whom worked in the Pulverraum line, were able to smuggle the gunpowder and pass it to the resistance. Innovative in hiding it, they tucked it inside their bras if they were lucky enough to have the surreptitiously constructed undergarment; knotted it in their headscarves; fitted it into the seams and hems of their dresses; hid it in the mess tins rigged with double bottoms; tucked it into sardine cans or shoe polish cans; and even pushed it under their fingernails. They had to be ever-vigilant. They were regularly searched, and Anna Heilman recounted that when they saw from a distance that they would be searched, they would let the powder out onto the ground, and mingled it into the soil so that it could not be seen.[25] They even hid the powder among the dead bodies transported in carts and lorries to the crematoria for disposal.

The smuggling of explosives was a carefully coordinated operation. According to Heilman, "[t]hree women could accumulate approximately three teaspoons of powder in one day. Once successfully smuggled out of the factory the gunpowder was handed off . . . 'through Marta [Bindiger] to Antichka who was working in Birkenau. She ran between Auschwitz and Birkenau and passed it to Roza Robota.'"[26] Robota and Hadassa Zlotnicka gave the material to Godel Silber (Zilber), a native of Ciechanow, who in turn "passed the contraband on to a member of the Sonderkommando and then the material finally reached [Borodin] the Russian 'Sonderman.'"[27] Other sources state that the material was delivered to Kanada and from there picked up. They also mentioned that Robel (Wrobel), a Polish Jew and member of the Sonderkommando assigned to a special detachment, received the explosive material from Robota and passed it to Borodin. "Forbesky, the electrician, whose work granted him access to the Sonderkommando, served as the liaison between the people involved."[28] Possibly it was Forbesky who transferred the powder from Robota to Robel (Wrobel).

Two other leaders of the Sonderkommando, Israel Gutman and Jehuda Laufer, were also workers in the munition plants. They received small quantities of explosives directly from the Ciechanow Jewish women and at the same time cooperated with Robota. Anna Heilman in "Anna Heilman—Part I," attests that a "fourth girl [not named], who was executed, was the one who used to give it directly to the man who worked in the crematorium."[29]

Shlomo Venezia, a Greek Jew, reports on a remark made by Shlomo Dragon concerning five Jewish women who passed along the gunpowder to Robota. Important in this account is the naming of "Sarah, a Greek woman," who worked at the Union Metallwerke in Weichsel, near Auschwitz. The name Sarah is also mentioned in Teller's film *The Revolt of the Greek Jews*.[30] Dragon, a Polish Jew whose wife Simha was from Salonika, comments, "There were definitely times when we didn't want to continue working. But alongside that feeling, we always continued to hope. Maybe despite everything, we'd be able to escape. Maybe we'd survive. . . . There were several cases where people among us would 'run to the fence.' I was one of those who put together the plan. . . . Henryk Fuchsenbrunner of Krakow helped me organize it; he knew the area well and could plan the escape route."[31] This plan, like several others, had to be postponed, mainly due to the attitude "of the non-Jewish participants in the main camp, Auschwitz. . . . The Sonderkommandos were ready for the uprising. But our friends outside of Birkenau thought the time had not yet come. They said, 'Not now, the time isn't right yet. We have to be careful. We aren't ready for an uprising yet.'"[32] Moreover, the situation was more dangerous since so many inmates were aware of the resistance.

Soon after the revolt, the SS apprehended four of the five women. Sarah, for some reason, was not caught. Bennahmias speculates: "As far as is now known, what happened is that five Jewish women were arrested by the SS in the Union armament factory nearby. These women were horribly tortured, but none betrayed either persons or plans. *Four of the five* were executed . . . after the revolt [on January 6, 1945]."[33] If five were tortured and only four executed, what happened to the fifth? An entry in "Prisoner Revolt at Auschwitz-Birkenau" notes, "The SS identifies five women . . . who had been involved."[34] Again, was Sarah the fifth? Finally, on January 6, 1945, at 8:00 P.M. the four women were hanged in front of the *blockovas* (women inmates), and the sister of one of the condemned women was present at the hanging. The sister tried to commit suicide by jumping from the top floor of the block. Heinz Salvator Kounio, who had to work late, had "the unfortunate opportunity to witness this frightful scene, another proof of the cowardliness of the Nazis. I can still describe in detail, even after all these years. It was something I will never forget, as long as I live."[35] Before the trapdoor opened, Robota boldly yelled, "Be strong and be brave." Mallenbaum speaks for the world in the following tribute: "Róza Robota, Estusia Wajcblum, Regina Safirsztein, Alina Gartner, the nations of the world must remember you, and our nation can never forget you! That is the reason for Yom Hashoah VeHagevurah [Holocaust and Heroism Memorial Day]."[36] Rose Meth's son, Jack Meth, informed me by email in the fall of 2015 that his mother "currently resides in New York with him, his wife, and children. Over the next decades, she raised three sons. All attained higher education, both in Yeshiva and secular institutions. Her husband passed away in 2005."

Asked by Greif to talk about the Sonderkommando uprising, Eliezer Eisenschmidt stated that among others, he was assigned to produce mines and hand grenades. He also sharpened long knives. In time, the men divided the hand grenades and knives among themselves. He further explains, "The Sonderkommandos obtained the explosives from women who worked in the munition plant. The women put the gunpowder in a place that we worked out in advance and from there it was taken by the Scheisskommando people (shit squad who worked in the latrines). . . . They concealed the explosives between the strands of the ropes used to pull the carts or trolleys with dead bodies."[37]

As mentioned above, in March 1943, along with others, Adam Krzyzanowski, leader of the Polish resistance, planned the destruction of the gas chambers and a mass escape. Krzyzanowski's confidant comments, "Yeshaya Eiger was entrusted with organizing a fighting unit and preparing the explosives. Eiger enlisted the help of his friends who worked in various sections of the camp and they, in turn, were able to recruit conspirators working in essential camp plants, such as the explosives factory, or in strategic points, like the area near the gas chambers." In addition to Eiger, there were Jews from Radomer, Poland, who were central to the preparations for the revolt. These included several men and women, among them Godel Silber and two women, Bronka Glatt from Radom and Dorka Saperstein from Sosnowiec. The two women worked in the munitions plant "and smuggled gunpowder into the camp daily in small portions. Colonel Borodin, a Russian prisoner and expert pyrotechnist, built powerful bombs, which were entrusted to Handelsman and Warszawski, because of their jobs in proximity of the gas chamber. The plans called for destruction of the camp in October."[38]

PARTICIPATION OF THE ASHKENAZIM AND SEPHARDIM IN THE REVOLT

The heroism of the Ashkenazim in their participation in the Revolt of October 7, 1944, is recognized by both scholars and survivors. So must the participation of the Greek Jews, heretofore scarcely recognized, receive praise. For instance, the Sephardim have hardly been mentioned in the collecting of gunpowder, yet they directly obtained it for the Sonderkommandos. They played a great part in leading the revolt, manifested unselfishness and heroism, and lost hundreds of their brothers and sisters of faith in the October revolt. I spoke with Jacko Maestro of Bat Yam, Israel, by telephone on February 25, 2013, about the position of the Sephardim in general and especially that of the Greek Jews in the revolt. Even though advanced in age and in poor health, he was gracious enough to answer all my questions. He repeated some of his answers to be sure that I understood him:

IJL: How did you receive the gunpowder? From the women who worked in the munitions factory?

JM: No. I was given the dynamite in addition to the gunpowder from those who worked on the roads and in the mountains. They bombed the mountains for passages and building the Union-Werke. They brought me the dynamite and powder when they returned from work in the afternoon, and I immediately gave it to the women, who in turn passed it through three or four hands to those in the revolt. Uzavan la dinamita para konstruir kaminos. Avrian kaminos por las montanyas i ansi tomavan la dinamita (They used the dynamite to build roads. They opened roads through the mountains, and in this way they procured the dynamite.)

IJL: To whom did you give the dynamite?

JM: As I said before, I gave it to the women, and they, in turn, passed it to the men dealing with the revolt.

IJL: What part did you play in the revolt?

JM: Just obtained the dynamite; that is all. [According to some Sephardic sources, Maestro was more involved since he had unrestricted access to the Sonderkommando, permitting him to deliver the dynamite and gunpowder directly to them.]

IJL: Who was involved in the revolt?

JM: The Greeks. They were the ones who truly initiated the revolt. There was nothing before them; hardly anyone wanted to help. It was the Greeks who had enough courage to do it. Avia mas de un lider. Yosef Baruch era uno de eyos. Otro ke dio animo fue Errera, de komo lo mataron! (There was more than one leader. Josef Baruch was one of them. Another person who gave some encouragement was Errera, and how they killed him!)[39]

IJL: I spoke to Leon [Reuven Cohen] every time I visited Israel; he told me that it was he who was supposed to burn the mattresses and start the fire. Now, was he in another crematorium when it happened?

JM: I am not sure. A lot of the Sonderkommandos ran away to the "arvoles" (woods), most of them were caught and killed. However, many survived, such as Shlomo Venezia and Leon Cohen.[40]

Yitzchak Kerem reports that the Greek Jew Jacko Maestro, who worked in the *Führer Barrack* (Commandant Office) of the *Arbeitsdienst* (Labor Service), and who was free to go wherever he wanted throughout Auschwitz-Birkenau, "received from some Greek Jewish female inmates gun powder in a rag wrapped within napkins and papers and he brought it to the *Schuh-Kommando* (Shoe Command) whence it was passed on to Birkenau to be later used in the revolt by Polish and Greek Jewish inmates on 7 October 1944."[41] In an email dated February 25, 2013, Kerem wrote to me, "We have Jacko on film depicting how he did this and he shows it on his lap," how the women wrapped the gunpowder within papers. When I asked Kerem in a subsequent email if he remembered any names of Greek women who handled gunpowder and possibly helped the men, he referred to Erika Kounio's work. Erika writes, "Many Greek girls worked in the 'Union-Werke'-Kommando. It was a munitions factory, and demand was increasing. Production had to be expanded, and they needed more workers. The girls who already worked there recommended their 'sisters' and 'cousins.' . . . Many men also worked in the Union-Kommando."[42]

Marcel Nadjari reflected that for those in the Sonderkommando, the "only thing that kept them alive was our desire for revenge and the organized attempt to escape."[43] They had some financial sources. The Canada Kommando

Figure 3.1. Josef Baruch, officer in the Greek army, leader of the revolt. Courtesy of the Jewish Museum of Greece Photographic Archives.

searched the clothes of the newcomers and found in addition to food, dollars, gold, gems, and purses which they "managed to hide . . . giving up only things of little value to them [the Germans]." Among the Sonderkommandos, *der Zahnartz*, the dentists, such as Leon Cohen, hoarded gold from the mouths of the corpses. With it, Nahmia declared, "Paying a handsome sum in dollars we acquired dynamite from the Union factory, transported it in a little wagon that carried soup every day to all *Kommandos*, and buried it in the courtyard of the crematorium."[44] Leon told me in one of our interviews, "It was difficult to carry out this duty and to keep some of the loot, but it was worthy." I asked him why. Leon explained, "We exchanged it for food, for medicines, to save us from some beating and the ovens." I questioned him if gold had anything to do with the revolt. "Indeed," he said, "we used it to obtain gunpowder." I tried to find out the means to get it. In a cagey manner, he said, "We had our way. Some of our girls [meaning Greek ones] in the factory took a chance and got us some. I believe they delivered it to us through the kitchen."

Once the Greek Jews received the gunpowder from the women, they hid it in their mattresses. Some for safety stuffed it in the walls and in the pillars that supported the roof, just as the Ashkenazim did. Bennahmias relates that Shlomo Venezia showed him where the explosives he was entrusted with had been moved from the former hiding place to another since someone had betrayed the original location.[45]

Salvatore Katan, who had been in the Greek army and whose large family, except for one brother, was murdered in the camp, also provided gunpowder to the Sonderkommandos. When asked by the Germans, "What was your job in Greece?" Katan replied, "Mechanic." The Germans told him that he could be used in the munitions factory, the Union factory where he would build bombs. In the interview conducted by Sidney Bolkosky, a historian at the University of Michigan, Dearborn, Katan stated that he had the opportunity to take refuge in the mountains with the partisans but chose to stay with his family. Katan also recounted how he had obtained the dynamite from the factory and had given it to the women "to explode the Krematoriums." Katan took his own revenge against the executioners of his family and of his coreligionists: he sabotaged the machinery, causing shutdowns and delays in production. Just before the end of the war, his job was to build crates, put the machines in them, and seal them up. While other workers stood guard, Katan packaged the machines and then damaged them with a hammer before sealing the crates. Katan explained why the Greek Jews were selected to work in the crematoria: "The Germans used Greek Jews in the crematoria because the Greek Jews there no capable to talk German, they no capable to talk Polish. Just Greek or French or Italian, but also . . . Spanish, old Spanish [Judeo-Spanish]. . . . So that is the reason the Greek Jews were working in the Krematorium. And the Greek Jews were the ones who blow up Krematorium, with no help."[46]

Henryk Mandelbaum, a Polish Sonderkommando who was assigned the task of stripping his fellow Jews of valuables—sometimes hidden in noses, in ears, and, in the case of women, in their vaginas—participated in the rebellion of October 7, 1944, with Modechaj Halelli and Israel (Yisroel) Gutman as leaders of the group. Hermann Langbein compiled a list of participants that included Emanuel Mink and David Szmulewski, who were active in the resistance movement. They in turn named Józef Warszwski as one of the organizers of the resistance. As Langbein notes, David Szmulewski and Daniel Czech also added several individuals who worked in the Höß as leaders of the mutiny. In "Sonderkommando Revolt: Auschwitz-Birkenau, 7 October 1944," Chris Webb reports that during the revolt, "[m]ost escapees from Crematorium II [old system] were shot down mercilessly. Two hundred and fifty prisoners died in this exchange," among them some of the leaders.[47] While no mention of Greek Jews is made, Edward de Wind learned from the Salonikan Jew Kabeli, a Sonderkommando, the names of some Greek Jews who participated in the uprising—Josef Baruch, Burdo (Bourdo), Carasso, Michel Arditi, and Jachon (Dahon).[48] These five Greek Jews joined the two or three hundred Greek Jewish Sonderkommandos who were part of the revolt.

Eliezer Eisenschmidt, a member of the Sonderkommando, was assigned either to Crematorium 3 [IV] or to Crematorium 4 [V]. His testimony is important even though there are some inconsistencies, which might be due to the way in which Greif conducted the interview, to the sequence of questions, resulting perhaps in Eisenschmidt switching from one topic to another or changing focus. Eisenschmidt recalled even the minutest incidents in the camp. He remembered the names of inmates with whom he came in contact, their origin (from Europe to North Africa), their preferred foods, and their skills. Moreover, he remembered the conversations of the prisoners, the *Kapos*, and the Germans—and the social and political maneuverings within the groups. He recalled the diaries by Zalman Gradowski and the Maggid of Makow Lajb Langfus concealed in bottles buried in the ground; and the artist David Olère, who sketched the images while in the camp that were later published in *Witness: Images of Auschwitz*. He remembered the flyover of American aircraft to bomb the German factories near Gleiwitz, rather than dropping "a few bombs on the crematoria of Birkenau," and especially the preparation for the revolt and participation of fellow Sonderkommandos. Regrettably, Eisenschmidt's acquaintance with the Greek Jews in the camp was limited to a few details such as the arrival of a short man from Athens, Piccolo, who was well educated and who "looked for the children's bodies only, went into the gas chambers and pulled out their bodies. . . . He'd pick up the bodies and carry them to the pit or the furnace."[49]

Eisenschmidt also recalls, "When Jews came from Greece, they brought something that we'd never seen—olives, [and] corn bread. Almost all of them had bread and olives."[50] Eisenschmidt adds, "The Greek Jews spoke French and Ladino. I spoke French with them. Most of our people spoke Yiddish." Eisenschmidt continues, "After the Warsaw ghetto uprising some Greek Jews were forced to destroy the ghetto buildings and to gather up belongings in the ruins. They used Greek Jews for this work, and not Polish Jews, because Polish

Jews might make contact with other Jews who were in hiding."[51] Eisenschmidt remembers that an "exceptional event that many of us still remember" involved two Greek Jews from Athens and three Jews from Poland, guarded by two SS men and a Lithuanian, selected to throw the ashes of the victims into the River."[52] In an ensuing struggle with the Germans, "the Polish Jews didn't help the Greeks. They stood aside and didn't lift a finger. They were helpless." Eisenschmidt, without mentioning the names, refers again to two Greek Jews who swam toward the opposite bank. Of one of the Greeks, he said, "I can still picture that strong, healthy guy. . . . He grabbed me by both hands and picked me up like a feather." It is unbelievable that Eisenschmidt could remember so many facts and names, including the name of one of the Polish Jews, Arcik (Aharon) Lubowicz, who refused to join the mutiny and "stood aside and didn't lift a finger." He even remembered that after the liberation, Lubowicz relocated first to Bnei Brak, Israel, and later to Canada, where he died. Eisenschmidt recalled the particular strength of the Greek army officer, but not his name, Errera, the name of a hero. He also affirms, "Since they couldn't speak Polish and didn't know anyone in the area, they were captured and executed."[53]

Eisenschmidt was assigned to the same crematorium where several hundred Greek Jews were also located, yet neither he nor any other Ashkenazi mentions them. Eisenschmidt recalls that two Greeks swam to the other bank; actually there was only Errera. Not speaking Polish or knowing any local people had nothing to do with Errera's death: it was the SS that found him, and they either killed him on the spot or took him to the camp, where he was tortured and thrown in the oven while still alive.

During my telephone conversation with a survivor living in Bat Yam, Israel, who participated in the revolt, I tried to verify Eisenschmidt's statements. I asked him if Errera had any part in the uprising. He replied,

> No. Alberto ya avia muerto una muerte terrivle. Los SS lo izieron sufrir asta el ultimo momento. El era eroe, sus aksiones desharon un gran impakto en todos mozotros. Todo el campo lo admiraron por ser el uniko de aver matado un miembro del SS i ferido un otro. No. No estuvo propio en la revolusion, ma lo ke el izo dio gran impetu para estar prontos para la lucha.
>
> (No. Alberto had already died a horrible death. The SS made him suffer until the last moment. He was a hero; his actions left a great impact on all of us. The whole camp admired him for being the only one to have killed one member of the SS and wounded another. No. He did not participate in the revolution itself, but what he did gave impetus to our being ready for the fight.)[54]

My interviewee added, "It seems that the one who told the story was not aware of what really took place, or, as it was normal among the Ashkenazim, we hardly mattered. They took credit for everything."

There are several versions of the story about Albert Errera's daring act during the disposal of the ashes of the Hungarian inmates in the Vistula River. Some statements differ according to who is telling the story: the composition of the group assigned;[55] the number of SS killed; how many Jews swam to the opposite bank for safety; where in the body Errera was shot; and whether he was returned to the camp dead or alive. Shlomo Venezia, commenting on Erreras's attempt to escape, states that he was captured and transported back to Auschwitz, where he had been a *Heizer* [a member of the Sonderkommando] assigned to the disposal of the ashes of murdered prisoners in the Sola River, actually the Vistula River. Michael Molho gives another version:

> A small squad of five Greek Jews, including Aleco Alexandrides, *alias* Albert Errera, deported from Larissa, Ugo Baruch Venezia, Henri Nahama Capon, escorted by two S.S. officers [in September 1944], were assigned to empty into the bank of the Vistula River the ashes brought in a long convoy of trucks. While emptying the trucks and receiving terrible blows, one of the SS, in order to hurry them up, uttered some macabre jokes, "*Schnell!* Hurry up! Do not wait until the ashes of your brothers reach Israel. The waves of the Vistula will take them straight to Palestine. *Schnell. Schnell!*" Aleco was brave. . . . He could not stop his anger. He held up his shovel and split the head of the sarcastic teaser, he tripped the second soldier and abruptly threw him in the river. Errera saw a way to escape and asked the other prisoners to make a break. They refused, instead of saving themselves, they pulled the drowning SS German and tended to his wounds, and returned him to the camp, where they were beaten furiously and paid with their lives.[56]

Jean Cohen recounted, "Errera tried to escape by swimming but a guard of the SS caught up and shot him in the legs with the famous bullets 'dom dom' which were built to explode inside the body, causing severe wounds which lose much blood . . . eventually, a time when Errera stuck his head out of the river to breathe, [the second guard] shot him in the head."[57] Molho continues: "Still bleeding he swam to the other bank and hid in the woods. But the next day, the Germans and their dogs hunted him down, he tried to fight. He was tied and brought back to Crematorium II. He was exhausted by his wound, by fatigue, and hunger. They beat him without mercy, interrogated him, and skinned him alive. The body was totally dismembered and disfigured . . . extremely agitated the Germans exhibited him on a table and forced everyone to pass in front. Then they carried him into the ovens still panting."[58] His fellow brethren recited the Kaddish before burning the body. "Nobody ever talks about this episode, since nobody has really carried out a study on the fate of the Greeks at Birkenau."[59] With the brutal murder of Errera and the sadistic display of his body, the "seeds of revolt had been sown. The time was ripe. The revolution did not take long to break out."[60]

The news of the brutal execution of Errera circulated not only throughout Auschwitz-Birkenau but also in other camps. He was highly revered by his people and respected by the German guards and by the Russian prisoners of war who worked in the kitchen. Leon Cohen added, "The whole story was recounted by a prisoner from the Warsaw [Ghetto] who had watched it all."[61] Errikos Sevillias praised Errera's valor and proudly stated that Alberto Errera's bravery was spoken of for weeks in the camp.[62] Bowman, referring to the account, writes, "This story is an important part of the folklore of Greek Jewish survivors, and it reportedly had important repercussions for the Sonderkommando revolt."[63] Nonetheless, the death of a hero, a Greek son of Sepharad, was immortalized for his courageous action. While his life seemed to be the theme of a Greek myth, it truly was the account of a real life lived with courage and resoluteness, a life that gave impetus to the uprising.

From the Ashkenazi perspective, as Eisenschmidt points out, just before the uprising took place the Germans announced that several dozen workers were needed for outside labor. No one volunteered, and the Germans chose thirty inmates, including Eisenschmidt, who belonged to the underground movement. It should be noted that at least two Greek Jews volunteered for the same duty, and one of them was Shlomo Venezia. Plans were already made for an attack. The head of Eisenschmidt's movement was a Russian Jewish major, taken prisoner in Stalingrad, who was for the attack and encouraged them to act: "There are eighty thousand prisoners in the camp. Even if the Germans shoot half of them, forty thousand will survive. That's a horde. These people have nothing to lose."[64] The plan was that the revolt was supposed to start in Crematoria 3 [IV] and 4 [V]. The free Polish partisans had promised military aid but refused to participate, since they wanted huge sums of money, which was usually smuggled out to them by the messenger Alter Sajnzylberg. They demanded that the uprising be postponed. Even members of the Jewish Military Resistance Movement, who were not part of the Sonderkommando, refused to collaborate and urged that the 1944 coup be postponed until a later date, so as not to jeopardize the lives of those in the main camp. The demand was turned down. The Russian officer said, "It doesn't matter whether they join or not, we're going ahead."[65] The chief arsonist, Yosl, a man from Bedzin, and a few men from the Sonderkommando were to set fire to the bunkers and the mattresses first, and the rest were supposed to kill the SS, grab their weapons, and move forward. "That was the signal for the start of the uprising."[66] Using the new system for designating the crematoria, but in Roman numerals, Eisenschmidt continues:

> The building had a wooden roof that caught fire easily. . . . All that remained of the building were the stone walls and the smokestacks. When the men in Crematorium I saw the fire, they realized that the uprising had begun, and they went into action. They killed Karo, tried to set the building on fire, and began to escape. It was easier to escape from there because the building bordered the outer fence of the camp. A few of them were able to jump over the fence. Eventually, however, all of them were caught. We were locked up there for half a day. By then the uprising had died down and they made us cremate the bodies. That was the only work left to do, since no new transports of European Jews arrived anymore.[67]

Asked to describe the murder of Kapo Karol, Eisenschmidt said the men in Crematorium 1 "killed Karol" using the knives that he had shaped. Moreover, there was a quarrel about who would kill him. After some discussion, Eisenschmidt lost and the killing was left to another comrade, who drew a knife, "grabbed the German Kapo in the corridor, and stabbed him so hard that the blade went right through his body and got stuck in the wall behind him. Afterwards, his body was thrown into the furnace. That was that."[68]

Salmen Lewental recalled the bravery of the inmates who "showed an immense courage refusing to budge from the spot. They set up a loud shout, hurled themselves upon the guards with hammers and axes." Lewental, in "Sonderkommando Revolt: Auschwitz-Birkenau," describes how members of Crematorium IV (3) listened to Staff Sergeant Busch read the selection list, and they attacked. "The men of *Kommando* 59-B [3] using the explosives in hand blew up the crematorium, which burst into flames. After cutting the barbed-wire fence, the prisoners got away into the nearby wood. At the sound of explosion and fighting the members of *Kommando* 57-B at Crematorium Number II [1] started the revolt. The *Reichsdeutsche Oberkapo* and a soldier were thrown into the burning furnace alive, another SS man was beaten to death. . . . The prisoners of squad 58-B in Crematorium III [2] and 60-B in Crematorium V [4] do not revolt because they were not informed of the plan to take up arms and since SS reinforcements quickly stifle any further resistance."[69]

Several hundred inmates from Crematorium II [1] who escaped into the woods grabbed some weapons and, as mentioned above, cut through the barbed-wire fence enclosing the crematoria and the adjacent women's camp, and fled in a southern direction. Instead of going toward the Vistula River, they took refuge in a barn in the village of Rajsko. The SS chased them and caught them. The prisoners tried to fight, but the barn was set on fire by the SS, and a large number of the prisoners were burned alive. Those who attempted to escape were shot . . . 250 prisoners from Crematorium II [1] died in this exchange, "among them the organizers of the uprising [Gradowski, Warszawiski, Deresinski, Kalniak, Langfus, and Panusz]."[70] Three German noncommissioned officers died, and fourteen were injured. Meanwhile, the prisoners of 59-B were killed, and a "fire-fighting squad from the main camp put out the fire of Crematorium IV [3]." As in other cases, no mention was given of the Greek Jews who were also from the same crematoria.[71]

In "On Holocaust Day We Forget," Allan E. Mallenbaum observes, "The Jews of Sonderkommando Squad 59-B [3] revolted against their slave-masters." He gives credit to "Zalman (Salmen) Levental, who had been in the Sonderkommando since 1942, for coordinating the plans for the uprising and to Noah Zabludowicz, from the town of Ciechanów, a male member of the camp underground, for initiating the revolt, once he made contact with a trusted young woman [Robota] he knew from home."[72]

In our telephone conversation on March 12, 2015, I asked Mallenbaum if he was aware of the planning and participation of any other groups in the revolt. His response, which appeared verbatim earlier in "On Holocaust Day We Forget" was the following: "*I realize that many details were lost in the ashes, and other details were subject to disagreement by historians* [my emphasis]." I then asked him if it was possible that only the actions of the Greek Jews were lost in the ashes. His only recollection dealing with the Spanish Jews was what he already had said above, "the heroic deed of the Jews from Greece who chose death rather than accept the Germans' dirty work of murdering and burning of their fellow Jews." He was referring to those Jews from Corfu and Athens who gave their lives rather than work in the crematoria. Again, I asked him if the Greek Jews participated in the revolt; "None that I recall" was his answer. As in the case of Eisenschmidt, Mallenbaum could remember only insignificant details concerning the Sephardim, and he was not aware if they took part in the uprising, "on that day in that vast Jewish cemetery called Auschwitz, at the killing factory called Crematorium IV [3]."

When I contacted the Auschwitz-Birkenau State Museum in August 2016 to inquire if the annals of the camp reported any action of the Sephardim in the revolt, especially by the Greeks, the response from Dr. Piotr Setkiewicz, director of the Centre for Research in Auschwitz, was discouraging. In my second try, his response was that the museum did not consider the Jews as belonging to different groups. "They were all Jews," he wrote. In a subsequent email, I indicated that I agreed with him, since all Jews suffered equally in the camps and there was no need to differentiate among them. However, since my research dealt with the Sephardim in the Holocaust as a forgotten people,

I had to consider their particular situation as opposed to that of the other groups. Dr. Setkiewicz was kind enough to continue his search. In a following email, he wrote, "The tendency of overestimating the role of the Polish resistance movement is clearly visible also in some testimonies by the Polish survivors. Eyewitness accounts, especially those made many years after the war, require particular attention."

To the best of my knowledge, none of the non-Sephardi survivors or Holocaust writers mention the inmates' high esteem in Auschwitz and other concentration camps for the heroic fight and deaths of the Greek Jews. With the assistance of a colleague, I was able to reach by telephone a Sephardi survivor and former Sonderkommando living in Southern California. I asked him why the Spanish Jews were not mentioned in any of the early reports on the revolt. He answered, "I do not know. I have always been amazed, I have questioned time and again why our people were left out in so many studies, as if we had never existed. I attended a few lectures on the subject, and not one speaker mentioned us. Don't they realize that we lived and worked together in the hellhole of Auschwitz? Nothing was different. We, the Sonderkommandos, Ashkenazi and Sephardi, knew that sooner or later we would be selected to die in the oven. Yet they claim that only their people suffered and fought, but it was us who in the final hours decided to fight under the guidance of our own leader [referring to Baruch]. We did it without any assistance; we rebelled and paid with our lives."

His words troubled me. I found myself wondering again if the Ashkenazim were aware that thousands of Sephardim were in the camp with them and hundreds of Greek Jews were assigned to the four crematoria. I wondered if they were not cognizant that Leon Reuven Cohen, alongside Kapo Kaminsky (Kaminski), Lemke Chaïm Pliszko, Josef Baruch, Marcel Nadjari, and Alberto Errera took part in planning the two earlier uprisings that failed due to a betrayer.

Their descriptions of life in the camp and especially in the crematoria hardly differ from those of the Sephardim. However, the Ashkenazi brothers and sisters do not acknowledge the presence of the Sephardim. In their accounts only the names of Ashkenazi leaders and other participants are mentioned. Granted, they played an important role in Hitler's Hell, but so did the Sephardim.

CONTRIBUTIONS OF THE SEPHARDIM TO THE REVOLT

Important for understanding the suffering of Sephardi Jews, those who died in the Nazi concentration camps and those who survived the calamity, are the photographs, published sources, and oral and written descriptions of the eyewitness. The publication by Photini Tomai and the DVD by Marios Sousis and

Tomai under the same title, *Greeks in Auschwitz-Birkenau*, both of which rely on survivors' testimonies and archival research, and Tomai's twenty-three-minute DVD, produced by the Greek Ministry of Foreign Affairs in 2009, support and complement the accounts published about the surviving Greek Jews.[73] Their portrayal of the "Greek Holocaust in the tragedy of the Holocaust," honors the heroism of 77,377 Greek Jews and some Greek Orthodox victims who shed their blood "on the altar of the Hitlerian minotaur."[74] The impassioned testimonials are from those who with heroic intent embraced their motto, "Freedom in Death."[75]

I disagree with Gideon Greif when he writes, "Since there were no surviving eyewitnesses to the uprising and no documents related to it, the course of the uprising is shrouded in many doubts and much vagueness."[76] Indeed, Greif contradicts himself in the next sentence when he notes that he interviewed survivors about the uprising. Both Greif and I interviewed witnesses to the uprising. There are also documents left behind, mostly by Ashkenazi, with a few by Sephardi Sonderkommandos. However, I do agree when Greif states that some accounts lack precision, and that the "story is told in several versions, especially in regard to the heroism of the participants and the symbolism of the act."[77] Steven Bowman observes, "[T]here is the Greek perspective told in repeated detail that suffers from occasional inaccuracies and partisan memory."[78] Hermann Langbein rightfully points out that "[n]o matter which version is correct," the revolt existed in reality. "The plan of a joint revolt in all four crematoriums failed in any case."[79] The differing accounts may also be due to the varying recollections of the survivors and the change of memories with the passage of time.

Victor Frankl, an Austrian neurologist and psychiatrist, and survivor, wrote after the liberation, "I am aware of the limitations of one survivor's efforts to give an objective presentation of people in Auschwitz and their problems. Each of us harbors his personal biased memories and has experienced 'his' Auschwitz."[80] The variation in these individual accounts is entirely understandable, for, as I have explained, the prisoners were transferred from one crematorium to another, often in an instant; they were under incredible stress; and they had different personal experiences and thus had their own recollections, which may seem to be at odds with those of others. Additionally, the time span between the liberation and when the recollections were recorded would account for variation in the narrative.

Rebecca Fromer explains the state of mind of the inmates in critical situations, "moments of pandemonium, moments of hesitation, and then the intermingling of fear and hope." Fromer continues, "Pockets of memory are lost, and pockets of memory await retrieval; pockets of memory freeze into photo-stillness, and pockets of memory are thrust into the dungeons of the mind, too dangerous for freedom or parole."[81] Bowman writes of memory, "Much material and novel facts of the story can be recovered only from memories. A memoir immediately after the event has a different value from one written decades later; yet there is a phenomenon of forty-year memory that occasionally recalls events and conversations more accurately than a memory closer in time to the event. Some individuals have better memory than others, some have photogenic or aural genic memory. In other words, some individuals are better witnesses than others."[82]

Moshe Shaul, a prominent Israeli radio host and editor of *Aki Yerushalayim*, conducted a Judeo-Spanish gathering in Tel Aviv, where I spoke. A participant, who was a survivor, recounted, "The uprising had its initiation in Crematorium 1 [new system] and from there it spread to the other crematoria." Daniel Bennahmias remembers hearing the cries of the Nazi guard who was thrown into the oven: "We heard the screams in Crematorium 2, '*-a-a-ah! A-a-a-a-ah!*'"[83] It seems that the new numerical system was used in the above entry. Apparently, there is an error in recording that the "Sonderkommando in Crematorium 2 breaks through the wires of the camp," when in fact it was those of Crematorium 1. Crematorium 2 did not participate in the uprising.

Heinz Salvator Kounio wrote, "In the two years that I was at Auschwitz, there were only two major attempts to revolt against the SS." The first one was in October of 1943, when an Italian heroine entering the gas chamber refused to completely undress. "An SS officer stopped her from entering. He pushed her back violently, ordering her to undress. . . . She refused to comply. Suddenly, she grabbed the gun out of his holster and began to shoot at all the SS soldiers, officers and guards who were standing nearby. The Italian Jews seized the opportunity and grabbed guns from the dead SS. . . . SS reinforcements surrounded the building. . . . What could 500 individuals do? . . . The SS surrounded them, armed with machine guns. The 500 were killed. As a result of this rebellion the SS executed 3,000 Jews in reprisal."[84] Heinz Kounio continues his account: "The second attempt happened in the fall of 1944. This revolt was more serious and better organized. As a Greek, I am proud to say that *Greek Jews* organized the second insurrection. Some Russians and Polish Jews . . . joined them."[85] Kounio, unlike his fellow Sephardim, uses the German numbering system of the crematoria and follows the account as told by the Ashkenazim: "They approached [Robota and] four other women who were working in the "Union" Factory where the weapons were manufactured. The women—no mention of any Sephardi—stole gunpowder and passed it on to friends of the insurgents to be used to blow up the crematories. They planned to set fires in crematory IV to cause a distraction, enabling them to surprise the SS, take their guns and then blow up the remaining crematories. A large quantity of gunpowder was stored in crematory IV and it would be blown up. Only one crematory would remain untouched, number V. According to the plan, it would be set on fire after the first three."[86]

The plan was set for noon, but nothing happened. Something had gone wrong. Someone had betrayed them. Still they decided to go on. When the whistle sounded, "the fires were set and crematories I and II burst into flames, exploding. So much damage was caused that the crematoria were useless for some time." SS reinforcements arrived quickly: "The insurgents were confined to one block, where crematories II and III were located. The crematories were on fire, and they were trapped inside. The SS besieged the exits and would not allow them to flee. The insurgents decided to risk everything. It would be freedom or death. They attempted a heroic exit. However, few were able to survive the bursts of machine gun fire. Of the 1,500 who made up this section of the Sonderkommando, only 250 survived."[87] The survivors were spared in order to burn those who had been machine-gunned. Kounio lists eleven names of "the brave Greek Jews" who participated in the revolt; only Isaac Venezia and Daniel Bennahmias survived. Kounio, who was aware that more Greek Jews took part, stated that "unfortunately their names are lost to history. Their act will be remembered by those of us who lived through the horrors of the camp."[88]

Albert Menasche, who published *Birkenau (Auschwitz II)* in 1947, did not have the benefit of consulting with his fellow survivors or access to published accounts that appeared later. His account of the revolt is brief and incomplete. He admits that he "is not in a position to give exact details either on the type of explosives used or on the manner in which the *Sonder* obtained them." As other commentators had related, Menasche also told how a German *Kapo* and a sentry were killed and thrown into the furnace. "But, from Crematorium III (3), the revolt spread to the other crematoria."[89] Mensache continued, "A few minutes later, machine guns and pistol shots were heard. The entire *Birkenau* garrison estimated at 2,000 SS soldiers went into action." The workers in Crematorium III tried to escape, but they were overcome by the SS troops swarming toward them. Menasche concluded, "Singing the Greek National Anthem, *three hundred Greek Jews* buried themselves beneath the debris of their crematorium. The revolt lasted all afternoon. The entire Sonder was massacred."[90] Crematorium III was destroyed.

A woman who worked in Kanada II is in accord with Menasche. The Greek Jews, she recounts, "died as true heroes, singing the Greek National anthem and waving the Greek flag made from pieces of their uniforms." Many critics have questioned this account. However, in his communication to me dated August 23, 2016, Piotr Setkiewicz wrote, "Please forgive me. I have just spoken to a charming lady [most probably the same lady as above] who claimed that during the Uprising, prisoners from the camp could see the Greek white-and-blue flag waving over the crematorium." Her message follows:

> Στις 7 Οκτωβρίου 1944, ημέρα Σάββατο, οι Γερμανοί επιχείρησαν να απομακρύνουν επιπλέον 200 Έλληνες και Ούγγρους που είχαν επιλεγεί για εξόντωση. Στις 14.30 το μεσημέρι μια ομάδα των SS έφτασε με τους ονομαστικούς καταλόγους για τη δεύτερη διαλογή. Σύμφωνα με τις διαθέσιμες μαρτυρίες, τα γεγονότα διαδραματίστηκαν ως εξής: Όταν άρχισαν να εκφωνούν τα ονόματα των Ελλήνων, κανείς δεν απάντησε. Σε κάποια στιγμή ακούστηκε μια φωνή στα ελληνικά: «*Θα γίνει ναι ή όχι το ντου*». Αμέσως όρμησαν στους Γερμανούς φρουρούς, τους αφόπλισαν και οχυρώθηκαν μέσα στο Κρεματόριο IV αναμένοντας βοήθεια.
>
> (On October 7, 1944, a Saturday, the Germans attempted to remove an additional 200 Greeks and Hungarians who had been selected for extermination. At 14:30, a group of SS arrived with their list of names for the second screening. According to available testimonies, the events took place as follows: When he began to read aloud the names of the Greeks, no one answered. At some point a voice in Greek, possibly that of Baruch, was heard: "This attack we were talking about. Will it happen or not?"[91] Immediately they rushed the German guards, disarmed them, and barricaded themselves inside Crematorium 3 waiting for help.)

When I asked a survivor for the translation of the phrase, he said, "I believe I heard something like, 'Είναι η εξέγερση, ας πάμε'" ('It is the rebellion, let's go!').

As time passed, the reports released by surviving Sephardi inmates added new details. With few exceptions, the oral material I collected from them and from their published autobiographies gave virtually the same information. The account of the October 7, 1944, uprising is solidly based on a concurrence of opinions. The inmates, realizing that their lives were at stake, decided to rebel against their oppressors. It is also said that a Russian Jewish officer participated in the rebellion. A Salonikan Jewish survivor told me, "Los otros ke ya savian de la revolta refuzaron de partisipar, kreyeron ke ivan asegurar sus vidas, ma no lo pudieron azer" (The others who already knew of the revolt refused to participate. They believed that by doing so, they would secure their lives, but they failed). Piotr Setkiewicz related to me on August 23, 2016, that the members of Crematorium 3 were "waiting for the fellow inmates to make the next move; unfortunately, even though they knew about the revolt, the men of the Crematoria didn't do anything."

There are those who cast doubt on the participation of the Greek Jews in the revolt because of the language barrier. These writers mistakenly assumed that because many of the Sephardim could not speak German, Yiddish, or Polish, they could not be part of the uprising. Moreover, the editor of *In Memoriam, Sho'at Yehude Yavan*, posits that Robota and the Greek Jews could not have communicated with each other because of the language barrier.[92] Bowman, however, argues that "the situation in the camp was much more complicated" and that some Greek Jews knew Polish and German as well.[93] The editor of the Hebrew version of *In Memoriam* was mistaken in assuming that the Greek Jews did not take part in the collection and smuggling of the munitions. He adopted the stereotypical view that the Greek Jews could not communicate with Robota because they did not speak her languages. Moreover, he stated that the Greek Jews credited themselves with the explosion of Crematorium 3. Unfortunately, the editor also displayed an ignorance of the facts, and he relied on previous accounts without verifying them.

There is ample evidence that several Sephardi inmates knew German, and some could also speak Yiddish. Morris Venezia's brother knew both languages. Leon Cohen spoke German and conversed with German officers when a transport of Greek Jews arrived in the camp. Leon Yahiel served as an interpreter in the registration section. Shaul Senor could also speak several languages. According to Shabetai Hanuka [Chanuka], Shaul Senor had lived in Palestine before the war; he returned to Salonika for his bride and was caught by the Germans and sent to Auschwitz.[94] After having been interned in Auschwitz, Senor was sent to the Warsaw Ghetto. According to Kerem, "The Salonikans, as foreigners who had no knowledge of the Warsaw Jewish past, were the first group sent from Auschwitz to Warsaw to clean up the place and build an Auschwitz satellite labor camp. The Salonikan totaled some 1,000 of the 3,683 Auschwitz inmates who were sent to the Warsaw camp in 1943."[95]

Jacko Maestro, a fourteen-year-old Salonikan Jew, spoke fluent German. He served not only as translator in the Arbeitsdienst (Labor Service), but also in the office of the Politische Abteilung (Political Department), the most important political division in Auschwitz, where he had contact with high Nazi officers and with members of the Gestapo. His duties were to coordinate and assign work for some 16,000 Jewish inmates "in the area of the large Auschwitz-Birkenau camp complex. . . . He was free to go wherever he wanted throughout Auschwitz-Birkenau."[96] After the liberation, survivors who knew him praised his compassion and loyalty to his people. Jacko often took chances in sparing inmates from medical experiments. Shlomo Venezia recalls, "Jacquot [Jacko] Maestro was a lively, cunning youngster who'd often transmitted information to us in the camp."[97] Yitzchak Kerem and Eduardo Retyk praise Maestro for assisting his people:

Jacko took people from the gas chambers, prevented some from appearing for the death selection lineup, helped people in the infirmary, supplied crucial medicines and salves to people in need, changed work places for those who lacked strength, took and placed people in or out of work selection lineups, checked on the weak and the sick, bribed the castration of Shabetai Chanuka [Hanuka], helped Salonikan women in Block 10 who were there for heinous medical experiments, covered for people intentionally missing in the lineups, acquired gun powder for explosives and passed it for the future revolt and made contact with his sister, Esther Maestro, who on three occasions personally rescued a total of 181 girls from Block 25 destined to be gassed. Jacko would visit sorting warehouses in Auschwitz I and II (Birkenau) to obtain diamonds, gold, money, and cigarettes needed for future bribes and trades that would benefit in easing and rescuing [not only] fellow Salonika Greeks, but also other Jewish prisoners.[98]

Shabetai Hanuka also found Jacko Maestro to be a savior to many of his Greek compatriots. In 1990, when I interviewed Hanuka in Tel Aviv, he told me that while he was in the hospital awaiting a medical experiment for castration, Maestro had bribed the guards to prevent it. Hanuka praised Jacko Maestro:

Es komo mil malahim. Este salvo muncha djente de todo lugar. Izo muncha buendad. Tenia muncha influensa en Auschwitz. Este salvava djente de ser matada. Era ayudante del Sekretario Djeneral, avlava en sus lengua.

(He is like a thousand angels. He saved a lot of people from all over the camp. He performed a great deal of good deeds. He had a lot of influence in Auschwitz. He rescued people from being killed. He was assistant to the Secretary General; he spoke in their language [German]).[99]

I asked Hanuka what made it possible for Maestro to behave as he did. He replied,

Era kerensiozo kon todos. Kuando posivle, mos azia saver lo ke pasava en el kampo. Saviendo Aleman desde chiko, sentia lo ke dezian en el buro [for *bureau*], avlava kon los grandes, i munchos de eyos tenian konfiansa en el. Ansi es ke pudo salvar munchos de mozotros.

(He was affectionate with everyone. Whenever possible, he kept us informed of what was going on in the camp. Knowing German from his childhood, he listened to what was said in the office, he spoke with important people, and many of them trusted him. Thus, he was able to save many of us.)

Heinz Salvator Kounio came from a family that spoke German. His mother was born in a German-speaking area of Czechoslovakia, and his father also knew the language.[100] His sister, Erika Kounio-Amariglio, who died in 2013, was assigned to the Politische Abteilung to work as a translator and interpreter. Jacko Maestro and Erika Kounio-Amariglio were in excellent positions to know either directly or through special connections what was taking place in the office and in the camp.

According to Elie Cohen, a survivor, there were other inmates from Greece who wrote and spoke perfect German. In our interview in Tel Aviv in 1982, Cohen told me of an incident that took place in Auschwitz. He said that the Greek inmates used to attend concerts. On one occasion they were absent, and the commandant inquired from a soldier why they did not show up. Elie explained,

> [S]tan djugando marionetas i ke la una marioneta se asemejava a su persona. "Scheiße das konsert," le dize [el komandante]. Le esta diziendo, "Konsierto es medra." Los gregos izieron sinema kon personas chikitikas?
>
> (They are playing with marionettes, and one of the marionettes looks like you [the commandant]. "Shit the concert," the commandant tells him. He is telling him [to the soldier], "the concert is shit. The Greeks put together a film with small people?").

The commandant wanted to see the concert and invited all the important officials and their wives to attend. Elie continued, "I fizieron un bien grande i traduzieron el teksto de las marionetas en aleman. Avia ayi uno de Molho, el savia alman i el lo izo." (And they put together a wonderful show and translated the text of the marionettes into German. There was a Molho there who knew German, and he translated it).[101]

Several inmates dared leave "their memories [diaries] of the shocking testimony to the crimes committed against the Jews." These included the Ashkenazi Zalman Gradowski,[102] Lejb (Lajb) Langfus, Chaim Heman, and Zalman Lewental, as well as the Sephardi Marcel Nadjari, the lone survivor.[103] However, no other Sephardi was mentioned. During his internment, the Sephardi Yomtov Yakoel, a member of the Sonderkommando, also wrote an account of what was happening in the crematoria. He stuffed his notes into several bottles and buried them. His intent was to publish his memoirs, *Dans l'Enfer* (In Hell), about life and death in the crematoria. Sadly, he was executed in September 1944. Leon Cohen also wrote of his experiences, and he, too, buried his account. Ya'akov Gabai, an inmate in Crematorium 2, wrote a detailed "diary beginning on his first day with the Sonderkommando and kept it until January 18, 1945. The journal covered the most ordinary events that occurred every day in the Sonderkommando. . . . A few of my friends knew, but it was kept secret."[104] Unfortunately, fearing reprisal from the Germans, who searched the inmates meticulously for any written materials before leaving on the Death March from Birkenau to the west, Gabai was forced to leave his five hundred pages without burying them. Fortunately, he was capable of communicating valuable information orally to Greif. Another unfortunate case was that of Abraham Mevorah, the son of a rabbi from Kastoria. "Every day for months he wrote down his experiences in the camp. He held his diary [during the Death March] until the last moment when he went insane, forgotten inside the sealed wagon of the train [packed with 120 people], choking from suffocation."[105]

There were other means for the Sephardim to spread word about what was going on in the crematoria. The Germans placed the Sonderkommandos in rooms above the ovens to keep them isolated from other inmates because they didn't want them to tell about what was happening. However, the Greek Jews of the Sonderkommando were able to communicate their miseries in song. In testimony to their suffering, they sang verses they had created in Greek. They used the well-known melodies from the popular Greek singer Markos Vamvakaris, whom the Germans liked, and changed the words to convey their message about what was happening to the Sonderkommandos. Thus, by singing they were able to circumvent the restriction against talking outside their group. Berry Cassuto Nahmia, who worked in the Canada Kommando, reported hearing the following song by an unknown Greek inmate from Crematorium IV:

> Girls—Greeks—who listen to me,
> I say everything by singing, so you will understand.
> Here the chimneys you see are the biggest factory of death.
> Thousands of Jews, old, young, children
> Fall into the arms of the flames.
> I know they will burn me too.
> After a while, I will not be around
> To describe what my tired eyes have seen.
> Do you hear me? Believe me.
> It's true, horrible, I live it every day.
> Girls—Greeks—I beg you.
> If you get out of here alive,
> Tell the entire world the story I sing to you.[106]

Berry Nahmia said that she would remember the song until the day she died.[107]

In addition to the written and oral materials, Tzipora Hager Halivni reports that the four blurred photographs of Auschwitz were taken in secret in the vicinity of Crematorium 4 [V] by an unnamed inmate on August 1944. Two of the photographs (Nos. 280 and 281) "show the cremation of corpses in a fire pit, No. 282 shows a group of naked women just before they enter the gas chamber, and No. 283 is an image of trees."[108] Alter Fajnzylberg, who had contact with the resistance and collected explosive powder for the revolt, identified the individual who took the pictures as Alex, a Greek Jew.[109] Several writers, including Steven Bowman in *The Agony of Greek Jews, 1940–1945*, and Alter Fajnzylberg, state that Alex was known by his code name, Alekos Alexandridis, and that his real name was Albert (Alberto) Errera of Larissa, a former Greek navy officer.[110] Also attributed to him were the names Alex Errera and Alexander Errera.[111] Georges Didi-Huberman analyzes the photographs from Auschwitz in *Images in Spite of All* and attributes them to a Greek Jew.

Albert Menasche recounts that 212 members of the Sonderkommando were moved from Birkenau in August 1944 to Auschwitz and gassed there by the Germans themselves with the greatest secrecy. Menasche continues, "The news spread, however, among the remaining *Sonder*. The idea of the revolt was taking root and was to crystalize towards the middle of September 1944."[112] Henryk Porebski remembers that a member of the resistance movement "urged them to avoid staging an uprising at any cost."[113] According to Porebski, Kaminsky, two Greek Jews (Errera and Baruch) with whom he had previous discussions, and possibly some Russians still went ahead with the organization of the revolt, which was to take place on August 15, 1944, on the feast day of the Virgin Mary, "a more relaxing day when they could overcome the guards," but it was aborted due to a betrayal.[114] Kaminsky said in a whisper that it was a Polish *Kapo* named Mietek Morawa who reported the planning.[115] Two other reasons for the failure to act were given. "The Polish underground decided that they would not do it because the Russians are already coming very close and there was no reason for more bloodshed."[116] Moreover, some Jews, Russians, and Poles were opposed to the date of the uprising. Ironically, the Russians by-passed Auschwitz.

Otto Mohl, the commandant of the crematoria, announced in August 1944 to the Sonderkommandos of Crematorium I that Kapo Kaminsky, together with Romani, had been cruelly tortured and executed by a firing squad. Jean Cohen, quoting Filip Muller, adds that Muller accidentally found the corpse of Kaminsky with two bullet holes, one in the back of his neck and another above his left eye. A survivor of Crematorium 2 told me, "Esta matansa mos atristo muncho i desidimos tomar vengansa de estas kruelas bestias" (This murder saddened us, and we decided to take vengeance on these cruel beasts). According to Langbein, Kaminsky and Errera "did not live to see the day on which the uprising began."[117]

Meanwhile, the Sonderkommandos had begun to prepare for the revolt: they smuggled into the crematoria carpets, containers of diesel, oil, gunpowder, and some weapons. Leon Cohen informed me in 1985 during one of our walks in Bat Yam that everyone had a task. His was to burn the mattresses, but he failed then to mention where he was, or which crematorium was to be burned. In his 1996 book, *From Greece to Birkenau*, he gave some clarification: "With the help of two other inmates, I was supposed to burn the beds and mattresses in Crematorium 2, and by so doing this setting fire to the entire crematorium."[118]

Nahmia writes that Kaminsky was arrested and killed. His death "meant the end of our plans."[119] Baruch became the "spark of the revolt." In "No Other Jews like Them," Leah Aini quotes Tomai as saying, "According to the Greek Foreign Ministry, it would appear that the revolt organized by the Sonderkommando on October 7, 1944, was planned and executed completely by Greeks, led by Yosef Baruch and his two lieutenants, Joseph Levy and Maurice Aron," with the assistance of Isaac Baruch, Sam Karasso, and Yomtov Yakoel.[120] As mentioned previously, Erika Kounio-Amariglio, who worked in one of the most important offices in Auschwitz, the Politische Abteilung, was in a position to notice that her office was in turmoil. The Germans were running about angrily. Something had gone wrong. It was later that she learned that the Sonderkommandos "had blown Crematorium IV and had mutinied." Erwin, a Polish political prisoner, who had come from the men's camp, told them that the Sonderkommandos had mutinied and that "[t]he Greeks were in the front line of the uprising. The Greeks, our own people, had raised their heads and stood up to them." Erika was elated that her fellow Salonikans rebelled, and though they could not escape, she felt proud of them: "I thought, 'but what a noble death! . . . They have chosen death in the way they wanted!'"[121]

The Greeks were unable to get assistance from the partisans and other Sonderkommandos. Nadjari, commenting on the possibility of non-Greek cooperation, realized, "The Poles who worked in Crematorium IV [3] behaved worst of all. They could have helped us more with our plans and at the same time warn us because they had ways to do it. But they preferred to go on with their macabre work and die."[122] Dario Gabbai believed that there was a lack of collaboration during the struggle in Crematorium 3. In his interview he said, "And then I remember they were telling me that the partisans were not cooperating enough and letting the Jews do the job."[123]

Abandoned, the Greek Jews in the crematoria decided to start the rebellion by themselves. Nadjari explained that the Greeks were resigned to act alone. "The job was indeed delicate, but we were determined no matter what. The plan was exactly the same for Crematoria 3 and 4."[124] Leon Cohen told me during our second interview, "No teniamos otra opsion; era bivir o morir. Dinguno kijo ayudarmos. Ansi es ke todo kedo en muestras manos" (We had no choice; it was life or death. No one wanted to help us. So everything was left in our hands). Despondent, Leon Cohen continued, "Mos abandonaron. Ma no podiamos darmos por vensidos. No podiamos konfiar en dinguno. Dependia en mozotros el atake" (They abandoned us. But we could not give up. We could not trust anyone. It was up to us to make the move). Leon Cohen expands in *From Greece to Birkenau* about the continuation of the plans to start the revolt: "[F]rom then on, only Greeks were allowed to take part and if anyone else came along, we quickly changed the subject. Josef Baruch, the man chosen to lead our revolt, was determined to contact prisoners in Crematorium 1, who, in spite of everything, had remained loyal to our cause. We advised him to be careful but gave him a 'free hand.' In the end, we agreed with the Greeks of Crematorium 3 and 4 on a final plan."[125] While they waited for further developments, they decided to continue rehearsing and to keep in touch with others through the kitchen staff. Leon continues, "One morning, on 7 September 1944 . . . we felt that something unusual was about to happen. Could it be what we were all waiting for? Suddenly we felt we were ready for war, all of us!"

On October 7, 1944, the organizers of the revolt told the Sonderkommandos that the Nazis were making plans to kill them. However, the leaders of the Jewish Military Resistance, who were not part of the Sonderkommando, refused to join forces. They cautioned them to postpone the coup until a later date: "The uprising had to be avoided at all costs."[126] However, the Greeks were aware that two selections had already taken place and that several Sephardim had been cremated. According to Leon, this act strengthened their determination to fight. They, too, expected the Germans to get rid of them as soon as possible.[127] However, the Poles, especially Orer and Hersz Strassvogel, insisted that they do nothing, as "it would be futile."[128]

At 14:30 Sergeant Busch, a senior Sonderkommando officer, as well as some men from the SS, came as forewarned to the courtyard in front of Crematorium 3 with a list of names for transfer to another camp in Poland.[129] Morris Venezia declared, "When those officers came there, there were Greeks, almost 200, 300 Greeks. And the Germans started to call numbers, so, and so, and so. One 100, 150 numbers."[130] All prisoners were told to line up. Busch began to count. Those not selected were sent back to Crematorium 4. Busch started to call two hundred Hungarians, who, following orders, stepped on one side of the courtyard. When Busch called the names of the Greeks, no one answered. To protect themselves the Hungarians tried to disarm the Greek Jews but failed: subsequently they were sent to the bath (shower) of the Gypsy Lager. Morris continues, "So the Greeks, who were more courageous, knew that they were going to kill them." The Greek Jews in Crematorium 3 declared that they would not go like lambs to the slaughter. Led by Josef Baruch, they proceeded with their plans. Their aim was to fight for themselves and the captives in the main camp. The Greek Jews could not be stopped. As told by Morris Venezia, their enemy knew that it was fighting with the Greeks. "So, one of the Greek guys, he had a shovel in his hand and hit the German right on the head. The German holding his head run out and start screaming. . . . How did I know that? I was in Crematorium 2."[131]

While the guards were busy with their routine, Leon Cohen said that he and his friends "started slitting the mattresses lengthwise. We removed all our loot from its hiding place; knives, medicines, padded clothes, everything we had collected when planning to start hostilities on August 15."[132] Unfortunately, Crematorium 1 failed to send the signal. The inmates wondered, "What had happened in Crematorium 1? Were they ready?" Meanwhile, "the sound of bullets were getting closer. . . . Suddenly we saw black smoke out of Crematorium 3 (or was it 4?)."[133] Leon added, "It was difficult to locate [where the smoke was coming from]. Then the smoke turned to bright flames. Yes, this was a fire, a real fire! . . . At the same time, unnoticed by us, the courtyard [as well as Crematorium 1] had filled with soldiers, their fingers on the triggers of their machine guns." Leon continued, "Hell, we were trapped. In the middle of the uproar we heard bellowing: 'A-N-T-R-E-T-E-E-E-E-N-N-N' [assemble, line up, in German], repeated by the *Kapo*." Leon Cohen, amazed, looked at a friend, who said in Greek: "'*Pame*, let's go, God help us!' We rushed to push the mattresses and blankets back all higgledy-piggledy. We managed to join the end of the queue, just as the *Kapo* was calling us for the second time to wake us up (!). Pretending to be half asleep, with tousled hair, yawning widely, we came down to the courtyard which was filled with SS and soldiers."[134]

Another voice in Greek was also heard: "'*Apamo*' (onto them)." Elias Lampropoulos, pastoral assistant at the Greek Orthodox Cathedral of the Annunciation in Atlanta, Georgia, proposed that the two terms *andrizethe* and *pame* could be combined into Άνθρωπος πάμε (*Ánthropos páme*), "Men, let's go." It was the signal for the revolt. Leon notes, "The Greeks immediately responded by jumping on their two guards to snatch their guns."[135] Unfortunately, they did not get the assistance of the non-Greeks, who turned their backs on them.

The Germans, notified by the wounded soldier in Crematorium 3, surrounded Crematorium 3, fired a hail of bullets and grenades, and ordered the prisoners to surrender. The prisoners set the building on fire. Leon Cohen recounts, "Within minutes, Crematorium 3 was engulfed in flames and all the Greeks were wiped out. The others had run away and sought refuge in Crematorium 4 before the doors were locked. Needless to say, they were all gunned down inside the crematorium. They had mistakenly believed that by dissociating themselves from the Greeks they would be reprieved. Unfortunately for them, they paid a higher price than they expected."[136] The Germans were furious and massacred everyone in Crematorium 4. Leon Cohen recalls, "Albert Nadjari, if I am not mistaken, was overcome by smoke, and when he fell outside Crematorium 4, he broke his leg and passed out." Later in the day he was brought to Crematorium 3. He was saved and survived the tragedy.[137]

Shlomo Venezia notes that the smoke seen from Crematorium IV (3) came before the assigned time. Danny (Daniel) Bennahmias related that "a Crazy Hungarian," who did not know of the plot, had consciously set his pallet on fire. Danny and the others in Crematorium 2 did not see the smoke on that day; they had no way of learning about its precipitous cause; they were in no position to know either one or the other."[138] It was much later that Danny learned from Isaac (Isaacquino) Venezia what took place in Crematorium IV (3). Meanwhile, we learn from Morris Venezia that Isaacquino, an eyewitness, "[s]aw the flames coming. He went to the second floor where he was hiding, and the flames were coming. He went into some kind of bathroom . . . and started kicking the floor with his feet so hard kicking, kicking, kicking and he broke the floor up, the ceiling whatever, and he come down. . . . [He got entangled in an electrical wire but was able to free himself.] He went to Kanada Kommando, it was near to him. So the women, when they saw him, they got him and they hide him 1, 2 days. When the German went inside they told him, 'We got a guy.' This German, he did not kill him, he brought him to us in Crematorium 2. And he was working with us."[139] Morris smiled, knowing that they had fooled the German. Danny Bennahmias's version is that Isaacquino "had managed to escape through the forest separating Crematoria 1 and 2 from 3 and 4, was able to mingle with and be absorbed by the surviving men in the Sonderkommando from Crematoria 1 and 2. . . . [He informed Danny] that 400 Sonderkommando prisoners from Crematoria 3 and 4 were made to lie naked, face down to the ground, and in rows of five, a standard German line-up procedure, before being shot [in the back of the head] and killed. As to the actual disposition of the bodies, we are led to conjecture that they were burned in the huge, open pit adjacent to Crematorium 4, since none of the Sonderkommando was assigned to cremate them."[140]

According to Shaul Chazan, it was Raoul Jahoun, not Isaacquino Venezia, who escaped from Crematorium 3 "and came to us, where his brothers were. . . . Raoul told us that the Sonderkommando at Crematorium [3] torched mattresses and set the whole building on fire. It looked like they'd all been executed. Afterwards, the Germans came around in their usual way to do a head count. They noticed that there was one prisoner too many. After they discovered Raoul, he was shot right there."[141] Chazan recounts that Raoul's brothers picked up his ashes and bones and placed them in a crate along with Leon Cohen's letter. When Chazan visited the camp after the liberation, he was not able to locate it, since everything had changed.[142] In addition to the burning of the mattresses, Hunter Mayes writes, "The members of Crematorium 4 placed demolition charges into the oven rooms and detonated them in a defiant suicide."[143] Subsequently, "Four SS men were killed and several wounded."[144]

The men in Crematorium 1, who were in the midst of the revolt with those in Crematorium 3 or 4, panicked when they saw the area surrounded with dogs and SS armed with machine guns. Danny in Crematorium 2 was informed that something had gone wrong. Within seconds they heard the first shots and the cry of someone nearby shouting, "*It's on! We're going to move.*" There was a second shout "*Let's move! Out! The revolt's started!*"[145] Bowman relates that in the third and fourth crematoria, "the Greeks were able to overcome the guards," and they blew up "the furnaces and smokestacks before they were finally killed." They killed approximately twenty guards, destroyed one crematorium, and caused "extensive damage to the second, thereby halving the 'production' of the death factory."[146]

On April 6, 2015, I called Dario Gabbai, then residing in California. I asked for more information on Crematorium 2. At first he apologized for being old and not being able to recall what truly had happened. I kept prodding him on the participation of the Greek Jews in Crematorium 2. After a while, he recalled, "We were surrounded by the Germans and a lot of dogs; we could not help at all. We heard guns and shouts and someone screaming for help." It was the voice of the sadistic Oberkapo Karol that came from Crematorium 1, where he had been pushed into the oven. Morris Venezia recalls, "We were only 100 in Crematorium 2, they did not touch us. They took us to Crematorium 1 to burn the dead people that escaped. They needed us at this time. That is why they couldn't kill us."[147] Among the 100 were Aaron Barzelai, Daniel Bennahmias, and Shlomo Venezia. They were used to remove and to dispose of the bodies of the escapees who fell on the barbed wire.

CONCLUSION

For a few minutes, the inmates were free. From their disempowered state, they attempted to seize power. Though many were killed inside the crematoria, or surrounded and killed once they had escaped, theirs was a moral victory. The uprising in Auschwitz offered some hope to the other prisoners that they would see the end of the war. The ever-present horrors persisted. "Forty-eight hours after the revolt, the horrible chimneys again belched forth their eternal and sinister flames. The bodies of the heroes were burning," writes Albert Menasche.[148] Word of the revolt passed to the other camps, and the Greek Jews were praised for their courage. "This extremely unusual event for a Nazi concentration camp, the Birkenau Revolt, held a profound moral significance for us all. The Germans weren't invincible, even against us."[149] Of the death of all "who were sacrificed on the altar of freedom, their sacrifice was a small victory over hate and war. Their courage will never be forgotten."[150]

4
Medical Experiments

In 1942 Heinrich Himmler along with prominent German military officer SS Major-General Karl Gebhardt and physician Carl Clauberg (Karl Klauberg) decided to implement medical experimentation in Auschwitz. They also undertook medical and genetic experiments in Dachau, Buchenwald, Ebensee, Mauthausen, Natzweiler, Neuengamme, Ravensbrück, and Sachsenhausen. There were some sixty-five to seventy programs inflicted upon approximately seven thousand prisoners by two hundred doctors, the most horrendous of whom was Josef Mengele (1911–79), called the Angel of Death.

Peter Tyson notes that Nazi doctors conducted as many as thirty different types of experiments on concentration camp inmates. They performed these studies without the consent of the victims, who suffered indescribable pain, mutilation, permanent disability, or, in many cases, death. "Many of the subjects died . . . while many others were executed. . . . Those who survived were often left mutilated, suffering permanent disability, weakened bodies, and mental distress."[1]

The medical experiments were to help "the survival of military personnel," to test drugs, and to advance "Nazi racial and ideological goals."[2] The purpose of the experiments was supposedly to research diseases such as typhoid and cancer or to conduct trials of new drugs produced by the pharmaceutical company Bayer, which was part of IG Farben. In effect they perpetrated mass castration and sterilization to prevent the reproduction of what were deemed to be racially inferior people. The experiments were performed without anesthetics or antiseptics. Doctors Josef Mengele, Horst Schumann, Herta Oberheuser, and Carl Clauberg, among others, selected a great number of women and men for atrocious medical experiments, including sterilization.

An entry by Hermann Langbein concerning Carl Clauberg's experimentation states, "When the Jews from Greece arrived in 1943 many were chosen as his guinea pigs, most of whom would die before liberation of the camp in January of 1945, adding to the statistics of Greek Jewish losses. On April 28, 1943 (as specifically noted in the Archives of Auschwitz) 128 Greek Jewish women are transferred to Block 10, the experimental block."[3]

Erika Kounio-Amariglio writes, "As transports from Greece were arriving one after another at that time (1943–44), and from these transports they [Dr. Mengele (PhD and MD) and Professor Dr. Clauberg] chose young girls, 'virgins,' barren women as well as young married ones—particularly from Salonika. Among others, they placed them in one wing of Block 10 where experiments were performed in hopes of finding ways to sterilize men and women faster and more effectively. This was basically Dr. Mengele's specialty, Dr. Clauberg would bring as many twins from the transports as he wanted to the block. I don't know what his criteria were. They were known as 'Clauberg's twins.'"[4] After the liberation, Erika tried to find out what happened there, "but everything was concealed under an air of mystery and nobody 'knew' anything. We did not know how many Greek girls there were, nor did we know their names." After the liberation Erika met some girls from Block 10, even some of the men. Hardly anyone wanted to talk. After some probing, she found out how horrible and traumatic the experiments were. Erika concluded saying, "I regarded the inmates with awe and did not dare to ask any further questions."[5]

Of the known experiments, "the Greek Jews constituted about a quarter of the victims."[6] Even though the majority of the victims were from Greece, the Sephardim from the Dodecanese islands and the Balkans were also subjected to these brutal medical experiments. During my interview with Salomon and Rene Bivas in Tel Aviv on June 7, 1982, Rene told me, "As soon as the trains arrived in Auschwitz, Dr. Mengele and his cohorts were there to select their prey." Salomon noted that the Germans chose only virgins. "They particularly preferred 'Jewish girls from Greece. . . . The Germans had no qualms in manhandling us. They considered us the lowest of the low. They had no problem in selecting us for their exams rather than animals since they were scarce and tasteful to the palate." Salomon sadly added, "There were a series of experiments performed on Jewish men and women from Greece." One of them was his sister, Flor Tabo, who survived and moved to the United States. He continued, "Unfortunately she was not exterminated; rather, her health was destroyed due to several experiments performed on her by Doctor Mengele. Even today she suffers." Rene, referring to her sister-in-law, added, "They took her and several other young ladies from Greece and performed all the experiments that doctors do on *hayot* (animals), on beasts. When the Germans located living bodies, there was no better way for them to perform any experiment." I asked Rene to explain more. In visible distress, she answered:

Komo dezir? A las mujeres les echavan injeksiones en las partes privadas para no parir: esterizasion. Otros eksperimentos uvo ke les echavan injeksiones para ver komo kurar la tuberkulozis. Otros eran para komo salvar a los askerlikes ke mandavan a las frontieras. Para esto tomavan ombres tambien. Les kitaron todo. Aki los operaron de una parte, aki los operaron de dos partes. Desharon un guevo, aki no desharon nada. I otra eksperiensa era ke los seravan en unas sierras [kamaretas] en las kualas el yelor no se de ke grado para saver komo va somportar el soldado alman. Los kitavan de ayi, el ke rezistia salia bivo, el ke no, salia muerto yelado. Si era bivo, prokuravan de salvarlo para ansi poder salvar a sus soldados. Izieron tantos eskperimentos ke uno no viene a kontar.

(What can I say? To women, they gave injections in their private parts to prevent them from getting pregnant: sterilization. There were other experiments, they gave injections to find out how to cure tuberculosis. Other ones to see how they could save the [German] soldiers that they sent to the front. For these tests they chose men also. In general, they would remove everything. One time, they operated on one side, another time, they operated both sides. They left one testicle, now they removed everything. And in another operation, they locked them into certain rooms, of which I do not know the temperature, to find out how the German soldiers would be able to stand it. They took them out of the rooms, the one who stood the cold came out alive; the one who did not, was frozen dead. They tried to save those who were still alive in order to save their own soldiers. They performed so many experiments that one can hardly count them.)

According to Dr. Isaac Aaron Matarasso, in addition to virgins, the "German doctors selected women according to categories . . . *uniparae* (women who gave birth to one child) and *multipara* (those who had given birth to more than one)." Matarasso reports that the different procedures were "performed by the murderous doctors."[7] In the section titled "Medical Experiments on Hostages," which he submitted to the Tel Aviv Medical Society, dated February 1, 1946, Matarasso comments on "observations collected through direct interrogations of the victims." For example, "on March 27, 1943, 99 women, who had just arrived from Salonika, were taken directly to the infamous Block 10. Soon thereafter they were subjected either to a surgical procedure, radiation, X-rays, injection or a combination. They injected toxins into the uterus that caused excruciating pain, long-lasting adverse medical effects, and sometimes death. For instance, the Germans chose a 43-year-old mother and her 19-year-old daughter. Within one month, both were subjected to several injections. The daughter not only was given various injections, but underwent a surgical operation for removal of the ovaries. Both women subsequently suffered from amenorrhea, menses and hot flashes."[8]

Matarasso also reports on a short list of men who were subjected to medical experiments.[9] While subjected to a series of multiple experiments, the Sephardim were intensely concerned about the sterilization of men through high doses of radiation and castration, and of women through radiation, incisions, and injections in their reproductive organs. The results of such medical crimes were a perpetual tragedy throughout the lives of the survivors. Not being able to have children devastated the women.

A survivor from Greece who received some intravenous injection at first felt well, but in a short time she experienced abdominal pains and vaginal bleeding. The German doctors exposed her to an overdose of radiation. Her situation worsened, "No podia ni levantarme. Grasias al Dio ke me enviaron a la baraka i no al krematorio. Kon la ayuda de mi amiga de Atemas poko a poko me enfortesi" (I could hardly stand. Thank God, they sent me to the barrack and not to the crematorium. With the assistance of my friend from Athens, little by little I regained my strength). She continued, "After the liberation I noticed that I was not menstruating. I went to a clinic in Tel Aviv, and the doctor told me that I was sterile as the result of the radiation. I felt dejected, I cried. To calm me down, the doctor said, 'I feared that the amount of radiation given to you could have caused vaginal cancer.'"[10]

One of the most sadistic of the Nazi doctors, Aribert Heim, was known to perform the cruelest experiments. Except for Adolph Eichmann, he became the most sought-after war criminal. The inmates referred to him as the "Butcher of Mauthausen and Dr. Death." He was charged with murdering more than three hundred individuals in a grotesque manner. He removed organs without anesthesia, butchered his victims, and "poisoned prisoners with various injections directly into the heart, including petrol, available poisons or even water, to induce death. [On one occasion], he gave the prisoner anesthetic and then proceeded to cut him open, castrate him, and take out one of his kidneys. The prisoner died and his head was cut off, boiled and stripped of his flesh. . . . Then he allegedly used this young man's skull as a paperweight on his desk."[11] After the war, Heim moved from country to country and finally settled in Cairo, Egypt, under the alias of Tarek Farid Hussein. Heim converted to Islam. He died of cancer on August 10, 1992.

In "No Other Jews like Them," Leah Aini states that in Blocks 10 and 11 in Birkenau, Germans carried out "the most horrifying acts ever enacted by people upon their fellow human beings. Many of the women tortured were young Jews from Greece. The purpose of the experiments was supposedly to research diseases such as typhoid and cancer or conduct trials of new drugs produced by Bayer. In effect, however, what was perpetrated there en masse was sterilization. The devil for 200 Greek Jewish women was Dr. Carl Clauberg, who removed their ovaries in terrifying ways, without anesthesia or antiseptics. Let us remember the names of some of his victims: Rivka Ari, Dora Cohen, Buena Bitran, Rachel Mordoch, Bella Malach."[12] To this list, I include the following women: Aliza Sarfati Baruch, Mazaltov [Fofo] Behar Mordoh, Lili Katan, Julia Sophie Elze, Flor Tabo; and men: Ovadia Baruch, Salvatore Katan, Alexander Katan, Sam Molho, and Asher Varon. Violette Fintz added, "Those who were selected were terrified. They were aware that they would end in Block 10 from where only a few returned. The experiments were brutal and agonizing. In several cases the inmates were called again and again for more tests, some within a few weeks. Those who refused to obey the orders were not successful. They had no option; it was either submit to further unknown medical experiments and hope that they would survive and not be sent to the crematorium. If perchance they survived, they were sent back to Birkenau looking like ghosts, as if they had returned from the grave." Hermann Langbein concurs: "The inmates were afraid of the surgical procedures. Many women underwent these procedures for self-preservation believing that after them they would not be transferred to Birkenau. 'Perhaps they will let us live afterwards!' Only one group of Jewish women who already had one operation refused another and preferred a transfer to Birkenau. Where they faced extermination."[13]

In Aini's article, Elvira Kolado, from Greece, declared that the Germans "pulled my womb down and performed experiments. Afterwards I could never have children." There was no end to their investigations. "They chose . . . Greek Jewish young women with long noses. . . . Afterwards, I saw several types of masks fitted to the face, a month later the young women were put on a train and never returned. People said they had been mummified."[14] Many of them died before the liberation.

The suffering of Sephardic men and women from medical experiments, *los olvidados* (the overlooked), during the Holocaust has not received much attention. As with their Ashkenazi sisters, "the women suffered indignities, degradation, and the worst atrocities; they were dishonored and their sense of femininity was robbed; they were forced to disrobe before men, to be part of brothels where they were sexually abused [by the Germans and elite prisoners]."[15] The order for the *pure* Germans not to interact with those of the lower classes did not stop them.

Doctor Albert Menasche, a member of the orchestra for the camp, described the hospital:

> [E]quipped with all the instruments necessary for good diagnosis; well-equipped laboratories, modern operating rooms, X-ray equipment. Only the remedies were at fault. The entire hospital had been created not to save lives, or to alleviate the suffering of the sick, but . . . to permit a young S.S. doc-

> tor, who was the hospital head, to successfully complete his insane experiments: or to work beside doctors on Jewish patients who had no right to object to any operations.
>
> Millions of young men were castrated or sterilized by X-rays, millions of young girls were rendered sterile. . . . Innumerable appendectomies were performed. . . . Only twins found themselves in the good graces of this monster [Mengele]. . . . Eighty-four Jewish doctors comprised the personnel of this Lager.[16]

From the totality of my interviews, I know that no Sephardic twins were part of the diabolic experiments.[17]

There were some Sephardi doctors in Block 10. In some cases, when not watched by the German doctors, these White Angels tried to protect some of their own. "One such case was Mazaltov Behar Mordoh, also known as *Fofó*, from Salonika, a brave seventeen-year-old who, when selected for radiation, begged Dr. Samuel (Shmuel), a Jewish doctor also from Salonika, to spare one of her ovaries, which he did without informing her. He was not worried of the consequences. Unfortunately, Dr. Samuel was not able to fool Dr. Shumann, the German doctor, and he paid with his life. After the liberation she gave birth to a son and named him Samuel."[18]

In Tel Aviv on June 16, 1982, Aliza Sarfati Baruch told me that no matter how sick they were, they resisted going to the clinic, knowing full well that "[k]ualker akto de febleza era direkto para los ekperimentos o avria la puerta del krematorio. Djente ke no podia lavorar no tenia futuro" (Any act of weakness was straight to the experiments or opened the door to the crematorium. People who could not work had no future). Aliza's husband, Ovadia, recounted how they had met. For stealing some soup, he and his friend Moshe Gabai were "caught and punished with forty lashes on their behind." He was so beaten that he wished they would kill him. "The Germans kicked me in my private parts, and I started screaming, 'Oh Madre! Oh Madre!' Aliza was walking nearby . . . and recognized the words in Ladino [Judeo-Spanish]. She asked the *Kapo* if she could meet him. She risked her life in meeting him." They found out that they were from Salonika, fell in love, and kept it secret. They lost track of each other until two years later. At first Aliza would not divulge to Ovadia what had happened to her in Block 10.

During the interview, Aliza interrupted Ovadia, adding what happened to her after the first operation: "De verdad ke yo estava muy, muy hazina porke estuve onze mezes en la kama kon la tripa avierta. . . . Me desharon ayi, venia el doctor i me mirava" (Truly I was very, very sick because I had been in bed for eleven months with my stomach opened. . . . They left me there, the doctor would come to check on me.) Some months later, many women who were outside Block 10 were taken, possibly to the crematorium. By chance Aliza being inside was safe. "What spared me is not that I was inside but also that I was going to be operated again later." A French female Christian doctor tried to protect her. When she realized that Mengele would make a list for a second experiment, the doctor hurriedly included Aliza's number (41444) at the bottom and urged her to move to the back. When her number was called, she answered present without showing her face. Since it appeared that Aliza had not been previously operated on, she was not taken. Four months later those operated on for the second time returned; most of them soon died.[19]

Aliza was saved temporarily. In a Yad Vashem deposition, Aliza and Ovadia related that a German doctor [Mengele] called out three numbers; one was Aliza's. "Aliza heard that she was summoned, God gave her tremendous strength. She pushed the beds, barricaded herself and started screaming. Dr. Schumann pointed his gun at her, 'I'll kill her!' and Aliza said, 'Go ahead, kill me, kill me.' Dr. Schumann said, 'Bullets are too valuable for using on Jews. Jews deserve the crematoria. You will come down to the operating room. You will have to slither in like a snake and I'll operate on you last.'" Aliza was lucky, because while they were operating on the first girl, a siren blared. Dr. Mengele sent the staff to the bomb shelter and left the second girl and Aliza to be operated on by Dr. Shmuel, who was left alone with another doctor. "Dr. Shmuel sabotaged the sterilizations that the SS doctors were performing. He cut their bellies open, removed this and that, and sent me back to the department." Each day, Dr. Shmuel would come to change Aliza's dressings, and Aliza would admonish him: "You Satan, you wicked man! I am sixteen and half, why did you operate on me?' And he would tell her in French, 'Aliza, try to stay alive. One day you'll understand what I have done. Try to stay alive.' Unknown to her, she was not left sterile. Several weeks after Aliza's operation, she heard that Dr. Shmuel was caught through an informant and executed."[20] Due to his intervention, several women managed to get pregnant after the war; however, most women were not able to conceive.

In my interview in Tel Aviv in 1982, I asked Aliza for clarification about the death of Dr. Shmuel:

IJL: Why did they hang him?

ASB: La razon ke izo sabotaj. Ke los doktores ke vieron ke kuando deshavan la koza en manos del doktor djidio, el doktor djidio no kompletava el dirito [el orden] ke le dieron. Azia kozas de otro modo. A mi, el savia lo ke el aleman le disho. No me korto lo ke devia de kortar. (The reason is that he committed sabotage. The [German] doctors noticed that when the matter was left in the hands of the Jewish doctor, the Jewish doctor did not carry out the order given to him. He performed differently. As for me, he knew what the German told him. But he did not cut what he was supposed to [the ovaries].

IJL: Were they also experimenting for other things?

ASB: For many other things.

IJL: Have you heard of other women?

ASB: Well?

IJL: To you also?

ASB: Not to me. They did something else to them. To them they did something inside the womb, to women who were already married and had given birth. Unfortunately, the babies were sent to their deaths with their grandmothers, while the mothers stayed alive.

It was then that sadly she told me that her sister had given birth to a boy in Salonika five days before the deportation. She, the baby, and the entire family were cremated.

IJL: Do you know women who were given injections in the womb?

ASB: Yes, there were some.

IJL: What were their reactions?

ASB: The same. These women did not have children. They did not do the same to them. They vomited, not because of the injections.

IJL: Radiation?

ASB: Yes, radiation. Only due to the radiation.

IJL: How often they administered the injections?

ASB: Well, each two months, each three months they gave them a shot. They died because they were infected. It was like they treated us; few of us stayed alive.

IJL: The others died?

ASB: All of them died. They kept us in a room, laying down and looking at a running faucet: we were thirsty. To those they gave water, to those who asked for water, they checked the spinal cord. We were then afraid to ask for water. We could see these women struggling, and after an hour, two, they were dying, they were already infected. I was infected up to my stomach. They placed some rubber tubes with pins, English pins, to hold the tubes in place. That is how the pus was coming out.

IJL: You were left there?

ASB: The Germans waited until the person was fully recovered and then killed him or her. At other times, they waited for the scar of the operation to be healed, and then they sent the inmate to work or to undergo another experiment.

It was after the liberation that Aliza learned that the "experiments performed by the doctors on young girls—'I was the youngest, fourteen [sixteen] and half years old'—were to do away with the Jewish race." She continued, "Those who were fortunate not to be operated on eventually lived a normal life. However, the others, such as me, as the rest, were afraid, we were suspicious even of the young men who loved us. Unfortunately, you had to explain to them what took place."

Aliza switched to a different topic, a personal one. She spoke of her second encounter with Ovadia: "It was in 1946, after the liberation. I went to the community Council in Salonika to register, and he was there." Soon after, Ovadia proposed to her. While initially in the camp, she had not told him of what had happened in Block 10; however, before accepting his proposal, Aliza had to clarify her situation: "What I told him was that the young girls who got married lived a good life, because they first informed the men what took place in the camp. The men realized that it was not the fault of the girls. Telling them was the great miracle. Since he came from a large family, I wanted him to know that he would not have children. He answered, 'I never thought of having any. I know what happened in the camp, and we are going to get married.'" She asked him to declare it in the Ketubah (marriage contract). In 1946 they were married. With the financial assistance of the Joint Distribution Committee, and the efforts of the Jewish Brigade, they illegally immigrated to Mandatory Palestine. One day her belly got big, and she thought that she had caught a disease from a lady who had allowed her to take showers in her house. They took her to Beilinson Hospital, Rabin Medical Center, to be checked, and they found out that she was three months pregnant. Yaakov was born in 1947. Fourteen years later a girl, Lily, was born. She was named after Ovadia's sister who had died in Auschwitz.

During our discussion in Brussels on July 23, 1984, Violette Fintz, from Rhodes and Cape Town, South Africa, told me the following: "During an *appell* a German woman came to the barrack and asked if there is someone pregnant, we are going to give her double rations. A certain Israeli lady from Rhodes stepped out and said she was. The German *Kapo* took her away and disappeared. Two or three weeks later, we saw her, weak, sick, and hardly able to walk. She told us that they opened her stomach, removed the fetus without anesthesia, and left her stomach opened. Soon she died from an infection." I asked Violette if there were any other such cases among our people from Rhodes. Without any hesitation she said, "Here. We were told by an older lady that her daughter was pregnant. They took her. She was awake during the delivery and saw everything. She could neither cry out nor talk while they were operating on her without the use of anesthesia. Imagine her shock when the Germans placed the fetus in a bottle with some liquid in front of her."

The Germans also deceived Salvatore Katan, a survivor from Salonika. He recounted to Sidney Bolkosky, who interviewed him in 1981, "Then on Sunday in the afternoon while we were washing the clothes, there was an *appell*. We had to look everything clean and so forth, all right. A German doctor came and asked, 'Who wants to have a good job? It's going to have more food and it's going to be better off, not hard work.' And myself, I raised up, I raised my hand and volunteered." Katan was chosen with five other inmates; they were taken to the hospital. Some Polish guys who were laid up in bed warned him not to move. "Greek, Greek! Don't go, don't go. . . . Don't go because they're going to take you away. And they told me why. I said, 'That's a good job.'"[21] The doctor told another one, "'You're good. This way.' When he came to me, he said, 'You're no good, go back.' So this was my luck." Later, when he was assigned to another gang, he was called and taken to the hospital, where he was operated on. Even though he was in pain, the Germans sent him back to work. After the liberation, once in Milan, Italy, he reported to a hospital. The doctor checked him and asked, "'What's the matter with you?' I say, 'I don't know. I have a pain. . . . I can't put my feet down.'" Katan felt that he was paralyzed from the waist down. During the surgery the doctors in the camp implanted a bone in his hip, which caused a serious infection. The bone was removed, and he recovered. When asked if there were any other kinds of horrible experiences, Katan replied, "Yeah, and then they gave shots like they give you shots here, the doctors for, you know, polio. . . . And there was inflammation. The arm was three times big, and then it got bigger like a moon."

Salvatore Katan and Alexander Katan (1899–1943) were related only in their ancestral origin from Spain, when their forebears left the Iberian Peninsula during the Inquisition. Salvatore's family took refuge in the Ottoman Empire, while Alexander's took refuge in the Netherlands. Salvatore was born in Salonica; Alexander, in Rotterdam. Salvatore was of normal stature, but Alexander was born with spondyloepiphyseal dysplasia, a rare congenital disorder of bone growth that results in short stature. They both were arrested for being Jews. Both were subjected to inhuman medical experiments. Salvatore was liberated from Auschwitz in 1945 to tell the world of his suffering, while Alexander perished in Mauthausen, Austria, on January 27, 1943. If they'd imprisoned Alexander in Auschwitz, he probably would have survived, since the dwarfs subjected to Mengele's experiments often survived the Holocaust, while those from Mauthausen did not.

Alexander Katan had been formally educated; he spoke six languages, was a translator, an accountant, and a teacher. He married Julia Sophie Elze, a dwarf; and in 1930, they had a son, Alphons. The Germans arrested Julia and sent her first to Ravensbrück and then Auschwitz, where she died upon arrival. When Alexander arrived in Mauthausen on November 3, 1942, SS Dr. Eduard Krebsbach (1894–1947) was the chief physician in the camp. He considered the Jews worse than animals, and he executed those he judged unfit or unable to work. Based on his physical disability as a dwarf with a bent spine, Alexander was considered "the embodiment of Jewish degeneration" and thus was "subjected to a number of experiments. Among other treatment, they photographed him first clothed in his concentration camp prisoner garb, then naked." Dr. Krebsbach and his subordinates administered "lethal injections (*Spritzen*) of phenol directly to the heart."[22] The inmates called Krebsbach "Dr. Spritzbach" (Dr. Injection). Tried by a US military tribunal in Dachau on May 13, 1946, he was executed on May 28, 1947, at the Landsberg Prison. Asked by the prosecutor if he knew what he was doing was a crime, Krebsbach replied, "No. I carried out my work to the best of my knowledge and belief because I had to."[23]

On January 27, 1943, SS-Sturmbammfür Dr. Karl-Joseph Gross "ordered Alexander killed with an injection of phenol to the heart. Alexander died immediately."

> His body was then skeletonized, with every step of the process documented by a photographer. The skeleton was taken to the SS Medical Academy near the University of Gratz and then reassembled for display. . . . Following the end of the Holocaust . . . four photographs of Katan were kept on prominent display in the museum: Katan dressed in his concentration camp prison garb, a frontal naked photo, a rear naked photo, and a photo of his skeleton. To his horror, Alphons Katan saw the photographs of his father on display at Mauthausen when he visited in 1994. In these images, he saw his father naked, and then "stripped of flesh." With the assistance of the Dutch government, the Austrian Interior Minister instructed the museum authorities to remove the photographs from display. He tried to find his father's remains in order to give him a decent burial [but the University of Gratz] alleges that they were unable to locate the skeleton.[24]

René Molho, a survivor from Salonika, tells of another case of brutality. His brother Sam was quite sick and had to be taken to the hospital. Three days later he recovered. One night Mengele selected his brother and ten other prisoners, ages twenty to twenty-five. No one heard anything of them. Finally, when Sam returned to the barrack, he told his brother of his suffering: "The doctor took X-rays of his genitals and removed them without using anesthesia. He tells me that the Germans are experimenting on the vitality of sperm and on the ovaries of women. He also told me that they were experimenting on the resistance to cold and that many prisoners were sent to freeze in chambers. Sam felt as if he was an animal and that he had been dehumanized. After Sam recuperated some, the Germans took him for more experiments. A pharmacist who worked at the hospital told me that Mengele continued to operate on the body of my brother and removed his testicles. My brother died. I never saw him again."[25]

Asher Varon, from Rhodes, when interviewed by Yad Vashem, said that due to endless hours of work in the mine, often fourteen to sixteen hours per day, many of his fellow workers committed suicide. He, too, fell sick. When the Germans noticed that he had scarlet fever, they moved him to a hospital, which was divided into two parts. From the description given to me by other inmates, one side of the hospital was for sick people, and the second for medical experiments. One day "after going to the toilet outside, I went to the other home [section of the block]. I heard my name . . . but I could not see the person because his face and chest were covered with chalk, he was covered with plaster. I asked him what was wrong with him." He told Varon that he was all right and that the "doctor came every morning and afternoon to administer some injections and give me some medicines." Varon visited him for two days, and on the third someone informed him that his friend was taken away. "I think they were doing more experiments."[26]

In 1987 while she lived in Cape Town, South Africa, Violette Fintz sent me a letter with further information,

> This topic was not easy to treat then or now. Even those who survived were not willing to talk about it. What I am sending you are ideas that I was able to put together. There was a total silence. Those affected by it believed that talking about it would bring shame on themselves and their families.
>
> Women who came pregnant were immediately sent to the crematoria. The infants and the young who arrived to the camp were snatched by the miserable SS officers from the mothers' arms, mistreated, and when satisfied killed them. I saw an elderly woman give a child to a young one believing that he would have a chance to survive; the Germans sent the young lady and the baby to their death. Many mothers chose to die holding their precious children's hands. The mothers who were about to deliver were forced to abort, while the infants who were just born had their head either bashed against the wall, were shot or drowned. No mother should experience such calamity, not even our enemies. . . .
>
> No one was safe. Our women, especially the young and beautiful, were harassed and forced to work in *bordellos*. They were abused and raped by the Germans and the kapos, and some elite inmates. Woe if the woman got preg-

> nant and gave birth. In such case both the baby and the mother were killed secretly.[27]

It is ironic that the Germans, especially the SS, committed such sexual atrocities, while at the same time they were prohibited by law from mingling with the prisoners.

In my recent telephone conversations with Sephardic survivors in their eighties or older living in Greece, Israel, and the United States, I became aware that most of the survivors knew about the medical experiments but didn't want to talk about them. They began talking about their involvement in the experiments when they realized that I was a Sephardi, one of them, and that I knew many survivors. Such is the case of an eighty-two-year-old survivor who settled in Bat Yam, Israel. By my encouraging him about the importance of his statement, he relented and said, "The medical experiments performed on me and fellow internees were the most harrowing to remember." Reluctantly, he continued:

> Lo ke izieron es inkonprensivle. Los eksperimentos en las partes privadas, dinguno puede imajinar, no ay manera de deskrivirlo. Mos rovaron la manseves, mos desharon sin porvenir. Mos tomavan bivos, mos malograron sin piedad, mos mandaron atras a la baraka o al orno. I lo ke izieron kon las desfortunadas mujeres i presiados krios! No ay lugar para estos desgrasiados ni en geinam. Eran brutales, deskorasonados, monstruos. Es imposivle imajinar, aun en esfuenyo lo ke paso en los maldichos kampos.
>
> (What they did is incomprehensible. No one can imagine the experiments performed on the private parts: there is no way to describe it. They robbed our youth [innocence], they left us without any future [progeny]. They would take us alive, damage us, and without any compassion, return us to the barrack or to the furnace. And what have they done with our ill-fated women and precious children! There is no place in hell for these despicable ones. They were brutal, heartless, monsters. It is impossible to imagine, even in a dream, what took place in the accursed camps.)

The survivors of the medical experiments in the concentration camps were in a real sense double survivors. They survived the trauma of Auschwitz and the diabolical experiments of Dr. Mengele and others. The cruelty was carved onto their bodies and into their souls, and almost became part of their collective DNA.

5
The Death March

As World War II was coming to an end and the Red Army and Allied troops were advancing on all fronts, the Nazis were preparing for the evacuation of prisoners from concentration and slave labor camps in order to conceal evidence of the mass murders and atrocities they had committed.

In January 1945 Heinrich Himmler, who coordinated the murder of millions of Jews, issued the order to dismantle the gas chambers and dynamite the crematoria: "The mass graves were dug up, the corpses cremated, and Polish farmers were induced to plant crops on the sites to give the impression that they had never existed. Local commanders continued to kill Jews, and to shuttle them from camp to camp by forced 'death marches' until the last weeks of the war."[1] Martín Hazan recounted, "In their retreat the Germans would take with them all those [prisoners] who remained alive at the time of departure. It was a mass evacuation that was being talked about. . . . It was the March of Death."[2] It was the dead of winter. Albert Elkoubi recalled when he and others were taken from Auschwitz: "They walked us several hundred kilometers through Poland in search of a camp. . . . They placed us in open wagons . . . in January . . . in the cold regions of Germany, . . . [and] Austria, without eating, without drinking during some number of days, and I knew that we understood that we were surely going to our inevitable death."[3] The Germans figured out that with hardly any provisions for food and with inadequate clothing, most of the inmates would die, little by little, on the frozen road. If perchance one survived, "A bullet in the temple or chest would end so much exhaustion."[4]

The problem was what to do with the thousands of physically weak prisoners and those in the infirmary from Auschwitz I and II, Monowitz, and several nearby subcamps. In a panic to save themselves, the Germans decided to entrust them to pro-Nazi Polish guards in Auschwitz to carry out the exterminations. Besides, Martín Hazan reports for David Galante, a survivor from Rhodes, that the Germans figured out that "[i]t was impossible for them to survive in this state without food until the arrival of the Russians. . . . Without food and in a delicate state of health, survival was impossible. . . . It was better to leave them there and not delay the march of the caravan or to waste ammunition unnecessarily."[5] Of the sixty-six thousand prisoners taken from Auschwitz between January 17 and 21, 1945, under heavily armed guards to the West, some fifteen thousand died during the Death March. It was the intention of the SS to use some of the survivors to continue the production of military equipment in the new camps and save some of them as "hostages to bargain for a separate peace in the west that would guarantee the survival of the Nazi regime."[6]

On January 27, 1945, when the Russian 322nd Rifle Division entered Auschwitz, they found around 7,500 prisoners and about six hundred corpses.[7] Sami Modiano was among the weakened inmates. At the age of thirteen, he was taken to Auschwitz. With tears in his eyes, he told how "difficult it was to see thousands die, die, die. I couldn't believe it. . . . My job was to cut wood, carry wood, and pull the dead from the electrified wire. It was cold, very cold." On October 12, 2013, at the "Giornata della memoria" (Remembrance Day), Modiano told the students of the Middle School of Caster, Italy, how he was saved in January 1945 from the Germans:

> It was a sad and unforgettable past. The March of Death dealt with the prisoners being taken from Birkenau to Auschwitz, only 3 kilometers away. . . . Because I had just given several pints of blood for the German soldiers, I could not walk, I fell, and my brains were not functioning. I was almost dead. I was forced to walk. Before reaching Auschwitz, about 800 meters, my forces gave up. I fell down, put my hands over my head waiting for the coup de grâce because the Russians were coming and the Germans had orders not to leave anyone alive. Something happened, something I cannot explain. . . . Two prisoners, Jews like me, with pajamas like me. How can I define these two persons, two angels? I did not even know them. . . . Before reaching Auschwitz, they bent, they raised me up, and they dragged me up to Auschwitz. They made a tremendous effort to carry me. Many would have not done it because they, too, did not have the strength. I reason, they probably said to themselves, "What are we doing? This one is almost dead, he does not weigh much." The march must continue. On January 15, 1945, it was 25 minus degrees under zero. These two men noticed a group of frozen cadavers under a tree: they decided to leave me there where I could not be found by the Polish guards.[8]

On January 27 when Modiano opened his eyes (woke up from a coma), he found himself with a Russian woman doctor working on him. The hospital staff was "quite compassionate in tending for our welfare." He wondered why he was so privileged to stay alive. He believed that he should have been among those who died. He kept asking, "Why, why, why? Why did God choose me, and why not my sister and father, who died when he was forty-five?" During our telephone conversation on May 6, 2016, Sami Modiano, originally from Rhodes and now living in Rome, informed me that the Russians were interested first in repatriating their own soldiers. Even though he was well treated by them, he wanted to return to his own people. Guided by a Jew from Rome, he escaped on foot across Europe until they reached Italy. After two years of insecure employment and bad housing in Rome, Sami, seventeen years old, moved to the Belgian Congo (1947–72). Although economically successful, he returned to Italy due to the outbreak of the civil war in the Congo. His wish was to be near his beloved Rhodes. "Once in Italy I felt close to the memory of my father Giacobbe and sister Lucia, both murdered in Auschwitz, and to my mother Diana, who died in Rhodes before the deportation." Modiano decided to spend the summers in Rhodes. On May 6, 2016, Carmen Bella, the director of the Jewish Community of Rhodes, originally from Volos, Greece, and married to a Jew from Rhodes, told me on the telephone, "Sami, while in Rhodes, spends his time at the Kahal Kadosh Shalom Synagogue, where people from all over gather to learn about the tragedy of the community. Sami feels that he is the one to keep the story alive, to tell the story on the spot, which is Rhodes, the community in which he was born, and was wiped out in 1944."

The story of the March of Death is also known as "The Long Walk" and "The Death March across Germany," and by the Sephardim as "El kamino a la muerte" (The road to death) and "The Road to Martyrdom." It was also called "The Great March West," "The Long Trek," "The Black March," and "The Bread March." As appalling as it was for those left behind in Auschwitz, the March of Death, which started at five o'clock in the morning, was disastrous for those transferred west. In addition to the cruelty perpetrated by the Germans, the prisoners also had to fight the weather, which was extraordinarily cold in January and February 1945.

As told in the following testimonies, many prisoners died from lack of clothing, from hunger, and from exhaustion. Daniel Bennahmias, from Salonika, writes, "By January 18, 1945, the front had moved closer; the artillery fire pronounced, and the men could now see the bursts of sporadic explosions. . . . Pandemonium broke loose."[9] The Germans were ordered to leave the camp. A senior officer told the Sonderkommandos in Block 13, "Everybody, take your things! We are going to leave! *Alle antreten!*" The Sonderkommandos had a sad premonition that something horrendous was to take place. At the first opportunity they dispersed among the other prisoners, realizing that following the practices of the SS, they would have been killed to prevent them from telling what had taken place in the crematoria. The Germans seized every opportunity to trace the members of the Sonderkommando. "From time to time, during the night, a German passed among the prisoners and yelled, '*Wer hat im Sonderkommando gearbeitet?*' (Who worked in the Sonderkommando?) Of course, nobody replied."[10]

Marco Nahon, a medical doctor from Dhidhimoteichon (Dimotika), Greece, describes in a contemplative and touching style the brutalities he and his people suffered: "In 1945, the Germans began the evacuation of all camps in the region of Auschwitz." At the time, he asked himself, "Are they expecting a great Russian offensive?" True to their evil nature, on January 18, 1945, the Germans killed six thousand Jewish women, while the rest were sent to different camps in Germany. Nahon was sent first to Stutthof, near Danzig; then with the advance of the Russians to Echterdingen (Stuttgart, Germany), to a *Lager* at Klavinkel not far from Ohrdruf (Ohrdruf, a subcamp of Buchenwald), where he worked for a month at the hospital. As the Americans reached Erfurt and Gotha—just north of Ohrdruf—the prisoners were once again on the move. On the evening of April 6, they reached Buchenwald. Exhausted, they dropped on the freezing ground to get some rest. Their preoccupation was the sight of piles of dead bodies and of those stretched on the sides of the road. Nahon recounts, "A few steps ahead of me I see a prisoner collapse by the roadside. . . . It is easy to see that he cannot walk another step. An SS guard who has also seen him approaches and stands before him. Very quietly he takes his rifle from his shoulder strap, places the barrel a few inches from the poor devil's head, and shoots." From time to time, they would hear gunshots and know that some of their companions, who were "no longer able to drag themselves along," had been shot. Thousands of such quick executions were performed. Those who clung to life were forced to walk, "almost to run, forty miles a day without ever resting. Sometimes they make us stay at the same place in a forest for several days. Then the march goes on again, always faster and faster."[11] As Leon Cohen told me, "Dinguno podia somportarlo. La muerte era preferivle. Munchos desharon las filas i se estiraron en el kamino. Venga lo ke venga" (No one could bear it. Death was preferable. Many left the ranks and stretched on the road, come what may).

Nahon reflects on the punctuated suffering—walking, then being loaded mostly in open freight trains, then walking again: "When we leave Buchenwald, the SS convoy takes us to Weimar, five miles away, where we take the train. We cover about forty-five miles by train in three days and then we continue on foot. Later we cover another few dozen miles by train in three days, down to Dachau." Finally, on April 27, they arrived at the Dachau concentration camp on foot, the end of their long odyssey. But the questions resounded: was it really the end? "Will all the suffering of these last days—the hunger, the thirst, the rain, the blows, and the wounds on our feet—have been in vain? Tomorrow or the next day, if we have to leave Dachau, almost all of us will be killed."[12]

Berry Nahmia from Kastoria, who was eighteen years old in 1944 when she was deported by the Nazis to Auschwitz, well remembers the "Road to Martyrdom":

> On this Death March we walked in rows of five, and an armed guard with one or two dogs was stationed every three or four rows on each side for the entire length. It was impossible to escape or even change rows. The guards, young soldiers with pistols, machine-guns, and dogs at their heels, became our most ruthless dictators and clearly demonstrated they were not joking.
>
> "Whoever, man or woman, can no longer walk shall be shot on the spot," they said. "No one shall stop for any reason. Only onward."[13]

Berry Nahmia recalls the terrifying spectacle of meeting thousands of Jewish prisoners on the road, dressed in rags, with bleeding feet in clogs or with feet wrapped with rags because they had no shoes. Every two or three minutes, someone fell half dead in the snow. At their fall, the guards finished them off with one shot. Nahmia describes the vast snowy landscape, the excruciating freezing weather; the unbearable fatigue; the unending shouting of *schnell, schnell*; the guards pointing their machine guns; the scenes of prisoners debilitated, shoved, beaten, slaughtered, and left on the side of the road to rot or be devoured by animals. As she said, she became "aware that my mind had completely escaped reality and had drifted off somewhere far away from that horrible environment. I was walking like a robot as if I were not there." During one of the marches, they could see villages, peaceful settings with joyful inhabitants surrounded by their families, hardly aware of the outside world. For a moment the inmates longed for their own communities. However, as Berry Nahmia expresses, they never escaped from the reality of starvation, exhaustion, and death: "At the entrance of each town were young children, ten or twelve years old dressed in military khaki and stripes with whistles and caps. Pitchers in hand of hot beverages, they were serving various refreshments so the guards could quench their thirst. . . . We wretched people asked them for a sip also. I remember well, how those small children answered us in the most repugnant manner: 'Nothing for you, never, *verfluchte . . . Schweinejuden* . . . damn, Jew pigs.'"[14]

Berry Nahmia remarks, "The march was horrible. The shootings by the German guards became more frequent. . . . They killed those who were the most wretched and exhausted in the lines. Those who had no strength to take another step, themselves asked to die!" Nothing stopped the march. Nothing stopped the cruelty. They arrived in Prague, Czechoslovakia, and soon they continued their long crossing through fields and snow-covered mountains. They spent the night in the open, afraid to close their eyes, afraid to freeze "from the severe cold. Shivering until dawn, we remained sitting on dead bodies." A few days later, they were fortunate to get into a truck bound for Ravensbrück, Germany. Berry Nahmia continues, "Others were boarded onto locked trains where approximately 120 people to a wagon were packed and forgotten for several days like trapped mice. Few survived. . . . In the road, we left behind frozen corpses whose human limbs were torn to pieces by the wolves and wild animals that came down from the mountains at night to eat them." Three days later the prisoners were separated. Berry and her friend Gita went to Retsov.[15] After some days with nothing to do, Berry volunteered to work in a small factory owned by two kind Germans. At night she was able to return to the barrack where some Greek girls from Ionnina and Athens were. Life in Retsov was tolerable. They felt more secure: there was no crematorium, there was hardly any work, and they were allowed to have contact with other inmates. The SS men and women suddenly grew nervous: "The general situation was rapidly changing. They were primarily concerned about themselves and their families. . . . The camp atmosphere was electric." The Americans, British, and Russians were hitting Retsov, the faces of the prisoners shone with pride, which irritated the Germans, who, continuously incensed, turned on them even worse than before, and they and their dogs attacked the inmates ruthlessly for no reason at all.[16]

On May 1, 1945, what a joy for the inmates, the camp gates were open, and so were the storerooms. The camp was deserted, the enemy gone. "Incredulous, unable to grasp the reality," Berry and her cousin ran out to the road, the local people with their "wagons, cars, motorcycles, push carts, all full of thrown-together household goods, with children crying next to their parents, men, women, young and old, running everywhere." The townspeople were leaving now that the Russians were behind them and the Americans in front. Betty, some Italian boys she met, and other prisoners from France, Italy, Greece, and other parts of Europe came together and formed a group. Finally, they took refuge in a two-story German villa in Malhov [Malchow], a subcamp of Ravensbrück.[17]

On May 4 they were liberated by the Russians: their superior supplied them with bread, various foodstuffs, even chicken. They also moved them to a temporary military hospital, where Russian doctors and nurses took care of them.

With joy they heard the promise that "repatriation would begin! You are going home." Berry won a waltz contest with Giuseppe Lucarelli. He became her protector until he proposed that she go with him to Italy and marry him. Moved by his gesture, she still refused to change her religion: "From the time I was taken to the concentration camp, the subject of my religion was very painful for me and touching upon it now was very premature."[18]

With the passe-partout from the Russian commander in Malhov and the assistance of a German mayor, the group was able to receive food and accommodations. Once they reached Berlin, the mayor gave them lodging for a month in the Russian sector of the capital. In the lodging, Berry found eighty Christian Orthodox, impoverished Greek men and women, who had come to Berlin before the war looking for a job. They also asked to be repatriated.

In order to leave the Russian sector for the American, they had to secretly reach a camp supervised by the Americans. The Americans found a way to send Berry by bus first to Munich and then to Brussels, the last stop before repatriation by plane to Athens. All along, the Americans took complete care of the expatriates. They even provided them with some money. While in Brussels, Berry found people she knew in Kastoria and Birkenau, and had Greek visitors, both Christians and Jews from the city. The Rikanatis, an elderly couple with no children, wanted to adopt her. She even received a marriage proposal. Again, she declined both offers since "her first priority is to go back home to Greece, a free woman."[19]

On the day of repatriation by air to Athens, she was very upset about not knowing what to expect, alone as she was without family and friends. She thought "of all those countries and cities I was leaving behind. How many hardships I had endured on the way here! Sometimes by train, sometimes on foot, by truck, by bus, and now by American military plane." On the plane, she fell into a slumber, she brought to her mind everything that had happened to her in her life. She closed her eyes and "remembered the recent experiences of the camp, the crematoria of Auschwitz-Birkenau. I saw again that endless Death March, then Ravensbrück, Retsov, Malhov. All that suffering, each of which alone caused me so much pain." Suddenly, as if "a miracle touched her," the depressing images, the confusing feelings, her despondency, her solitude even as she sat next to her dear friend Paula seemed to vanish. There was much to be thankful for: she was alive, she had compassion for others, she had escaped Mengele's experiments, and her body was intact.[20]

Finally, Berry Nahmia was happily married, had two children, and eventually two grandchildren, as well as four great-grandchildren. She was the president of the Greek Survivors of the Holocaust Organization. She dedicated her life to honor the memory of the millions engulfed by the brutality of the Germans during World War II. She maintained a busy schedule lecturing so that the world would never forget the Shoah, and especially the loss of the Jewish community that held for a thousand years an important status in Kastoria.

AF1 (Stella V), whose real name was not given by Bea Lewkowicz, who interviewed her in 1994 and 1997, reported that when Stella, Vera K., and her daughter "had arrived in Ravensbrück. . . . It was very dirty. The previous day they put us in a block where there were a lot of people who were about to die."[21] She continued with a description of life in the camp, where danger was ever present, and food was scarce. "Patience, patience. If God wants we will live, if not we will die," she told her friends. She and friends stayed there eight days. One morning the Germans called "Zahlapped [*sic*] [roll call] and yelling 'You out, you out, you out.'" They were loaded on a bus, and about seven hours later they arrived in Malchow. A Greek inmate who knew German very well advised them to answer positively to whatever the Germans asked. By so doing, Stella was assigned to the Außenkommando and was able to survive. With the Russians approaching, the Germans left the camp on May 1, 1945. Stella and other inmates walked, hardly realizing where they were going. Taking refuge in a shed, they were able to sleep. Finally, on May 5, the Russians arrived.

Unlike Berry Nahmia and Modiano's positive account about the behavior of the Russians after the liberation of Auschwitz, Stella A. gave a different view: "The Russian soldiers did not acknowledge the plight of the women concentration camp survivors, they order them *работа, работа* [Russian: work, work]." She continued, "We had to peel potatoes and clean vegetables. After work we got some potatoes to eat, a bit of bread and we went to sleep in a room with blankets on the floor. In the middle of the night somebody bangs on our door. BUM, BUM. BUM. The Russians wanted women. They were drunk, they had been drinking a lot of Vodka. They all came to me. 'Chora, Chora' (Polish: I am a sick woman). One wanted me, one took another girl. Then came other soldiers. I said, 'No, no, chora, chora.'" Stella preferred death to being violated. Some old bearded Ukrainian soldiers threatened her. Scared and confused, Stella still refused: "The old men . . . took me to where the horses and the cows were and pointed the gun at my head." Stella continued, "When I woke up there was blood." The other girls found Stella "without shoes, knocking my head against the wall, like a madwoman." Not a single word came out of her mouth.[22]

The next day they left. Since Stella could not run as fast as the other girls, she found herself separated from them. She asked herself, "What am I going to do, all on my own?" Luckily, she met some French soldiers, prisoners of war, who gave her things to eat. "Together with the French POWs she was taken to a place where she could recuperate for the next couple of months." Late in September she was able to return to Salonika, only to find that her family had not survived. Of her ordeal in Auschwitz and the Death March, Stella A. remarked, "I will never forget this."[23]

Chaim (Haim) Refael, also a Greek survivor, told me in Tel Aviv on June 7, 1982, that "their torment in the camp lingered for months," and they often wished "that death would put an end to the tragedy." He described the Death March: "In the fall of 1944, I was transferred from Birkenau to a work camp near Breslau, and in January 1945, I was sent on a death march to the camps of Flossenbürg [Northeast Bavaria] and then to Ohrdruf. I tried to escape but was caught and transferred to Buchenwald and from there to Theresienstadt, where I was ultimately liberated." His eyes teared. For a while he could not proceed. Then, with profound sadness, he continued, "There are no words to describe the ferocity of the satanic guards with their dogs during our long journey from village to village, from camp to camp, walking or crammed into trains, some open, with no food, no water, and subject to constant beating. Woe, if one was exhausted, sick, stopped for a breath, or tried to escape. It was mortifying to see thousands of people, our people, men and women, old and young, shot or beaten to death, and left stretched out on the cold freezing ground. It was excruciating. At that point we longed for our miserable days in Auschwitz." In Theresienstadt (Terezin), Chaim was introduced to Esther, a woman from Corfu. Together they went back to Salonika, where they were married. In June 1946 they made *aliya* (immigrated) to the Land of Israel on an illegal ship called the *Haviva Reik*, named after a heroine Jewish parachutist who helped illegal Jewish immigrants reach Palestine.

René Molho reports that after a long and exhausting march, they reached Oranienburg. The Allies bombed the camp incessantly and destroyed it; German soldiers and some inmates died. Subsequently they had to evacuate them to Camp 11, one of the Dachau satellites, "where the SS assigned us to build bunkers: we had to carry heavy stones and bags of cement. We are very tired and hungry. We are not workers, rather slaves. We took the empty bags of cement and placed them under our uniforms to keep warm. Also if we were beaten, it would hurt less."[24] The main task of those in the satellite camp was to build German rockets in the underground factories from which the V8s would be launched.

The trip was to be long and difficult for those who were weak, sick, and old. Shlomo Venezia said, "We were dragging our feet, we were thirsty, cold, hungry, but we had to march, march, and keep on marching. Those who dropped from exhaustion were left behind and executed by the SS who brought up the rear."[25] When they reached Mauthausen, Melk, and Ebensee, they lived in barracks and were organized in three shifts of eight-hour work crews and subjected to regular *Appells*. While in Mauthausen, Bennahmias learned that 189 Sonderkommandos from Auschwitz had been gassed. Jack (Giacomo) Hasson of Rhodes and 150 additional inmates worked in the coal mines, quarries, and on the railroad. Without a place to sleep, many of these men were forced to stay in the mines for days on end, without seeing the sun.

The miserable lodgings in Auschwitz were "better than hotels" compared to the situation during the Death March. Now they had to sleep in the open, on freezing ground, and, if they could find it, cover themselves with straw. Asher Varon from Rhodes said that he, his brother, his uncle, and many prisoners worked in the Rizertau Charlotte Gruppe mines in Poland. As the Russians were advancing, they were moved from one place to another. A survivor from Rhodes told me, "La djente se aserkava, mos demandavan kozas ke no podiamos responder. 'Donde vos yevavan una ves ke salitesh del campo?'" (People came, asked us things we couldn't answer. 'Where did they take you once you left the camp?') Ni el Dio lo savia. (Not even God knew it). Era kaminar a pie, mos arastravan de un lugar a otro. No saviamos de donde veniamos ni a onde mos yevavan. Solo me akodro la ambrera, el yelor ke mos matava, i la matansa." (It was walking on foot, they dragged us from place to place. We did not know where we came from or where we were going. I only remember the hunger, the freezing cold that killed us, and the slaughter.) Asher Varon was assigned to work in construction at Auschwitz and then in the coal mines of Charlotte Gruppe. Regardless of the assignments, the situation was dire, and for many death was preferable. Escape was impossible since the consequences would be horrendous for them, for members of their family, or for the whole group.

The only option was suicide, and Varon witnessed several. However, as the Russians were advancing, there was no time for collective punishment, as Varon recounted:

> The Germans were in retreat, so they had to abandon the camps and walk for many days towards Czechoslovakia; right away, they put us in open carriages with other prisoners and took us to Mauthausen. I must say that if I survived it is thanks to the dead, dead of cold and hunger, who covered me the whole trip. When they cleaned the car they found me still alive under the corpses. . . . Around the 10th of March we had to abandon Mauthausen. It was a death march, many people died. We were dressed in rags and would have taken anything to put on our bodies, letters, and bags of cement. . . . If someone had died and the Germans noticed that someone was taking the jacket, they would kill him on the spot. . . . We walked and sometimes returned to the same starting point. For example, we were going to Denault, then returned to the same place. We walked from early morning and at night we stopped and slept. If someone during the march left the column to pick up something from earth, such as herbs, carrots, potatoes, he was shot. . . .

> We walked on secondary roads, there were 150 soldiers to control us, and we were . . . [not allowed to rest], but I did sit on the edge of the road next to 50 prisoners. The column passed and the soldiers forced us to get up and join them. I and 10 prisoners did. Those who did not were shot with a bullet in the head. We reached Linz, Austria. . . . A few days later we heard artillery fire. Then some prisoners and ex-soldiers announced that the war was over.[26]

By the time the Americans liberated him on May 5, 1945, Varon weighed 23 to 25 kilos (51 to 55 pounds). He couldn't walk or stand. The Americans sent him to a hospital, where they took good care of him. By following the prescribed dietary regulations, he survived. On the other hand, according to Varon and the testimonies of various ex-prisoners, those who did not follow the rules overate and consequently died. In addition to his uncle who went to Italy with him, Varon was able to locate his younger sister who came from Russia and an older one in Stockholm.[27]

Like Asher Varon, Giuseppe Coné also was sent from Auschwitz to a coal mine in Rizertau Charlotte Gruppe, where many died of hunger and cold. The work was difficult. Coné's task was to build tunnels and move large stones by hand. Subsequently he developed an immense bulge in the upper part of his leg that required his hospitalization. A Polish Jewish doctor cut the lump and eliminated the infection. However, many inmates, with their hands shredded and bleeding, died loading wagons with bricks. Escape was impossible, since the Germans always caught them. A fellow inmate from Rhodes, Elie Hugnou, tried to hide in the latrines; the Germans found out where he was and set the latrines on fire, thus killing him. Soon thereafter the group was moved again.

As the Americans and Russians were closing in, the inmates were sent to Mauthausen. Varon's story was no different than that of the other prisoners—open wagons, thin pajamas, bad weather, no food, no boots, sleeping on the side of the roads. "The majority of the prisoners died frozen, only the strong survived."[28] Coné kept walking with his friends from Rhodes: Joseph Hasson, Ner Alhadeff, and Joseph Menasché, who, when not able to walk any longer, was shot by the Germans and left to die in the snow. The column continued to Ebensee, Austria, one of the most dreadful German concentration camps. Coné continues:

> Again we had to work in the mines. Once outside, near the wagons, watched by a SS and his sheepdog, they served him a bowl of thick soup with bones and meat. . . . Once the guard disappeared, I threw stones and the dog run away. I took the bowl and swallowed its content. . . . There were times in

> which I was so hungry that I picked up dried bones of dead animals and chewed them with my teeth or picked up asphalt from the road and masticated it like chewing gum to last until the next meal. Hunger was terrible. . . . I heard the Americans arrived to liberate us. Many Germans managed to escape and others were taken prisoners. I heard that a German officer even tried to poison the inmates when he learned that the Americans were arriving. I also remember that many prisoners died after the liberation from eating too much. I also remember that an American gave my cousin a thermometer, my cousin believed that it was food, and being so hungry he ate it. He then died of mercury poison.[29]

Once liberated, Coné was sent to a hospital in Weimar. Only those who were young and strong survived. Among these were Jack Hasson, and David and Joseph Castavel. Coné's brother died in Mauthausen, his sister went to Palestine, another brother moved to the Congo. Once cured he went to Rome, where he was taken care by a group of Sephardic women. He married one of them. Mrs. Coné related that her husband had nightmares every night. As relief from the terror of their memories, the survivors met and exchanged stories about some of their experiences. Only telling the stories seemed to help him. Sad as he was, he looked at the future optimistically. Coné and his wife moved to the Congo, and as things did not go well, they moved to South Africa, where things went well, and they found happiness.[30]

In our conversations and letters, Violette Fintz informed me that after the long march from Auschwitz, she reached Brennero on the border of Austria and Switzerland, and then Dachau. She found her barrack, Lager 2, so filthy that the young women from Rhodes had to clean it with their own hands. Soon they were forced to march again, five kilometers "through freezing cold and snow as high as our heads" to Lager 8, where their new assignment was to place the dead bodies in pits. Afterward, she was sent to Bergen-Belsen. At first this was no different than Auschwitz: they were fed a slice of bread and some thin soup. With six or seven hundred young women joining her block, they were overcrowded. There was no space to lie down, and many slept on the frozen ground. The newcomers were all sick with typhus and cholera; and they were infested with lice. Diarrhea was so bad they could not even reach the toilet: "So they relieved themselves on other prisoners." Food became so scarce that they went fourteen days without eating. All that was heard in the block were moans of people dying. Hundreds died each day. They could not depend on anyone for help. Violette's sister, feverish, asked for some water. "Komo una loka kori de un lugar a otro para topar mizmo una gota de agua" (Like a crazy person I ran from one place to another to locate even a drop of water). "On her way she saw heaps of bodies lying on the ground, most of them black and decomposed. This situation even worsened until they were liberated by the British on May 15, 1945."[31]

As reported by several inmates, the march went on and on, they crossed from one country to another, from Poland, to Czechoslovakia, to Germany, and to Austria. They were shuttled from one camp to another: Gross Roken in Silesia, Bergen-Belsen, Buchenwald, Dachau, Ebensee, Majdanek, Mauthausen, Melk, Ohrdruf, Sachsenhauren-Oranienburg, Ravensbrück, Theresienstadt, Treblinka, and some subcamps. They were forced to walk thousands of kilometers, day in and day out, and transported in open train-gondola cars. Tens of thousands died during the journey. They crossed open fields, wetlands, villages, cities, and mountains. They took refuge in barns and cowsheds, in empty dilapidated houses, under trees, and on the freezing ground. They suffered from abscesses, cholera, dysentery, constipation, scarlet fever, typhus, tuberculosis, pneumonia, and scabies. In the final months of the war, seized with worry about losing, the Germans relished tormenting the marchers. A survivor from Macedonia told me, "Mos yevavan de lugar a lugar, ni tiempo para repozar un segundo. Avia hazinuras i suisidios devido a las kondisiones insoportavles, a la ambrera i al eterno kansansio por el duro kamino" (They took us from one place to another; not even a second to rest. There were diseases and suicides due to the unbearable conditions, hunger, and eternal fatigue due to the harsh road). The cold was insufferable; the clothing, worn out. There was no rest. Shlomo Venezia expressed it thus: "We marched for days on end, always five by five, through the icy cold. At night [we looked for a place to rest. Some found a place indoors]. The others had to stay outside. Many died of cold during the night, or their feet were frozen. If they could no longer walk, they were killed on the spot. Those who dropped from exhaustion were left behind and were executed by the SS who brought up the rear. Other prisoners had to their throw bodies into the ditches."[32]

While the survivors took the Long March mainly from Auschwitz, others were transferred from Warsaw. Yitzchak Kerem reported, "Salonikan Auschwitz survivors, from [the Warsaw Ghetto] Gensha camp, who had Auschwitz prisoner numbers tattooed on the arms, were at risk of being slaughtered by the murderous SS Dirlewanger and Kaminski [Brigades]."[33]

Henry Levy, self-described "messenger from the dead," was deported to Auschwitz in April 1943. His first assignment was to cut squares of grass from a pond outside the camp to beautify the *Lager* commandant's house and later to collect the seemingly endless number of bodies in the camp. Henry Levy stated, "In August 1943, 3,500 Greek Jews—Leon Yahiel, Shaul Senor, and Eliezer Sotto among others—were transported to Warsaw from Birkenau to remove the debris of the Ghetto and build the camp in that city. . . . Our first task was to remove the bodies of the SS and other German officers who died during the revolt of the Jewish Ghetto."[34]

With the advance of the Red Army, the Germans razed the ghetto, and the inmates were ordered to prepare for a move to the west. Of the 3,500 Greek Jews from Salonika, 2,466 were taken without food, water, or adequate clothing on the Death March. Henry Levy recounted, "We walked day and night without food, water, and proper clothing. Many ill-fated people were sick and there were no crematoria."[35] According to a Sephardic survivor, "To dispose of the dead, the Germans had them build large trenches and dropped the kadaveres, muertos, i medio hazinos. Metian tavlas i kadaveres, uno ensima de otro, echavan benzina i los kemavan" (cadavers, dead, and the half-sick. They placed wooden planks and cadavers one on top of the other, poured benzene and burned them). The survivors were first sent to Dachau and then to Mühldorf, where they were forced to carry heavy equipment, such as railway tracks. Morris Mosche, whom I had interviewed along with Elie Cohen in Tel Aviv on June 14, 1982, added to this account: "Kuando Hitler avia visto la fin de la gerra, dio orden ke a todos los reskapados ke estan a sus dispozision sean todos metidos en vagones, portados a destinasion de Chirosh andi ayi un transporto solo arivo. Kontan ke todos los ke arivaron ayi fueron metraliados" (When Hitler realized that end of the war was near, he ordered that all those who had escaped but are still at their disposal be put into wagons and taken to Chirosh [Shroff]. Only one transport arrived. It is said that those who made it were machine-gunned). The rest were sent to Feldafing. Elie Cohen interrupted Mosche to add, "When they put us to work, to destroy the buildings, we saw, in the mountain of the destruction, hands and feet sticking out, the Jews killed." Elie continued, "In Warsaw we worked one year."

Elie Cohen corroborated Henry Levy's story on the manner in which the Jews were killed. When I asked Elie if he had personally seen the burning of the bodies, he replied, "Karne asada" (Grilled meat). Life was not sure, only death was certain. "If a German soldier was killed," Elie recounted, "they would take two or three tramways of people and shoot them at the wall." When I asked for his comment on the "Marcha de muerte" (Death March), Elie said that they had to walk thirty kilometers per day until they reached Poznan, and in train to Dachau. "In each new camp they gave us a new number: in Birkenau was 136,994, in Warsaw 1,331, in Dachau 87,284. There was no name: we were not called by our name. The permanent name is the one they gave us in Birkenau. From Dachau they took us to Mühldorf [Mühldorf am Inn, in Upper Bavaria], where we had to build underground hangars for the Germans so that they could hide their V-2 used to bomb London. A year later, they grouped us according to wagons and were supposed to take us to the Tyrol Mountains and kill us, but we were lucky, the Americans showed up first."

In this camp there was a pregnant woman. Such women were condemned to death. The Germans soon found out that she came pregnant before the transport, and they let her live. She gave birth to a girl and named her Deutsch Stella. They were liberated, and the young mother married Izak (Isaac) Senor. An obituary published in the *Arizona Daily Star* on April 13, 2011, announced that on May 5, 1945, Isaac was liberated from Dachau concentration camp. After living in Cincinnati, Ohio, where he raised a family, he moved to Tucson, Arizona, to be near his daughters and their families. On April 1, 2011, Isaac Senor died at the age of eighty-six surrounded by his loved ones.[36]

Henry Levy said, "Along the march of death 1,481 lives were lost. Only 985 arrived in Dachau on the 28th day, they were weak, bleeding, exhausted, their clothes in tatters and without anything to protect their feet. The Commandant of Dachau was so shocked at our physical condition and ordered an investigation."[37] He detained all responsible, fed the inmates, and sent some to the hospital. This care did not last long: a week later the newcomers, guarded by sadistic overseers, were sent to Mühldorf-Waldlager. On the way, Henry Levy and his fellow Greeks were menaced not only by the Germans and their bullies but also by the constant bombing of the Allies. In the new camp, some were assigned to work in a cement factory, and the rest in an ammunition plant. To take revenge on their captors, they produced defective cement blocks and defective machine-gun bullets.[38] On March 17, 1945, they were moved again and spent thirty-three days in a train. Some 437 Greek Jews died due to the bombing by the Allies. Finally, on May 1, 1945, they were liberated near Munich by the Third US Army under the command of General Patton, and they were moved to Feldafing Displaced Persons Camp in Bavaria.

Once he arrived in Greece in 1946, Henry Levy learned of the death of his brother, Edgard, who "had been hanged for helping to blow up two crematoria in the revolt of September [October] 1944."[39] He was reunited with his wife, Ida, who had survived the Bergen-Belsen concentration camp. "On April 12, 1947, he was drafted into the Greek army and fought the Communists in the mountains of Ipirus until December 31, 1950. . . . Ironically, several Holocaust survivors died fighting for Greece."[40] Later on, he settled in Greater Hartford, Connecticut.

In 2015 when I visited the Jewish Oral History Project of Atlanta, Georgia, at the William Breman Jewish Heritage Museum, I located the testimony of Eliezer (Eli) Sotto, dated September 16, 2001.[41] Eliezer Sotto from Salonika was taken to Auschwitz-Birkenau at the age of fifteen. Upon arrival, his father, mother, and three sisters were exterminated. After a short stay in Auschwitz I, Eliezer, his older brother Charlie (Charlo), and Isaac, the youngest one, were sent to Birkenau. Finally, Eliezer and Charlie were transferred to Buna (Monowitz, Auschwitz III), where thousands of slave laborers were assigned to work in factories producing synthetic fuel and rubber. Isaac had to stay in Birkenau, because anyone younger than thirteen was not transferred.

In Buna, Charlie and Eliezer were assigned to different blocks. Six months later Eliezer and five hundred prisoners were selected for extermination in Birkenau. However, at this time thousands of Jews from Hungary arrived, and most of them were murdered in the ovens and open pits. The Hungarians were given priority for extermination. Thus, miraculously Eliezer was saved. He was "'put on reserve' and for the time being assigned to dig ditches, pick up empty bags of cement, bricks, and move lumber, stones, and all kinds of stuff."[42] A week or two later, there was another selection, mainly from among those who could not work. Eliezer was lined up with them; and as he recounted, he took a step to one side of the line while the rest went the other way. When they stopped the selection, Eliezer escaped from being sent to the ovens. "I was saved. I survived the gas chambers at that time," he added. Instead, he was sent to a barrack to register for a transfer to the Warsaw Ghetto.

On the way to Warsaw, Sotto stopped in Birkenau, where he found his young brother Isaac, who was also transferred to the Polish capital. They both left in a cargo train. Their task in the new camp was the same as described above. He recounted, "In 1944, the Germans evacuated the camp because the Allies was [*sic*] pretty close, and they took us to Dachau."[43] It took them two weeks of marching and traveling by train to reach Dachau.

> Then we transfer to another camp: Number 4. They had different camps, Number 1, Number 4 . . . I went to *Lager* [German camp] 7. I think that was in Landsberg [am Lech, concentration camp in southwest Bavaria]. Then to Leimeritz [concentration camp Arbeitslager Litoměřice within the Sudetenland]. That was in Czechoslovakia. . . . We worked in a town for five, six month. . . . Probably in March 1945, they put us in a cargo train. The train make many stops because . . . there was bombing so the train cannot continue. . . . The Czech civilians came, nuns and all kind of people and begged the Germans to take the sick from the [open-tops] trains, and because they were *Tsechia* [Greek Czech] and Polish, and Russians, they know the language. . . . They begged the Germans to get the sick people . . . so the Germans agree.[44]

When they saw that the nuns had succeeded in taking the sick people from the train on stretchers to a Catholic hospital, Eliezer Sotto and Isaac jumped off and mingled among the sick people. The nuns and people with the Red Cross took them to the Bulovka, a Catholic hospital in Prague. When they heard that Czechoslovakia was liberated, they went to the railroad station and boarded a train without even knowing its destination. When the train stopped, they got off to find something to eat. Meanwhile, the train left them behind, and they had to walk until they reached Ukraine. Along with some Ukrainian women, they boarded a train for Budapest, Hungary, where they located a Jewish community and school. Their goal was to "find out how to go home. From one train to another, so finally it took two months to go back home."[45] Asked by the interviewer, Sara Ghitis, how they managed without money, Sotto explained: "The number, just show the number. We don't have no money. Every place we go, there are some organizations, they give us food."[46]

In Salonika, Sotto learned about his family, "They are not around no more, they are gone . . . I feel bad. I don't know how we are going to make new lives."[47] He found means to open a fruit stand. A woman he met upon arrival introduced him to Lucy Levy, a Holocaust survivor. Three months later they were married. Failing to relocate in Israel, they moved to Atlanta, Georgia, where they found Congregation Or VeShalom, the Sephardic synagogue. A helpful person took him to find a job as a barber, a task he had performed in the camp. In 1954 he was able to buy his own shop, the Trim Shop.

In May 6, 1995, after forty-nine years of marriage, Lucy died. Eliezer was devastated. He was looking forward to their fifty-year celebration: "Since I lost my wife, I no have desires."[48] Depressed, he felt that he had to "continue working and go to the shop," and so he did until he was two weeks from his ninety-fourth birthday. Eliezer continues, "I have two dogs that is part of my life now." He told of his children Rachel, Viki, and David: "Are good to me. Thank G-d they are good to me. I have blessing to them." As for his three grandchildren: "That is all I have in the whole world, the children and my grandchildren."[49] He is also appreciative to the Atlanta Jewish Community, the Federation, and the Congregation Or VeShalom for having helped him in his days of need.

In spite of the tragedies in his life, Sotto was thankful for the many miracles that kept him and the Jewish people alive: "I survived five times from the gas chambers . . . and also for the Jews that survived, also, that is a miracle. What is happening here in the United States [and the world] is very serious. . . . I hope a miracle can come to solve these problems all over the world. . . . So many times, miracles happen in this world. That's how the Jews live now, with miracles. Do you believe that?"[50]

In February 2017, to clarify passages from the interview conducted by Sara Ghitis on September 16, 2001, I contacted the Breman Museum and Or VeShalom, both in Atlanta, to see if Eliezer or a member of his family was still alive. I was informed that Eliezer and his son, David, were living in the city. I got in touch with David, who told me that his ninety-three-year-old father was residing at Dogwood Forest Assisted Living in Dunwoody, Georgia. He spoke with me about some of the experiences of his parents in the camp and after the liberation. From a family of nine, Lucy and her brother survived the Holocaust. She died in 1995. Eliezer died in his sleep in Atlanta on April 13, 2017, two weeks shy of his ninety-fourth birthday.[51]

With the liberation, the American and British forces did everything possible to assist the survivors. The primary concern of the Allies was the physical and mental health of the liberated. After a physical examination, those found weak or sick were assigned to a camp hospital, where they spent weeks and months recuperating. Once able to take care of themselves, many were placed in displaced persons camps and houses under the supervision of caring people. The United Nations Relief and Rehabilitation Administration (UNRRA) gave them 3,000 liras every month and cards that allowed them to eat in popular restaurants. The Allies, Jewish organizations—the American Jewish Joint Distribution Committee (JDC) and B'nai B'rith—as well as the International Red Cross, and local governments did their best to place survivors with relatives or to repatriate them to their original homes.

Jack Hasson remarked that he was very weak, weighing twenty-seven kilos, hardly able to walk. The Americans gave him plenty of food, but he was fed like a baby, in small quantities several times a day. He stayed in the camp hospital for three months, until he recuperated. On June 21, 1945, the Americans sent him to Naples, where his uncle lived. He spent three years there. Meanwhile the American Jewish Joint Distribution Committee supplied him with food, cigarettes, and pocket money. On June 17, 1947, he moved to the Belgian Congo, and ten years later he met Rachel Soriano and moved to Salisbury, South Africa, in September 1957.

Stella DeLeon, who was originally from Rhodes, was interviewed by Leni LaMarche on May 20, 1982, in Seattle, Washington. She told of her background and her joyous life with family and friends until the racial laws were implemented on the island. Although existence was rough between 1941 and 1943, she had a good life. Her account of the tragedy in the camps is not much different from those of others who have been interviewed: the appalling treatment; the lack of humanity on the part of the SS, German guards, and *Kapos*; the language problems in the camp; the lack of food and water; the harshness of the climate; the guilt for stealing from someone else; and the uncertainty of life. Her only happiness in Auschwitz and in the march was being close to the young women from Rhodes. Being transferred multiple times was unbearable. DeLeon added that on a Saturday afternoon, "We heard cannons. About four o'clock we saw these guys [the British] with masks coming inside the building. We were liberated." Somehow that was her miracle, her prayers were heard by God, and once again she regained her faith in God.

DeLeon was grateful to the British for taking care of the sick and keeping them in hospitals until they recovered. The prisoners from Italy and Yugoslavia, who could take care of themselves, were not forced to move. Meanwhile, Stella's sister met two Jewish brothers in the hospital and some Italian soldiers. Together they went to Rome, where the family of the Jewish men lived. The older sister took it upon herself to take care of them. In Rome, Stella also met Madame Victoria Buchuk, originally from Rhodes. Victoria took Stella and her sister under her wing until they immigrated to the States. While they were in Rome, their aunt in the States sent them money. The sisters remained in Rome until May of 1947, when the Red Cross located some relatives in Los Angeles. Stella's sister came to the States in January 1947; and Stella, in June 1947, because she had to wait for the special quota. In 1949, after a visit to Seattle, she married Ralph DeLeon and had children and a successful family.

Most of the Sephardic survivors moved back to their original countries or to Israel. Others refused to return, since their homes and businesses were occupied by local, unfriendly people, and only unhappy memories awaited them. Many of the young from Rhodes stayed in Italy. Victoria Buchuk went every day to the railroad station looking for Rhodeslis. Because of her, Violette Fintz and many other young women were saved. For them Victoria was forever considered a saint.

6

Albania, the Mufti, and the Ustashas

DURING MY 1990 trip to Macedonia, Serbia, Croatia, and Bosnia Herzegovina, I stopped in Sarajevo, where I visited with the president of the Jewish Community, Isaac Levi. We met for over two hours, discussing the situation of the community during World War II and after the liberation. Mr. Levi was gracious and informative about the history and customs, especially of the Sephardim. We even took some time to enjoy a brunch "a la turka" (Turkish cuisine): black olives, cheese, and *guevos haminados*, along with a popular drink, a strong spirit, *raki*.[1]

Knowing that I was investigating the Holocaust, Mr. Levi told me that the Balkan countries were not exempt from the tragedy: "Muy pokos saven lo ke yevimos aki espesialmente kon los Ustashas. Guay si uno kayiva en sus manos! Estos monstrous eran barbaros, no se puede komprararlos ni kon los desgrasiados alemanes. El nombre solo mos venia temblor" (Very few know what we endured especially under the Ustashas. Woe if one fell into their hands! These monsters were barbarians, one cannot even compare them to the despicable Germans. The name alone terrified us). With his assistance, I got in contact with a few survivors, a painter of the Holocaust, and the military museums in Sarajevo and Belgrade. Their assistance made it possible for me to document the experiences of the Sephardim in the Balkans.

In April 1941 the German forces invaded Yugoslavia. "Italian, Hungarian and Bulgarian forces were also engaged in the operation. . . . The Yugoslavian army was defeated. . . . On April 17, 1941, the capitulation was signed."[2] The country was subsequently divided between the participating countries. The Italians and Germans annexed Kosovo to Albania. Soon after the annexation, the Germans and their collaborators victimized the Jews, Serbs, and Romani. According to Romano, "This meant that the Yugoslav Jewish community, with its membership of 82,500 people, had to face the darkest period in existence."[3]

Below I will discuss events in Albania proper; the mufti Hajj Amin al-Husseini and the Handschar Division that he formed and supported; and, finally, the Ustashas in Greater Albania.

ALBANIA PROPER AND THE KANUN

Albania was invaded by the Italians in April 1939. Italy's main goal was to occupy Greece. Unlike in Albania, they were defeated by the Greeks. In 1941 the government of Yugoslavia lost the war, and the Italians and Germans annexed Kosovo, parts of Serbia, Macedonia, Montenegro, and Greece. The Jews from Croatia and Greater Albania suffered the cruelties of the Germans and their Albanian collaborators. The four hundred Jews imprisoned in Pristina (Prishtina) were handed over by the Italians to the Germans and the Albanian Fascists and in the summer of 1944 were sent to Bergen-Belsen; only one hundred survived. The six hundred native and non-native Jews who lived in the annexed territories of Kosovo were also turned over to the Germans and perished in the concentration camps of northern Europe. Even in the occupied territories controlled by the Italians, those Jews who arrived with false papers were interned, yet the Italians treated them humanely and allowed them to practice their trade or profession. However, when the camp became overcrowded, the Italians turned half of the population of Jews over to the Germans, who in turn took them to a forest and killed them. "The Italians apparently felt guilty about this and smuggled the remaining Jews to Albania, which at the time, was occupied by the Italians."[4] Shirley Cloyes DioGuardi, in her "The Albanian Rescue of European Jewry," acknowledged that "Albania was the only country in occupied Europe during World War II where Jews were not victims of the Nazi killing machine. . . . [E]veryone, from officials to farmers, from every religion and economic class, had organized to save Jews."[5]

Harvey Sarner explained that the "delay in telling the story of the rescue of the Jews is due to the isolationist dictatorship that ruled Albania from the end of the Second World War until the early 1990s."[6] Sarner was amazed by the irrefutable hospitality of the Albanian Muslims and Christians to shield the Jews, and by the cooperation of a Jewish Albanian native well acquainted with the customs of his people. "Much that has been written is based on letters and conversations with Josef Jackoel," and on testimonies told by Christian and Muslim Albanians and Jewish survivors.[7] Sarner's book is a compilation of historical, social, religious, and cultural facts, many of which were not known before.

The history of the Jews in Albania was barely reported. Daniel Perez in "Our Conscience Is Clean" writes, "[T]he wartime history of prewar Albania's 156 native Jews has generated scant public attention and scholarly research both in Albania and abroad. . . . The dearth of primary sources specifically related to Albanian Jews makes it difficult to reconstruct even a basic narrative of the Holocaust in Albania."[8]

The Jewish population of Albania in 1930 was approximately two hundred, and by 1937 it was three hundred. With political tumult in Europe, Jews looked for refuge in Albania proper, which was under Italian occupation. Prior to May 1943, Albanian embassies issued visas to the Jews: two thousand Jews from Germany, Central and Eastern Europe, Austria, Greece, Slovenia, and Yugoslavia soon joined their brethren in Albania proper. Most took refuge in Tirana and Durazzo (Durrës); others found shelter in villages, such as Tre Vllaznit, and in the mountains with the partisans, while others went to the Italian zone along the Dalmatian littoral, including Split and various islands in the Adriatic Sea, such as Korčula, Hvar, and Brač.[9]

Of the resistance in Greater Albania, one person remarked to me that "not much is known about life in Greater Albania and how important women were. Little credit has been given to them." A second added, "They, too, joined the resistance movement. Muncho de los muestros murieron peleando por todo el pais" (Many of our people died fighting throughout the country). From 1941 until the end of the war, many were declared National Heroes for their bravery. "A remarkably large number of partisan women fighters, roughly half of 1,075 medical workers, were women."[10] Some were assigned to work in Croatian concentration camps for women and children, while others worked in partisan field hospitals. Friedenreich notes that several "were promoted to officer rank and received military decorations. . . . [O]ut of thirty-nine Jewish women physicians fighting with the partisans, thirteen lost their lives. . . . Among the survivors, Roza Papo became the first female major-general in the Yugoslav Army after the war."[11] Out of the thousands who served with the partisans, hundreds gave their lives. They served with distinction and were recognized as heroes. "In the Yugoslav People's Army 14 Jews reached the rank of general, two of them lieutenant generals, two major generals and 10 brigadier generals."[12]

In the Bulgarian-occupied zones, the goal of the Fascist Bulgarian forces, with the support of the Germans, was "the complete annihilation of all Macedonian Jews . . . while protecting the Jews in Bulgaria."[13] In Yugoslavia, Alexander Matkovski relates the stark change that accompanied the German victory on April 6, 1941. Germans began "immediately . . . to search Jewish shops." Matkovski continues, "The plundering continued on April 8 and 9, during which time the Germans ransacked the majority of Jewish shops in Skopje, as well as in other Macedonian cities." With the Germans came the anti-Jewish slogans that "spread through Macedonia." He notes, "The situation grew critical for the Jews after the collapse of the Kingdom of Yugoslavia. . . . The Jews faced the choice of either waiting quietly to be exterminated or of joining the anti-fascist struggle together with other Yugoslav nationalities. The help given by the Macedonian Jews [consisted] not only of food and money, but of offering many residences for the use of the liberation movement."[14] New laws were passed limiting the rights of the Jews. These directives sealed the fate of the Jews: final deportation and liquidation.[15] "It is known that despite the severity of the situation [in Serbia and Croatia], some Jews were saved from deportation" by Muslim and Christian individuals, families, and villages, as well as Catholic priests of Skopje and many other localities who hid them, especially children, for the duration of the war."[16]

An Albanian Jewish woman told us, "Si ke los Italianos formularon leyes kontra los djudios. Estas leyes devian limitar muestrsa aksiones. Ma los Italianos non eran anti-semitas i nunka trataron de azer maldades a los djudios. Al kontrario mos protejaron. Konosko a algunos de los muestros ke se fueron a Italia i eyos tambien se salvaron" (Yes, the Italians did formulate laws against the Jews. These laws should have limited our actions. But the Italians were not anti-Semitic and never tried to do any harm to the Jews. On the contrary, they protected us. I know several of our people who went to Italy and they too were saved).

When the Germans took over Albania proper from the Italians in September 1943, the Regency, the Italian administrative council, agreed that the Germans would have free movement across Albania as long as they did not "interfere with their internal affairs. This phrase 'internal affairs' was important when the Germans later [in 1944] asked the [Jewish leaders] and the Regency to provide a list of the Jews in Albania"; both the Italians and the Jewish leaders refused to provide it.[17] With cognizance of the positive attitude toward the Jewish people in Albania proper, the Germans did not vigorously maltreat, kill, or deport the Jews in this geographical territory. Still, this "did not mean that there was no danger to the Jews, or to the Moslems and Christians who protected them."[18] At times the Gestapo, for whatever reason, did arrest young Jewish men, but after the payment of a bribe, they released them.

The survival of the Jews who took refuge in Albania proper was due to the benevolence of the Christians, but mainly of the Muslims who opened their doors to give sanctuary to strangers and those in need. "When the people of Albania extended their traditional hospitality the Jews saw the contrast between Hell and Heaven."[19]Albanian generosity is based on the Laws of the Kanun, a fifteenth-century unwritten law that covers all aspects of social life. As Arben Cara and Mimoza Margjeka explain, "The application of the Kanun is a matter of honor, dignity and faith for Albanians. . . . The Kanun sets up very high standards for hospitality." Cara and Margjeka continue, "'A man is answerable, too, for his guest, and must avenge the stranger that has passed but one night beneath his roof, if on his journey next day he be attacked. The

Figure 6.1. Deportation of Jews from Skopje in 1943. Courtesy of the Jewish Community of Sarajevo.

sacredness of the guest is far-reaching.' The actual wording of the Kanun is somewhat dire, 'if your hospitality is violated, the Kanun gives a choice of two paths: [potential] ruin or dishonor.' . . . The key to the Kanun is a man's '*besa*' . . . where a man's promise or word of honor '*goes beyond the grave*.'"[20] For the Albanians, *besa* "is an oath that no man nor God can break."[21]

The safety of the Jews or gentiles—native or refugee (*refugjat*)—in Albania depended on *besa*, which was "most sacred to an Albanian." Norman Gersham in "Jews Saved by Albanians," explained: "We've had people say . . . to save a life is to go to paradise. I would sooner have my son killed than to break my besa. There is no way, no way, that anyone could break their besa. They would be ostracized in their village and probably even killed. I always asked these people 'What was it? Was it besa? Was it the Koran? What was it that you risked—you, your family risked everything to save Jews, in many cases, strangers?' And they would respond in different ways."[22]

The survivors were amazed by the commitment of the Albanians to endanger their own lives and those of the members of their families in order to protect not only the native Jews—considered Albanians—but also the emigrants. They were all *mysafirët* (guests) in their home and country, and guests had to be saved at any cost. They were given false papers, hidden in homes, farms, or villages and when necessary moved from one place to another. Ironically,

"Even those Albanians who cooperated with the Germans . . . did not violate the code of honor as it related to the Jews in Albania."[23] None of the Jews were betrayed. If anyone was arrested by the Germans, the Muslims, through their own contacts, did everything in their power to have them released. Even in danger, they comforted them and sustained them with the little they had.

Dr. Anna Kohen stated that her family from Janina "went into the mountains near Vlora, changed our names for Moslem ones, and blended perfectly with the Moslems who treated us like their own brothers and sisters."[24] Johanna Jutta Neumann, whose family in 1944 was in the hands of the SS, was saved when the partisans attacked. Neumann praised her rescuers: "We survived due to the courage, friendship, and hospitality of the Albanian people."[25] There are hundreds of such testimonies. Irene Grunbaum, who survived the war, also paid homage to the only European nation in the continent to have saved its Jews, and "to have given me so much, hospitality, refuge, friends, and adventures." She continued, "Farewell Albania, one day I will tell the world how brave, fearless, strong and faithful your sons are, how death and the devil can't frighten them. If necessary I'll tell how they protected a refugee and wouldn't allow her to be harmed even if it meant losing their lives. . . . Albania, we survived the siege because of your humanity. We thank you."[26]

Italian authorities either for political or humanitarian reasons transferred some of the Jews to Ferramonti di Tarsia in southern Italy. This camp was well known to the Jews of Rhodes due to the incident of the *Pentcho*, a decrepit boat, which in late 1940 sailed from Bratislava with 514 Czechoslovakian Jews to Palestine.[27] The trip was demanding and long. During our interview in Boston on October 27, 1988, Albert Alcalay informed me that neither the Czechoslovakian, Bulgarian, nor Turkish governments came to their aid: "Truly, they were a hindrance. When the boat was stuck in the middle of the Danube, in front of Belgrade, the Zionist youth [of which Alcalay was a member] supplied them with medicine and other things." When I asked if anyone came to their assistance, Alcalay said, "The Greeks at the port of Piraeus supplied them with food and water." The ship managed to cross the Black Sea and the Dardanelles before her boiler burst. "Drifting at the mercy of the winds the *Pentcho* finally ran aground on Kamilonisi, a barren island little more than a shoal," not far from Karpathos, south of Rhodes.[28] The Italian ship *Camogli* responded to an SOS, rescued the passengers, and took them to Rhodes.

Violette Fintz told me that the Italians helped the refugees from the *Pentcho* as much as they could, but it was left to the Jewish population of Rhodes to assist them with whatever food was rationed to them. They stayed in Rhodes until the spring of 1942, when it was decided that it would be better for Rhodes, due to lack of food, to transfer them to the internment camp of Ferramonti di Tarsia.[29]

The internment camp of Ferramonti di Tarsia was surrounded with barbed-wire netting and turrets, the guards were watching at all times, there were daily roll calls, and some restrictions. However, as a person from Monastir who had been in Ferramonti told me in an interview in Tel Aviv in the summer of 1990,

> La vida no era tan dura aunke avia algunas restriksiones. Mos permitian bivir en famiya. Eramos livres en el kampo. Avia de los muestros, de Gresia, de los Balkanes, de Makedonia. No teniamos todo, ma no mos mankava lo menesterozo. La vida era mas o menos normal, sin espanto.
>
> (Life was not so hard even though there were some restrictions. They allowed us to live as a family. We roamed free in the camp. There were some of our people—Spanish Jews, from Greece, from the Balkans, from Macedonia. We did not have much, but we did not lack the necessities. Life was more or less normal, with no fear.)

In her interview with Judith Itzhak, Julide Carbonara writes, "Ms. Itzhak's parents, Philipp and Muschi Kanner, had fled Poland for Palestine in 1940 but got stranded in Tripoli and from there they were taken to Italy."[30] Upon arrival, Mrs. Kanner gave birth to Judith in a hospital in Naples, and seventeen days later the family was moved to Ferramonti. In her report Judith expresses her good fortune for ending up in Ferramonti. Even though food was scarce and of poor quality, no one died of starvation. "Existence was fair" and "Every day [was] a good day," said Judith Itzhak. In general, they enjoyed several amenities: full autonomy, living quarters, kitchen, religious life, school, hospital, cordial relationship with local villagers, and a chance for young couples to meet and have children.[31] She also praised the Italians for keeping them safe: "In the spring of 1943, the Germans demanded that all the Ferramonti Jews be handed over. It never happened . . . because of the intervention of the camp's priest, Padre Callisto."[32] Another similar request was turned down by "Count Ciano, the Italian Plenipotentiary of Foreign Affairs and the son-in-law of Mussolini. He told the Nazis, 'You torture your Jews; we will torture our Jews.'"[33]

Professor Stanislao G. Pugliese from Hofstra University, who received many awards and honors, echoes the sentiments of my interviewee from Monastir and the information from Judith Itzhak. Pugliese discusses the Jewish situation in Italy and the state of the Italian internment camps in the country: "To their credit, the Italians can justly claim that until the Nazi occupation of the country in 1943, not a Jew—Italian or foreign—was deported . . . to extermination camps in Germany or Poland."[34] While Jews were fleeing northern Europe and Greater Albania, they took refuge in Italy even during the regime of Mussolini and the Fascists. With respect to those held in Ferramonti, they did suffer from malaria because of the surrounding marshes, and they did answer to roll calls. However, they were allowed to roam freely in the camp, and the Jewish doctors were allowed to leave the camp to take care of the villagers. They received some financial support from their families and from the government. "They were permitted to organize a nursery—21 children were born there—a library, school, theater and a synagogue." They were free to practice their own religion and have their own spiritual leader. Riccardo Pacifici, who was born in Florence, Italy, was the descendant of an "Italian Jewish family of ancient Sephardic origins, with roots in the Jewish Spanish and rabbinical traditions."[35] He served the Jewish community of Genoa as chief rabbi. Between 1942 and 1943, he visited Ferramonti in his capacity as a rabbi. During these times he performed marriages and shared in some of the activities of the camp. Tragically, after the capitulation of the Italians, the Nazis in 1943 took him from the synagogue in Genoa and sent him to Auschwitz, where he was killed. I should add that while he served as director of the Rabbinical College of Rhodes between 1930 and 1936, he visited my uncle Ruben Capeluto's house, and I, a child of four or five, was present on a couple of occasions.

THE MUFTI MUHAMMAD AMIN AL-HUSSEINI

In 1921 the British High Commissioner of Palestine, Sir Herbert Samuel, a Jew, bestowed the title of Grand Mufti of Jerusalem and Grand Mufti of Palestine on young Muhammad Amin al-Husseini, later known as the Führer of the Arab world, due to his role in the 1936–1939 Arab uprising in Palestine, which "portrayed the international Jews, including the Jews of the Maghrib, in a negative way."[36] In 1937 Damascus, Syria, was the center for anti-Jewish activities. By 1939, "When Hitler attacked Poland, and Britain and France declared war on Germany, the Mufti realized his well-known pro-Nazi activities could land him in a British jail."[37] He fled first to Lebanon and then to Iraq, Iran, Italy, and subsequently to Berlin. On April 3, 1941, as David Patterson recounts, "al-Husseini orchestrated an Iraqi government takeover, with Nazi support and financing. . . . He took advantage of the turmoil ignited by the coup to incite the slaughter of 600 Jews in Baghdad; 911 houses were destroyed and 586 businesses ransacked."[38]

On November 28, 1941, al-Husseini met Adolf Hitler in Berlin. To obtain the favors of the German chancellor, the mufti "proposed to rally Arabs and Muslims to the Axis cause in return for Axis support for his claim to leadership over the Arab world and the destruction of the Jews."[39] The Führer offered him the Office of the Grand Mufti (*Büro des Grosßmufti*), a lucrative stipend of thousands of Reichsmarks, an additional 25,000 in foreign currency, vacation places, and a radio station, supervised by the Germans, from which to broadcast to the Muslims of Europe, the Middle East, and North Africa. "The Mufti's radio broadcasts were some of the most violent pro-Axis broadcasts ever produced. He had at least six stations."[40] He used them "to appeal for martyrdom in order to help the Germans, as that would guarantee Paradise."[41] Hitler also promised to "recognize him as the leader of Arabs and Muslims worldwide."[42] In his propaganda he reminded his people that the fight against those who had subjugated them the world over was a holy mission. He stressed that the British repressed Muslims and Arabs and that, along with Russia, they "supported the Serb royalists whose militias, known as Chetniks, were carrying out mass killings against the Muslim populations of southern and eastern Bosnia."[43] In contrast, the Germans were fighting for their own existence, their culture, and the total destruction of the Jews. Only martyrdom would secure for them a place in Paradise.

Wisliceny stated, "The Mufti was also one of the initiators of the systematic extermination of European Jewry by the Germans and had been the permanent collaborator and adviser of Eichmann and Himmler in the execution of the plan."[44] In truth, both the mufti and Hitler, along with their henchmen, had initiated separately, years before their meeting in Berlin, plans for the destruction of Jewry.

While in Bosnia, Mufti Amin al-Husseini took the title of "Protector of Islam" and never missed a chance to recruit more of his coreligionists to the notorious Bosnian Muslim Brigades. He organized this as the Thirteenth Waffen Gebirgs Mountain Division of the SS Handschar [*Hanjar*] (First Croatian), which "slaughtered 90 percent of the Jews in Bosnia."[45] He also formed the Twenty-Third Waffen Gebirgs Division of the SS "Kama" (Second Croatian). Both units were known as the "Dagger" divisions. In 1943 they were made up of approximately twenty-five thousand Muslims, as well as German soldiers of the SS Division. They all swore obedience-to-the-death to Adolf Hitler. The Germans had to wear the same fez and uniform as the Muslims. According to Jennie Lebel, a prolific Israeli author, the mufti "helped in recruiting Bosnian, Albanian and former Soviet Union Moslems for the Waffen-SS divisions."[46] Every time the mufti visited Bosnia, he inspected his Handschar troops and praised them for their commitment to a "just cause," a cause immersed in the worst brutalities against the partisans, Serbs, Jews, and Romani. Indeed, even though the Romani were also brutalized and killed, they too, along with the Croatian Catholics, eagerly slaughtered Jews.[47]

A close friend of Eichmann—a fact that Eichmann denied during his Jerusalem trial in 1961[48]—and a great admirer of Himmler, the Grand Mufti further urged the Nazis "to accelerate the extermination measures." His goal for decades was the eradication of the "treacherous" Jew, whom he blamed for all the problems of the world. In November 1943 the mufti said, "It is the duty of Muhammadans in general and Arabs in particular to set themselves a goal from which they must not deviate, which they must pursue with all their strength. This goal is to drive all Jews from Arab and Muhammadan countries. . . . Germany is also struggling against the common foe who oppressed Arabs and Muhammadans in their different countries. It has very clearly recognized the Jews for what they are and resolved to find a definitive solution [*endgültige Lösung*] for the Jewish danger that will eliminate the scourge that Jews represent in the world."[49]

On March 1, 1944, Mufti Amin Al-Husseini made a speech in Berlin urging the "Muslim SS Nazi troops: 'To kill the Jews wherever you find them. This pleases God, History and Religion. This saves your honor. God is with you.'"[50] Also in March 1944, the Arabic voice in Berlin incited violence in Palestine. In his call to arms, Haj Amin "vilified Jews, as well as Britain and America. . . . He directly called on Arabs to kill Jews. These broadcasts went throughout the Arab world (North Africa, the Middle East), as well as Spain and Southern France."[51]

The Grand Mufti planned to marshal the support of the Muslim population and to use the military units that he had organized to fight not only alongside the Wehrmacht—the unified military forces of Nazi Germany that fought under the motto "Free Arabia"—but also with the Nazis, in order to liberate the Muslim Middle East from the colonial powers that had dominated the people for decades. In statements about the involvement of the Grand Mufti with the Nazi leadership, historians and commentators interject such phrases as "I heard say," "unsourced allegation," "little conclusive sources," "purportedly," "allegedly," "ostensibly," "it is possible," "according to my opinion," "based on hearsay," or "from most reliable sources." From my readings, I surmise that authors and critics themselves warily quote or paraphrase previous accounts, often not mentioning the source or clearly stating that in their view the story is false.

The International Sephardic Leadership Council (ISLC) recounts the visit of the mufti to Auschwitz and Majdanek (Maldanek), "It was said the Mufti visited not only Auschwitz but also Majdanek. In both death camps, he paid close attention to the efficiency of the crematorium, spoke to the leading personnel and was generous in his praise for those who were reported as particularly conscientious in their work. He was on friendly terms with such notorious practitioners of the 'final solution' as Rudolf Hess, the overlord of Auschwitz; Franz Zeireis of Mauthausen; Dr. Seidl of Theresienstadt; and Kramer, the butcher of Belsen."[52]

Trying to obtain the source of the mufti's visit to the death camp, I called Abraham Cooper's office at the Wiesenthal Center in Los Angeles and was told by his secretary that the information regarding the visit was taken from Ernst Verduin's report to Emerson Vermaat, "Dutch Holocaust Survivor—'I Saw How the Mufti of Jerusalem Paid a Visit to Auschwitz-Monowitz."[53] According to Verduin's testimony, the mufti and his entourage intended to gather data on the death camps. Following is the testimony as reported by Vermaat,

> I suddenly noticed a group of people who looked like actors. They were wearing long robes and strange headgear. Occasionally, internees did perform a play in the camp. I wanted to find out myself and as I walked towards that group, I was stopped by a high ranking SS-officer whom I did not know. He was from the main camp. . . . The officer asked me, "What do you want?" "I just wanted to know whether these people are actors or not." The SS-officer told me, "They are the Grand Mufti of Jerusalem and his retinue. . . . He is now paying a visit to Monowitz to see how the Jews worked themselves to death in the factories. He is also in Auschwitz to see the gas chambers. When we have won the war he will return to Palestine to build gas chambers and kill the Jews who are living over there."

It was known that the mufti had visited Auschwitz-Birkenau and Majdanek. "Verduin saw the Mufti in the second half of 1943. He saw 50 men wearing strange clothes and golden belts, accompanied by high ranking SS-officers from *Stammlager* (original camp) Auschwitz."[54]

These quotes support exactly the wartime conversation between SS Colonel Dieter Wisliceny and Eichmann in January 1942 concerning Husseini's visit to Eichmann's office in Berlin. Sells writes that Wisliceny could have *reconstructed* the statement in July 1946 and that "*K-W* [Rudolph Kasztner], *S-W* [Andre Steiner] . . . were soon followed by Simon Wiesenthal's 1947 *unsourced allegation* [author's emphasis] that Husayni had inspected Auschwitz and Majdanek in the company of Eichmann [and] observed the crematoria operations."[55] Tom Segev, in "Courting Hitler," writes, "It is equally implausible that Husseini was given a guided tour of Auschwitz gas chambers in operation, as [David G.] Dalin and [John F.] Rothmann maintain."[56]

In a January 1941 letter to Hitler, Amin al-Husseini asked the Führer to solve the Jewish question in Arab lands. In order to be successful, the Arabs "must learn the Nazis' techniques and obtain their technology." With this knowledge, the mufti would have been able to build death camps and crematoria in Nablus, Tunisia, and other locations. The next year, in February 1942, Fritz Konrad Ferdinand Grobba was named foreign minister for the Arab States and chief liaison between the Nazi government and the Arab exiles in Germany. He was the guide of the Grand Mufti. He knew the moves of the mufti and commented on them: "Grobba wrote approvingly of the Mufti's visit

[1942] with members of the Nazi elite to the concentration camp [Sachsenhausen, near] Orangeburg. . . . The visit lasted about two hours with very satisfying results."[57] There are different interpretations of this statement as reported by Grobba: either both Al-Husseini and Rashid Al-Kailani, an Iraqi, and their entourage visited the concentration camp, or it was Ali al-Kailani and one of Al-Husseini's nephews, Safwat al-Husaini, or perhaps Musa al-Husaini, who visited.[58]

There is no question for Klaus Gensicke, who maintained, "On 17 July 1942 the Mufti himself had visited Oranienburg concentration camp."[59] On the other hand, a video (Dec. 1941), "The Turban and the Swastika, Amin Al-Husseini and the Nazis," reports that once Eichmann disclosed personally to the mufti "the 'Solution of the European Jewish Question,' the Arab leader was very impressed and sent envoys to inspect Concentration Camp Sachsenhausen in summer 1942."[60]

In 1943 Mufti Amin al-Husseini met Heinrich Himmler. Having common cause—the annihilation of the Jews—they became good friends; it was then that the mufti was named prime minister of the Pan-Arab government with headquarters in Berlin. The mufti, eager to see the killing of the Jews, asked Himmler to visit Auschwitz; "Amin al-Husseini is given a private tour of the death camp accompanied by Himmler."[61] Arthur Pier (Asher Ben-Natan) confirms the visit.[62] Michael Sells references Pier's statement that according to "reliable friends"—possibly Israel Rudolph (Rezsö) Kasztner and Andre Steiner, who dealt with the Germans to save Hungarian and Slovakian Jews—he "received affidavits which contain information about the Mufti's connection with the notorious Eichmann, head of the Gestapo Jewish Department. The source of this information is Hauptsturmfurhrer SS. Dieter Wisliceny. Pier stressed that following Wisliceny's statement, "the Mulfti was the driving spirit behind the mass extermination of the Jews." Subsequent to his visit to Auschwitz, he was "very much impressed about the German efficiency to solve the Jewish problem."[63]

On January 31, 2016, I contacted the State Museum Auschwitz-Birkenau in Oświęcin, informing them that I was keen to obtain information on the Grand Mufti of Jerusalem. Specifically, I was trying to verify if the mufti, Haj Amin al-Husseini, and/or some members of his staff visited several death camps, mainly Auschwitz. On February 1, 2016, Dr. Wojciech Plosa, Head of the Archives, informed me, "I am sorry to have to tell you that in our archival collection there are no documents informing about the visit of Grand Mufti of Jerusalem in Auschwitz. There is no information about this event in any official camp document. Also there [is] no mention about it in postwar testimonies given by survivors and in materials from trials against members of SS staff from Auschwitz."

On February 11, 2016, Gideon Greif emailed me the following message in response to my request for information on the visit, or visits, to Auschwitz by the mufti and other high German officers: "Here is my opinion to the question about the visit of the Mufti in Auschwitz. It happened very often, that 'dignitaries' were brought to Auschwitz by the camp's authorities, to witness the 'Final Solution' in its making. Therefore, I was not surprised that Shaul Chasan [*sic*] remembered a visit of the Mufti. Such visits were not rare in Auschwitz-Birkenau. For the guests it was not more than a 'show,' an entertainment. From my experience, the memory of the Sonderkommando members was extremely sharp, even after many years, therefore the information about the Mufti and his family relatives seems to me authentic."

I contacted Jennie Lebel, author of *The Mufti of Jerusalem: Haj-Amin el-Husseini and National-Socialism*, for some clarification. She sent me the following email: "In any case, according to my knowledge, the Mufti himself also visited Auschwitz-Birkenau, but I do not have precise information about this visit, which happened only one time. To conclude, the visit of the Mufti and guests like him was a common phenomenon in the landscape of Auschwitz. I wish you good luck with your important researches."

On June 17, 1982, I interviewed Leon Reuven Cohen in Givatayim, Israel. During his internment in Auschwitz, he was assigned to the Sonderkommando. Questioned about the severity of the Nazis, he recalled the visit of SS Reichsführer Heinrich Himmler and Eichmann to Auschwitz in the summer of 1944. Leon stated:

> I was working on a ladder checking the furnaces when the *Kapo* who was at attention told me to leave. I did not understand what he was telling me. He kicked me. The hot soup that I was saving spilled on me, and I was burned. I stepped out and saw a bunch of officers. Eichmann was with them and Himmler—I did not know who he was until later. I knew that several people came every day also—when Himmler passed, a young boy called Tzvi was there. The young man was at attention. Eichmann, not Himmler, asked him, "What is your name?" He said, "Tzvi." "Who knows his last name?" [Himmler asked]. "How long have you been here?" "27 months," Tzvi replied. "They let you live 27 months?" Himmler asked. He shook his head and left. He went to furnace 3 in front. He took the boy and threw him in the furnace, himself, and [said], "This is the way we are going to kill all the Jews in the world."

To be sure, I asked Leon, "How did you know this?" His response was, "They were people inside. We were all together. They also told what happened."

In "I'll Get Out of Hell!," Ya'akov Gabai recounted that in July 1944, Eichmann and some officers came to the crematorium and ordered that six bodies instead of four be burned at the same time. Gabai added "Eichmann passed me twice, real close, just behind me, and stayed for a long time. He came to Birkenau twice."[64]

According to Gideon Greif, Shaul Chazan remained silent for years about his experience in the concentration camp. Chazan was, as Greif described him, a sincere and honest individual, eager to narrate not his own story but the story of his grief-stricken community of Salonika. Forty years after the liberation while Chazan and the interviewer Greif were "walking [in Auschwitz] from the ruins of Crematorium II [III] to the yard of the crematorium," Greif inquired: "Some high-ranking guests occasionally visited the crematorium to observe the killing operation. Do you remember any visit in particular?" Chazan replied that in August 1944, the mufti had stood next to him and that the *Kapo* had told him that he was the mufti. Chazan continues: "He wore a strange hat. He came to watch the cremations. Maybe he thought about doing something similar in Palestine. The Germans explained to him how the murder mechanism at the crematoria worked. They dressed him in German uniform except for the hat, which was his. I saw him outside, in front of the building. At that time, we were pulverizing the bones and the Kapo was working in the crematorium. I don't know how he blurted out that it was the Mufti."[65]

On January 20, 2016, I called Jacko Maestro. As previously mentioned, due to the requisites of his job, he roamed the camp freely and gathered copious information about the operations of the camp. I inquired if he knew of any visit of the mufti. Following is part of our conversation:

Maestro: The mufti was in Germany with Hitler, but I do not know if he was in Auschwitz. However, I recall that some people spoke of it, but I do not know.

IJL: Who were some of the people who spoke of it?

Maestro: I believe that they were some of the "*reskatados*" (Greek survivors) in Israel who mentioned it.

On the basis of Maestro's information, I called a member of the club of the *reskatados* that I had met in 1990 at the club on Lewinsky Street:

IJL: When you were working in the Sonderkommando, did you notice any foreign visitors?

Survivor: Once I saw a group of people in the *kemadero* (the furnaces). I think they spoke Turkish or some other language. They were talking with the *Kapos*. Some SS were with them.

IJL: Do you recall anyone in particular?

Survivor: No. Well, there was a man with a fez. Not a fez, a white hat. People were around him. That is all I remember.
IJL: When was that?
Survivor: Maybe in middle of 1944. I am not sure.

I surmise that the man in the white hat was the mufti, and that one of the retinue was his nephew, Mussa, who was known to accompany his uncle.

According to the information given by Vermaat, Leon Cohen, Gabai, Shaul Chazan, and Greek survivors, the visit of Himmler, Eichmann, and the Mufti of Jerusalem took place between July and August of 1944. They were all present in front of the furnaces, either viewing the extermination of the Jews or, in the case of Himmler, participating personally in the murder of one hapless boy.

After the liberation, with the help of the Germans, the Mufti of Jerusalem escaped by plane to Switzerland. Denied landing, he then took refuge in France in May 1945. Fearing assassination by the Irgun, he fled to Italy in 1946. From there, in disguise, he sailed on a British ship, HMS *Devonshire*, to Alexandria. He was welcomed by the Muslim Brotherhood and by the Arab nationalists and radicals. He held several important posts: leader of the Muslim Brotherhood, cofounder and president of the Arab League, and cofounder and president of the World Islamic Congress. Al-Husseini remained an anti-Semite to the end of his days, a sworn enemy of the Jews. His main goal was to cleanse the Arab world of Jews. The mufti died in 1974. In January 2013, Palestinian president Mahmoud Abbas named al-Husseini a pioneer martyr to the Palestinian cause. In sum, as a reader of my manuscript notes, al-Husseini was a "Nazi propagandist, an instigator of riots against the Jews in Palestine and Iraq, and the one responsible for the spread of" calls for extermination of Jews "through the Muslim Brotherhood and throughout the Muslim world after the Holocaust."

THE USTASHAS

The video *Croatian Nazis: The Worst Monsters the World Had Known* underscores the ruthless crimes committed by the Croatian Ustashas (Ustashe, Ustaše, Ustashis) during the Holocaust. Roman Catholicism and Islam were declared to be the national religions of the Ustashas. Even before the construction of the major concentration camps by the Nazis, Jesuit seminarian Poglavnik Ante Pavelić, the Slovenian Führer, in mid-April 1941 gave the "official order to establish a complex of camps (Gospić, Jadovno on Velebit, Stupačinovo, Slana and Metajna), and other execution sites."[66] He became the leader in the mass extermination of Old Catholics, Serbs, Jews, Roma, anti-Fascists, Communists, and those designated as unfit. His followers were well equipped to carry out monstrous deeds with the oversight of German soldiers, and the collaboration of the Catholic Church and Muslim clerics.

The participation of the Catholic Church in the genocide committed in the racist Independent State of Croatia (NDH), the most murderous of the Nazi puppet states, from 1941 to the summer of 1945, has been hidden due to political and religious reasons.[67] When I inquired from a Catholic priest from Atlanta, Georgia, what he knew of the cooperation of the Catholic Church and the Ustashas, he told me that he was not aware of any monstrous acts concerning the Church. On the contrary, he remembered only that clergymen saved Jews at the cost of their own lives. True, many members of the Church were opposed to the Ustashas, to their forced conversion of Jews and Orthodox Serbs to Catholicism, and to the endless violence against the people. These advocates of human rights were either defrocked, censured, or sent to concentration camps. The Vatican claims to have denounced the brutality, yet "[w]hile the killing was under way, the Croatian Archbishop (later Cardinal) Aloysius (Alojzije) Viktor Stepinać blessed the new regime and Pavelić was granted an audience with Pope Pius XII. A number of Franciscan monks participated in the killing. After the war ended, the Vatican helped Ustasha criminals evade capture and flee to South America" by issuing them passports, fake documentation, and financial assistance.[68]

In Tel Aviv, when I asked a survivor who was a Bosnian Jew to describe the Croatians, he replied, "The Germans were the children of the devil, and the Croatians the devil [himself]." Then he added in Judeo-Spanish, "El degoyar de los karneros por muestros shohetim no se puede komparar al modo mas kruel i inumano de estos desventurados barbaros" (The ritual killing of lambs by our religious slaughterers cannot be compared to the most inhuman and cruel way of these hapless barbarians). Avro Manhattan, a leading scholar on the atrocities committed in God's name during World War II, writes, "[U]nder the leadership of Archbishop Stepinać, the Roman Catholic Church in Croatia was complicit with the Nazis . . . and the 'Ustashi' were even more guilty than the Nazis, because they committed atrocities in God's name, with the blessing of their priests, their bishops and even of their so-called 'Vicar of Christ.'"[69]

Edmond Paris reports that 250 priests not only zealously participated in the brutality but also led the Ustashas in their endeavor.[70] The nuns also played a part in the extermination of hundreds of thousands of individuals. The following is a partial list of the members of the Catholic Church who collaborated with the Ustashas: Miroslav Majstorović, known among prisoners as "Fra Sotona" (Brother Satan); Father D. Juric Bozidar Bralow, known for his use of the machine gun; priest Bozo Simlesa; the above-mentioned

Archbishop Stepinać; Mile Budak, the minister of education and cults; monk Ambrozije Novak; and Father Srecko Peric.

These individuals and many other Catholic clergymen followed the sentiments of Mile Budak, who believed in the annihilation of the Orthodox Serbs, Jews, and Romani. In May 1941 in Gospić, Croatia, Budak declared "that the goal of the new Ustaše policy was an ethnically pure Croatia. The strategy to achieve their goal was one-third of the Serbs we shall kill, another we shall deport, and the last we shall force to embrace the Roman Catholic religion and thus melt them into Croats."[71] Mate Mogus, a Franciscan friar from Ubdina, in his homily on June 13, 1941, praised "16 brave Ustashas who have 16,000 bullets and who will kill 16,000 Serbs, after which we will divide among us in a brotherly manner the Mutilic and Krbava fields."[72] "Until now we have worked for the Catholic faith with the prayer book and with the cross. Now the time has come to work with rifle and revolver," he declared on July 24, 1941.[73]

In the midst of these horrifying killings, many Muslims and Catholics in the Independent State of Croatia that included Bosnia and Herzegovina protected Jews by hiding them in their homes and villages. Hanna (Hana) Montiljo Gasic, who was born in Sarajevo in 1949, in the film *My Spanish Bosnian Life*, states that her purpose is to share with us her pictures and her stories of a world that no longer exists. She reports that under the Nazi puppet state, most Jews were annihilated. Milan Bulajic, in his presentation "Jasenovac," reports that "the first mass slaughter of Jews (crimes of genocide—holocaust) was perpetrated in Bosanski Brod on 11 April 1941, the day after the proclamation of the Nazi Independent State of Croatia, that is while the Kingdom of Yugoslavia was still in existence, before the arrival of the Nazi occupation forces."[74] According to Hana Gasic, "On December 1941 some 2,500 women and children, from Sarajevo, Tuzla, and other cities, were arrested and they were put on trains and sent to an Ustashe concentration camp in the Croatian city of Djakovo. Over the next six months, 556 of them died in Djakovo of starvation and disease, including children, babies. After them around 2,000 were sent to Gradiska or Jasenovac." She added, "Not all of Sarajevo were rounded up, 384 joined Tito's partisans, and of those 302 of them died fighting."[75] Individuals such as Gavro Perkuvic, a Catholic Croat, protected her family. Serbs like Ranko Ristic from Blejina protected the Jews she knew, and Muslim Zeyneba Hardaga saved her Jewish neighbor, Josef Kabilo. Moreover, those Jews who were married to Muslims, such as Hardaga's sister, or Catholics were also protected from the Ustashas and Germans.[76]

As a survivor from Monastir (Bitola), Macedonia, told me in Rishon LeZion, Israel, on April 25, 1990,

Figure 6.2. Ustashas searching the belongings of Jews arriving at Jasenovac. Courtesy of the Jewish Community of Sarajevo.

> Los prizioneros en los kampos de konsentrasion de la Kroasha preferian estar en mano de los alemanes i no de los ustashas, espesialmente de los muzulmanos; eyos no solo aboresian a los djudios, tambien a los ortodoksos, i a los djinganos. Lo solo ke dezeavan era matar, degoyar, i brutalizar a los ombres, mujeres, i kriaturas sin piadad, komo si eyos proprios no tenian ijos. Ke manera de bestias eran? No tenian korason? Komo podian tomar plazer ver i bivir estas manzias?
>
> (The inmates in Croatian concentration camps preferred to be under the Germans and not the Ustashas, especially the Muslims; they not only hated the Jews but also the Orthodox Christians, and Roma. Their only desire was to kill, to slaughter, to brutalize men, women, and children without pity, as if they themselves did not have any children. What kind of animals were they? Didn't they have a heart? How could they enjoy seeing and living such atrocities?)

Indeed, they along with the Croatian Catholics eagerly slaughtered "90 per cent of Bosnian Jews."[77]

The reports of the atrocities committed by the Croatians, the Catholic clergy, and the Muslims of the Thirteenth Waffen Mountain Division are impossible to fathom. When I was told that the Ustashas used to put barbed wire through the eye sockets of the victims and take delight in gouging out the eyes of men, women, and children with special hooks, I simply could not believe it. I asked myself if such thing could take place in modern times. Could human beings—Germans, Croatians, Muslims, Albanian Fascists, or anyone—without regret, smash skulls with mallets, mutilate men's genitals, cut the breasts off women, kill women who were about to give birth, take babies from the womb and slay them?

Yet such barbarities were committed in Jasenovac and other camps in Croatia.[78] The number of victims can hardly be determined: records were not always kept or were destroyed; prisoners died on the way to the camps or were killed upon arrival. It is estimated that approximately 722,000 men, women, and children perished: 650,000 Serbians, up to 32,000 Jews, and 40,000 Romani.[79]

Lazar Lukajić, in *Friars and Ustashas Are Slaughtering* (Fatri i unstaše kolju) relates the testimony of a survivor of Jasenovac, Radomir Glamočanin, who on February 7, 1942, lost his mother, four brothers, three sisters, and thirty-seven other members of his family at the hands of the Ustasha soldiers led by the Catholic priest Tomislav Filipovic. According to Lukajić's testimony, except for his brother Milan, who was killed with a firearm after hitting a guard, the members of the "family were bestially murdered with knives and axes. . . . Ustashas murdered some 1,500 individuals [that day alone]."[80] Lukajić also interviewed "a precious and unforgettable witness" from Jasenovac, Borislav Ševa, a barber who was authorized to freely roam the camp. He described in detail the brutalities carried out by the Charkars [common Ustasha soldiers] and Romani. Both groups participated in digging large pits and smashing the heads of inmates. Borislav Ševa also reports that subsequently the Romani, too, were killed with mallets or were machine-gunned. While committing their savageries, the Ustashas drank, ate, sang, danced, and enjoyed themselves.

The following are some of the atrocities committed by the Ustashas:

> 1. Strong men were first separated according to their talents; however, once they became weak, their bodies were mutilated or grabbed by the arms and legs and thrown into the Brick Factory/Plant [flaming ovens] while drugged or fully alive.
>
> 2. Large massacres were carried out as soon as the Ustashas took power, for example, the Gina massacres of 1941, in which hundreds of Serbs were sealed off in a church and set on fire. Moreover, "Between April 12 and 15 and the night of May 31, 1941, mass arrests of promi-

nent Serbs were made in Zagreb, Sarajevo, Mostar, Banja-Luka, Travnik, Dubrovnik, Livno, and other towns and taken to the outskirts of the towns and shot. . . . The massacres continued intermittently until November 1942."[81]

3. Women and girls were violated, often in front of family members, or taken to Ustasha's caserns to be used as prostitutes.[82] Many were slaughtered or sent to the ovens upon arrival.

4. Women were thrown naked to the ground, their legs set apart, and their vaginas burned with cigarettes.

5. The Ustashas were masters at hitting, slapping, and beating the inmates to death.

6. Pairs of men were bound back to back with wire and thrown into the Sava River while still alive.

7. At the dam, near the Sava River, the inmates were beaten and killed with shovels, rifles, wooden spears, and mallets.

8. Inmates were thrown into huge pits or covered in mud while still alive.

The Germans ordered that the Jews be liquidated. "In Vinkovci 366 Jews were sent to the concentration camps because, among others, the Jews and their wives and children raised the prices of food stuffs and thereby corrupted our national Croat population."[83] In December 1943 all the Jews from Brčko "were tied with a wire and taken to the river Sava, where they were stripped naked and their children and their parents looked at one another as the Germans killed them with HAMMERS or SLEW them with KNIVES and threw them into the Sava."[84] Edmond Paris writes, "During 1941–1942 [in Jasenovac alone] crowds of Jewish children were burned alive in the old brick ovens."[85]

A Sephardi from Sarajevo, Cadik I. Danon, in 2001 passionately describes his life with his family and communities in Sarajevo, Gracanica, and Belgrade: "Before the war, the social and political atmosphere in the country the Jews had full rights and no anti-Semitic problems. This is because the Serbs were always inclined to be friendly to Jews."[86] Danon's ordeal began in 1941 when the Germans bombed Belgrade. The family then tried to move to Salonika, but with the disintegration of the Yugoslavian army, they decided to move to Tuzla, part of the Independent State of Croatia. A few months later, the Germans took the young into forced labor. Due to the action by the partisans, repression began and Serbian villages were burned. Danon and his sister tried to join the partisans, but they were rejected because their contact was tortured and killed by the Chetniks who had attacked the partisans' headquarters and slaughtered many. The Ustashas took Danon to a prison in Jasenovac, where his father and many Jewish adult males were. He recounts, "Of these 130 men I am the only one that survived that dreadful Golgotha known as Jasenovac."[87] Danon explained that Jasenovac, the biggest and cruelest camp in Croatia, "devoured about 700,000 people: 25,000 Jews, some Gypsies, and 650,000 Serbs . . . all innocent people who were taken solely on their origins."[88] Danon continues telling of life among the Ustashe:

> The Ustashe killed people in the most bestial manner. . . . They left the people without food. . . . The worst was when the Ustashe would grab someone in front of all of us, put his hand behind his back and slaughter him. I saw with my own eyes how one Ustashe, after slaughtering someone, licked the knife on both sides and said: "Oh how sweet Jewish blood is." . . . The young and strong were forced by the Ustashe to dig a pit. . . . After digging a pit, the Ustashe brought between 200 and 250 Jewish and Serbian children—exhausted, hungry with ripped and dirty clothing—and one by one brought them toward the pit. One Ustashe used a hammer to hit each child on the back of the head and threw him in the grave. . . . Watching all of this, I wept like a small child. Standing next to me was a Jewish man who was about 30 years old. He was obviously religious, and he turned his head toward the heavens and said: "God, if you exist send lightning from the clear sky and strike these criminals." The Ustashe continued to kill the children. You could hear the screaming voices of children who were to be hit, the heartbreaking fall of children into the pit. The man next to me again turned his back to this cruel picture, made the same plea loudly. He fell to his knees and wept like a small child: "God was silent and the criminals did their work."[89]

In case the children were not killed, they were sent to Catholic orphanages and converted against their will.

In their murderous actions, the Catholic clergy urged the Ustashas to fight without mercy, and the Ustashas relished killing thousands in Jadovno, the first death camp (1941), and then in Granik, Mlaka, Jablanac, Velika Kustarica, Stara Gradiska, Donja Gradina—the greatest killing place in the Balkans—culminating with the Auschwitz of the Balkans, Jasenovac, also known as "the Ustasha Camp of Death" and "the dark secret of the Holocaust." Thousands of strong inmates, men and women, were assigned to hard labor camps, working in the fields, on the dikes, or digging pits, before being liquidated. Hundreds of orthodox priests and lay congregants were burned in churches; hundreds of villages destroyed, synagogues were plundered and demolished; and the Jewish library and museum in Sarajevo, rich in sacred books and priceless Judaica, were burned.

In his talk at the Second International Conference on Jasenovac in Banja Luka, Bernard Klein stated, "I think that Jasenovac is a great distinction of a place where not only Jews were killed but non-Jews together with Jews. Usually it is only Jews who were killed, most of the time. But in Jasenovac, it seems there was no distinction made between Jews and non-Jews. They killed everyone: Serbs, Jews, and Gypsies, it made no difference."[90]

As mentioned above, there was no limit to the cruelties committed with sadistic pleasure by both clergymen and the laity. They also took pride in their tortures by utilizing crude tools: axes, spades, sledgehammers, hooks, knives, mallets, rifles, saws, shovels, wooden spears, guns, and pizzles (a whip made from a bull's penis). The tormenters looked on with delight and often celebrated joyfully their carnage to their holy personages:

> 1. In 1941 in the infamous complex of concentration camps of Jadovno, Slana, Metajna, and Stupačinovo, 1,988 Jews were exterminated. When a mother was put onto a truck leaving for the railway station, she asked an Ustasha to put up her two-year-old child on the truck. In response, he stabbed the child with the bayonet of his rifle and handed her the child impaled on the bayonet.[91]
>
> 2. On August 29, 1943, the Ustashas made bets as who could kill more prisoners by throat cutting in one night:
>
>> The Franciscan Pero Brzica [King of the cut throats] boasted of cutting the throats of about 1,360 new arrivals [Serbs and Jews] using a knife, known as srbosjek [a Serb cutter]. . . . Ante Zronuzic killed 600 inmates. . . . Mile Friganović admitted having killed 1,100 inmates. Brzica specifically recounted how he restored his grandest ecstasy by torturing Vukasin, an old peasant standing quietly watching Friganović as he killed his victims and how they died with the greatest pain. Then Friganović approached him and attempted to compel him to shout "Long live Ante Pavelić," which the old man refused to do. Although Friganović cut off the ears, nose and tongue after each refusal by Vukasin, ultimately, he plucked out the old man's eyes, tore out his heart, and slashed his throat from ear to ear, and threw him into a pit.[92] Lazar Lukajić states that this incident was witnessed by the Croat Dr. Nikola Nikolić, who is a Jew and medical doctor, and the author of *Jasenovac, Camp of Death* (1948). It should be added that "often AFTER gouging out their eyes, [they] were eaten as a delicacy by Ustasha figures. For

eating the most, Petar received a gold watch, a silver service, a roasted suckling pig, and wine as a reward for winning the contest."[93]

3. "Prisoners were killed by means of a nail which was put in the mouth and the chin [and] struck with an ax. [The Ustashas] stripped belts of skin from backs and then tightened the belts as the reins."[94]

To purify the Croatian nation, Serbian children were killed first, "even if they were still on their mothers's [*sic*] breasts. During the four years, April 1941 to May 1945, more than 74,316 children were killed in the Ustasha's NDH."[95] In "Brutal Second World War: The Ustashis," the anonymous author remarks: "If you thought that the German Nazis and SS were brutal, you haven't heard of the Ustashis. These guys enjoyed making the victims suffer before killing them. And they photographed the whole gory affair. In comparison the SS were saints."[96] The situation was so grave that Germans, Italians, and Orthodox Serbians were shocked by the atrocities committed by individual Croats and their government.

The main concern of Ante Pavelić, the Butcher of the Balkans, was "to make Croatia fascist, and ethnically homogeneous. . . . All alien elements within the Sovereign Territory of Croatia were to be eradicated."[97] To carry out his program, he selected the Fascist Ustashas. For Pavelić, the Ustashas were not quick enough. He approached Adolf Hitler to ensure that his planned program for purification would proceed swiftly. In turn, Hitler wrote Benito Mussolini to ask him to cooperate with the purification. However, the Italian Fascists, seeing the bestiality taking place in Dalmatia, remained defiant and refused to hand the Serbs and Jews to the Ustashas. General Mario Roatta, commander of the Italian Second Army in Yugoslavia, was known for his brutality directed against the Slovenian population, Croats, Chetniks, and partisans.[98] Still, he along with several of his officers, realizing that the Ustashas were the most vicious killers and more bloodthirsty than all others, "refused to hand over Serbs and Jews to the Ustashas" because they would end up in Jasenovac.[99] The Italian military governor at Trebinje (Bosnia and Herzegovina) "actually disarmed an Ustasha detachment emerging from a massive slaughter of Serbs and placed them under arrest."[100]

General Edmund Glaise von Horstenan, Hitler's plenipotentiary in the Independent State of Croatia, upon seeing the appalling conditions at Crkveni Bok, a village near Jasenovac, wrote to Berlin describing the horrors committed by the Ustasha troops besides their "scoundrel" camp commander. "This is enough to make a person vomit," he told his guide. "These camps [Jasenovac and its satellites] have reached the height of hideousness here in Croatia under the Poglavnik, installed by us. The greatest of all evils must be Jasenovac, which no ordinary mortal can glimpse." Glaise refers to the Ustasha murderers as "monsters." He concludes, "All the houses [at Crkveni Bok] were looted. The 'lucky' inhabitants were consigned to one of the fearsome boxcar trains; many of these involuntary 'passengers' cut their veins on the journey." Glaise repeatedly sent such reports to Berlin. In June 1941 he wrote, "According to reliable reports from countless German military and civilian observers . . . the 'Ustasha have gone raging mad,' and in the autumn of 1942, he referred to 'the unspeakable swinishness of this gang of murders and criminals.'"[101] Even the Orthodox Church of Serbia appealed directly to the Nazi general Dukelman to intervene and stop the Ustashi horrors.[102] German intelligence officers and the Gestapo were shocked to see Ustashas in an Orthodox Church "force worshippers to [lie] face down and [spear]them with bayonets like fish on a trident." The situation was so dire that the intelligence officer declared that "there won't be a Serb left in the country."[103]

The film *Jasenovac, the Cruelest Death Camp of All Times* (1983) conveys through images more than words can express. Through the historical photos and the words of the survivors speaking through their tears, one feels viscerally the ruthlessness and sadism of the Ustashas—neo-Nazi Croatians condoned by the Roman Catholic Church—whose horrifying religious massacres surpass all abominations. The film gives a vivid testimony of the horrific evidence destroyed by the Ustashas before they fled the crime scene in 1945.[104]

From the stretch along the Adriatic Sea from Albania to Croatia, a distance of approximately 550 miles, there was a moral separation of vast distinction. The Albanians were steeped in centuries and centuries of honor, of the Kanun and the *besa*. The Ustashas of Croatia were so base as to horrify the Italian Fascists and even the Nazis. How can there be room in the human spirit for such disparity? For such honor on the one hand, and such depravity on the other?

7
Jews from North Africa and Libya, the Invisible Jews

WHILE SOME SCHOLARS have recognized the inclusion of the Jews of North Africa in the Sephardic community, others have questioned the inclusion of the Libyan Jewish communities in a study dealing with the experiences of the Sephardim in the tragedy perpetrated by the Germans during World War II. I have no doubt that the Libyan Jews were part of the Sephardic community. Rabbi Hayim Kassorla of the Sephardic Congregation Or Veshalom in Atlanta, Georgia, in an email dated November 3, 2018, offered several possibilities for tracing their lineage, customs, and culture to the Jews of Spain and Portugal. He noted that in the eleventh century some rabbis traveled to Tripoli and greatly influenced the Jews. The Bet Din [Rabbinical Court] of Tripoli sent a number of responsa to the Bet Din in Salonika, referring to its members as "their brothers in knowledge," and stated that they "will not deviate from the rulings that they sent us." Moreover, a prayer book that Rabbi Kassorla possesses "reflects that the customs of the Libyan Jews and its style [are] the same as the prayer books of Spain, Turkey and Greece." Rabbi Kassorla concludes, "For these reasons and more the Jews of Libya . . . should be called Sephardim and not Mizrahim. They observe Judaism according to the Spanish rite which then spread to the Ottoman Empire and beyond."

The Reverend Rabbi Marc D. Angel, a distinguished scholar on the literary, religious, and cultural life of the Spanish Jews, in his response to my inquiry, wrote, "It would be fair to list Libya as part of the Sephardic/pan-Sephardic diaspora." In "The Customs of Libyan Jews," Yishak Sabban concurs: "The customs of Libyan Jews have much in common with the customs of the rest of North African Jewry and other Sephardic congregations." He adds that "due to historic and geographic circumstances, they have developed several unique customs which are of special interest."[1] In sum, the Jews of Libya are Sephardic and linked to the wider Sephardic diaspora culturally and liturgically.

I maintain that, in addition to the Libyan Jews, the Jews of North Africa are Sephardic. I know this from my discussions with North African Jews in Israel, Atlanta, New York, Montreal, and Toronto, and from my own recollections during my time in Tangier, Morocco, as a refugee during World War II.

The *invisible* Jews, those from North African countries and Libya, should not be neglected. The tentacles of the Holocaust reached approximately 450,000 Jews from Morocco, Algeria, Tunisia, and Libya in 1939. Sheryl Ochayon writes, "Whether they resided in North Africa or Libya, their situation varied from country to country, even within the territories subject to Vichy France, Germany, or Italy. Though anti-Jewish laws were announced in 1940 in all territories, they were implemented with different degrees of enthusiasm in each."[2]

Judith Roumani, scholar and editor of *Sephardic Horizons*, in an email to me dated November 12, 2018, writes, "I think that most Jews of North Africa will refer to themselves as Sephardi. . . . Some families can trace their origin directly back to Iberia. . . . Spain was more of a way station than an origin. Many Jews left Spain with the Reconquista in 1492." Thus, Sephardic *nusach* (liturgical rites), customs, etc. originated in Babylon/Baghdad, which passed the baton to Cordoba when the later caliphate became predominant. Judith Roumani comments on the lack of information concerning the Jews of North Africa and Libya: "Though the experience of North African Jews in the Holocaust has not received much attention until recently, Jews undoubtedly suffered, and hundreds died, through their treatment by the Nazi, the Vichy government, and the Fascist Italian authorities."

Mitchell Serels, in describing the situation of the Moroccan Jews in France, says that they were declared stateless, placed in the concentration camp at Drancy, and transported to Auschwitz, where they all perished, save for a few. He emphatically adds, "We, as Sephardim, must realize that the Holocaust was part of our history. We cannot pretend that the Holocaust was a European problem experienced only by Ashkenazi Jews in Eastern Europe."[3] I would add to Serel's comments that it was also a North African and Libyan problem.[4]

During my meeting in Jerusalem with Michel Abitbol, then director of the Ben Zvi Institute, we spoke about my time in Tangier, Morocco, as a refugee. He told me of the life of the Jews of Morocco, his birthplace, and the Jewish communities of Algeria, Tunisia, and Libya. I found his remarks and the sources he gave me invaluable and extended my investigation in Israel to the émigrés from Northern Africa and Libya.

Susan Gilson Miller, commenting on whether the study of the Holocaust in North Africa and Libya should be excluded or included in the "larger picture of Holocaust historiography," is in accord with Michel Abitbol's view: "In the process of developing a specific North African narrative, I find many points of comparison and crossover with the European experience of the Holocaust. Racial discrimination, radicalization, prison camps, forced labor, the texture of refugee lives, questions of anti-Semitism and racialization—all aspects of Hitler's Europe—were indeed also part of the Sephardi experience in North Africa."[5]

MOROCCO

Prewar Morocco had a Jewish population of approximately 300,000, including French and other foreign citizens. When the Vichy administration and the Nazi regime wanted to impose the anti-Jewish laws, Sultan Mohammad V refused to cooperate with them. Required to give a list of Jews in the country, the sultan responded, "There are no Jews in Morocco, only Moroccan subjects."[6] He saved his country's "250,000 Jews from persecution and death at the hands of France's pro-Nazi Vichy regime."[7] In spite of limits to his power, he ensured that there would never be roundups of Jews in Morocco. Royal Moroccan decrees, the *Dahirs*, "allowed for flexibility in the implementation of the anti-Jewish laws. . . . Jews could hold certain jobs, [and have] free access to the crafts and retail trade."[8]

Still, the Vichy regime issued anti-Semitic laws requiring Jews to move to ghettolike *Mellahs*, while those already living in them could not leave. The orders excluded Jews from public functions: limited the number of doctors, nurses, and lawyers; prohibited Jewish students from attending public schools, but not the Jewish ones of the Alliance Israélite Universelle; and restricted their activities in finance, banks, cinema, and journalism. The Vichy regulations obliged the registration of properties and permitted land expropriation and extortion: "10,000 Algerians Jews living in Morocco were deprived of their French nationality and relegated to the status of 'indigenous.'"[9] The Crémieux Decree 136 of October 1870 that granted French citizenship to the majority of Algerian Jews was suppressed. In spite of the anti-Jewish laws and the reaction of businesspeople who considered the Jews as their competitors, the Jews of Morocco were still able to work in such professions as medicine, law, and construction. By adding the name of a non-Jew to the business, they were able to continue functioning. Moreover, there were ways to profit economically by creating their own industries, such as those involving wax, soap, glue, fisheries, banking, and brokerage.

While most of the Moroccan Jews were not sent to the camps, approximately 2,100 refugees were interned in work camps located mainly in the southern Sahara. The main task of these camps was associated with the trans-Saharan railroad project, which "connected North African ports with ports in West African and sub-African mines and regions."[10] European Jewish and non-Jewish refugees, who were fleeing to Morocco to escape the upheaval in Europe, on arrival in Morocco were separated: "[T]hose who had money were sent to Mogador, Safi and Marrakech [where they either gave lessons or were allowed to peddle]; those who had none were sent to district camps and then to such labor camps as Bou-Afra, Berguent [Ain Beni Mathar], etc."[11]

The foreign Jews were interned in different labor camps: Agdz, El Jadida, Euh Ain Mellal, Ghbila, M'Rirt, Tadia, and Tamamert.[12] At Sidi Al Aryachi, seventy-five miles southwest of Casablanca, refugees mainly from central Europe, including the elderly, women, children, and disabled, were also detained. Conditions in the camp were difficult due to the harsh changes of temperature, sandstorms in the summer, poor bedding, insufficient food, overcrowding, and unsanitary shared toilets.

Berguent Camp was considered among the worst camps in Morocco. It was used entirely for Jewish refugees who had emigrated from Europe. The work was demanding: "The prisoners worked for long hours under constant yelling. . . . The sick were isolated without being treated. The punishments were severe and unjustified. The supervisors, many of whom were Germans, behaved tyrannically, with hostility and malice."[13] Among the most vicious officers was the notorious Major Jansen, who did not hesitate to send inmates to the "disciplinary camp" for any infraction: escape, reporting late to work due to sickness, protesting the insufficient amount of bread rations, and showing sympathy for other prisoners. His usual punishments were starvation, beatings administered with rifle butts, and shootings. His preferred castigation was to force an individual into the "tombeau" (tomb) for twenty-five to thirty days with no or limited food and water. The result of such tragic sentence was skin eruptions or frozen feet that in the long run were amputated; and in many cases emaciated skeletons were recovered.

In 1942 the Dirección General de Seguridad in the Spanish Protectorate International Zone of Tangier, Morocco, suspected that some Jewish and Arab youths sympathized with the Allies and worked for the British Intelligence Service. The Dirección kept them under surveillance. It alleged that the Jews played an important role in the preparation of the landing of the Allies in Morocco and had enlisted to serve in the Free French forces. "In May, hundreds of young Jews were arrested and sent to the labor camp of Khemis el Anjera (El Khemis des Anjra), some 19 miles south-east from Tangier."[14] From my recollection as a child in mid-1942, Jewish boys, among them school friends of mine, were arrested in the streets and deported to what I later learned to be Camp Khemis el Anjera, where they were flogged and "purified" (brainwashed). The Spanish authorities acknowledged that the boys were mistreated. I still recall the anguish among the parents looking for their children, and the Jewish community trying to learn what had happened. A few days later, upon the intervention of the British undersecretary of the Foreign Office and the head of the United States Legation, they were released, but they were kept under surveillance. They returned home frightened and with their heads completely shaved. I was spared because at the time of the roundup, I was attending the Sabbath morning prayers with our neighbor, the chief rabbi of Gibraltar Chocron, who took refuge in Tangier at the insistence of the British administration.

According to the Conference on Jewish Material Claims against Germany, the Jews who lived in Morocco during World War II were eligible for compensation, since they suffered under the Fascist Vichy Administration. The German government finally recognized that these Jews were eligible for payment.

ALGERIA

On October 24, 1870, as a result of the Franco-Prussian War, the Adolphe Crémieux Decree No. 136 granted some thirty-five thousand native Jews of Algeria French citizenship.[15] While the Jewish community had been autonomous, Decree 136 included some restrictions: "Jewish courts could only officiate over marriages, divorce and temporarily [over] liturgy."[16] This law was challenged by the French colonial settlers, who were anti-Semitic, hostile to acculturation, and opposed to any loss of political rights to a group they regarded as beneath them.

For centuries the Muslims and Jews coexisted in the country. However, there was a falling-out once Crémieux's Decree 137 codified that the granting of citizenship to the Jews did not apply to the Muslim Arabs and Berbers. Farah Souames declares, "Some Muslims felt betrayed, leading to the first significant rupture between the two communities."[17]

With the surrender of France to Germany on June 22, 1940, "The anti-Jewish laws promulgated by Vichy France were made applicable to the Jews of Algeria directly and mercilessly."[18] Some of the laws were harsher than those imposed on the Jews in Vichy France. The racial laws were established and enforced ruthlessly. The Crémieux Decree was revoked, and the Algerian Jews became stateless.[19] European nationals in Algeria tried to incite Muslims to act against the Jews.

On October 3, 1940, racial segregation was decreed against the Jews, and in March 1941 the Special Department for the Control of the Jewish Problem was established to apply the anti-Jewish laws, which included the following: requirement to wear the yellow badge; restriction against governmental employment; denial of teaching positions in public schools, except Jewish ones; exclusion of students from elementary and secondary schools and limiting the number of students at universities; and curbing the number of lawyers, nurses, doctors, and pharmacists who worked in their professions.[20] Moreover, Jewish positions in the financial profession—trading, banking, securities market, real estate, etc.—were eliminated. Also, an Office for Economic Aryanization—that did not even exist in Vichy France—was set up in order to "confiscate Jewish property and eliminate Jewish influence from the national economy."[21]

The Vichy administration deported about two thousand Algerian Jewish men to some sixteen labor camps. Their main task was to build the trans-Saharan railroad to carry coal across North Africa. Conditions at the camp were grueling. As in the case of the camps in Europe, the internees were subject to beatings, poor housing, and unsanitary conditions, and were barely provided enough food for survival. For any infraction of the rules, the guards sadistically inflicted unimaginable tortures. Many died from beatings, the austere climate, and exhaustion from the ten-hour workday. Many more would have died were it not for the invasion by the Allies in November 1942.

Another forgotten phase of the Holocaust was the resistance of the Jewish-Algerian underground that played a vital role in assisting the American forces in freeing Algeria from the Nazis in November 1942. Jos Aboulker, a member of an affluent family, refused to accept the Vichy laws of discrimination and organized a sports club named Go Grass, which was an armed group of his relatives, students, and friends for the purpose of defending his Jewish brethren from the cruelties planned by the French Fascists. The Americans needed some assistance from within Algeria for the landing. Jos Aboulker was General Dwight Eisenhower's facilitator. On November 8, 1942, the Jewish group, wearing uniforms of the Fascist movement and possessing fake warrants, took the Algiers police headquarters and the main radio station in fifteen minutes. They "issued faked orders misleading the Vichy regime and letting the Allies land. . . . During the next 24 hours, an American force of some 2,000 soldiers took Algiers with little resistance."[22]

The 1943 "Report on the Present General Situation of Jews in Algeria," compiled by the Comité Juif Algerien d'Études Sociales, remarks on the situation immediately following the Algerian armistice in 1942: "The racial legislation inspired by Hitler wrought havoc among the Jews in Algeria. . . . There was a semblance of changes, but it was not real. . . . Since the Allied landing, anti-Semitism grew enormously in Algiers. The misery of the Jews increased." Doctors and lawyers were still without work, military personnel did not receive their indemnities, and students could not attend higher education.[23] Preoccupied with the situation of his coreligionists in Algeria, Chief Rabbi Maurice Eisenbeth communicated to the governor general on November 17, 1942, his preoccupation concerning "the law pertaining to the status of Jews, and from the laws . . . which inflicted moral wounds upon us, [and] condemned almost the entire Jewish population to an ever-increasing misery." The chief rabbi and the Comité Juif Algerien d'Études Sociales tried "for the complete abrogation of all laws and regulations which affected the Jews of Algeria as 'Jews.'"[24] Henry Aboulker in his communication to Admiral Darlan dated December 9, 1942, apprised him that the Jews were "innocent victims of discriminatory legislation, from which they have suffered so greatly." He appealed to the governor general that "the laws and regulations" be immediately revoked in the name of justice and humanity. Aboulker further noted that with the disappearance of the Germans, "nothing happened."[25] Finally, in a letter to General Henri Giraud, the high commissioner in French Africa, dated December 31, 1942, the chief rabbi welcomed him as a great patriot and enemy of the Axis Powers and reminded him, "Since November 8th, no decree has been forthcoming abrogating the laws inspired by Hitler; they have actually become intensified by the military laws. . . . As a result there has developed an uneasiness which increased by the arrest of outstanding personalities of the Jewish community of Algiers."[26]

Unfortunately, "Some of General Giraud's recent amnesty measures benefitted the Fascist leaders who were still in their jobs." However, the Fascists continued to accuse the Jews of assisting the Allies and urged Algerian groups to support their cause.[27] Anti-Semitism ran rampant. Jews were conscripted as workers; Jewish Quarters were overrun; beatings, pillage, and murders continued; property was destroyed; charwomen were dismissed from their modest jobs; banking was forbidden; and clerks of the tribunals and of the Court of Appeals were dismissed. Ironically, a decorated Jewish veteran lost his right to drive donkeys and small carts in the public square.[28]

On March 14, 1943, Henri Giraud in a speech abrogated the Crémieux Decree.[29] The Crémieux Decree was reinstated on October 20, 1993, due to the lobbying of the World Jewish Congress, the American Jewish Congress, and the French Committee for National Liberation.[30]

In February 2018, Germany undertook to compensate twenty-five thousand Algerian Jews who had survived the Holocaust for their suffering under the Vichy administration, which had cooperated with the Nazis. Each survivor was eligible to a one-time payment of $3,183. While this small compensation was only symbolic, Ruediger Mahlo, the Claims Conference's representative in Germany, stated, "[T]he recognition is important and we will continue to fight until every survivor has been recognized.'"[31]

TUNISIA

On August 7, 2011, Reuven (Roger) Cohen, a highly respected journalist, commented on the Holocaust in Tunisia: "It took nearly fifty years before the Shoah Memory Foundation decided to evoke, first-hand, the horrors that the

Nazis inflicted on the Jews of Tunisia during the occupation of that country by their troops. This is also the new importance that historians of the Shoah attach to this six-month period during which the Jews of Tunisia have suffered directly from the Nazi occupation, a period that this generation tends to silence, obscure or minimize, but that history refuses to erase."[32]

In the early 1940s, Tunisia, with a population of eighty-five thousand Jews (eighty thousand by other accounts), was under the control of the Vichy regime. The Germans instructed the Vichy administration to make public the following anti-Jewish laws, which with the arrival of the Germans were increased: "Wear the yellow star; register their assets; confiscate apartments and businesses; prevent careers in commercial activities; set quotas on the number of lawyers, professors, and medical personnel; deny work in public positions; restrict students from attending universities, and teachers from holding jobs in public schools, except Jewish ones; prevent attendance to elementary and secondary schools; extort shop owners and plunder stores; constantly demand money, clothing, and furniture; and impose collective fines, ostensibly to compensate civilian victims of Allied bombings. The Jews were subjected to seizure, mistreatment, deportation, and sent to forced labor camps." In March 1943 pressure increased on Jews and non-Jews who were targeted by rightwing anti-Semitic French colonists. Approximately "5,000 Tunisian Jewish men were conscripted for forced labor."[33]

In 1942, as soon as the Germans occupied the country, the SS took charge of applying the anti-Jewish plan. On November 23, 1942, at about 11:00 P.M., Walter Herman Julius Rauff, "[h]omme de taille au-dessous de la moyenne, les mains et les pieds étonnamment petits, il est une homme bilieux, gonflé d'importance; d'une voix rauque" (man of below-average height, hands and feet surprisingly small, he is a vile man, swollen with self-importance, speaking in a hoarse voice), with several civilian and military aides, pushes into the house of Mr. Borgel, the President of the Tunis Jewish community."[34] The president and his son-in-law were arrested, as were other prominent Jews, among them Felix Samana and Cittanova, the honorary consul of Finland. They were held for four days. "The Germans wanted to know about the Jewish community, their ideas, their feelings, their possessions, their relations with the French, about the Muslims, and about the Chief Rabbi. In the office of the investigators one could see long lists with many names of Jewish notables. It was the intention of the Germans to arrest all of them, were it not for the President to take all the responsibility."[35]

The resident governor general, Admiral Jean-Pierre Estéva, was concerned about the situation of the Jews. He tried to intervene on their behalf, but he was not successful. "Rauff informed Estéva that the Jewish question was reserved to the occupation forces."[36] However, on November 29, 1942, Borgel was released and appointed to lead the Committee for the Recruitment of Jewish Manpower that selected Jews for forced labor. Due to the intercession of Borgel and Estéva, who disapproved of Vichy's anti-Jewish laws, "the other incarcerated Jews, except Cittanova, were released."[37] Cittanova, who had a heart attack, spent several more weeks in jail. Borgel was ordered to report twice a day with the translator, Maximilian Trenner, a Viennese Jew, and Chief Rabbi Haim Bellaich, who attended, dressed in his ritual attire.

The occupation of Tunisia by the German forces lasted from November 1942 to May 13, 1943. SS Obersturmbannführer Rauff, known for his brutality, was one of three representatives to rule Tunisia. Ochayon states, "Rauff was responsible for the murder of Jews in Poland and in Russia using mobile gas vans, precursors to stationary gas chambers later used at the death camps in Poland. He was transferred to an SD Einsatzkommando (SWAT Team) in Tunis in late 1942."[38] He was the commander of the Security Police. Under his command life for the Jews was harsh. One of his actions was to turn the Muslims against the Jews and to encourage them to kill and plunder. "But the wisdom of the leaders of the Muslim community and the long cohabitation between the Jews and the Muslims" defeated this nefarious plan. On December 9, Rauff "with his SS invades the Synagogue on the Paris Avenue, pride of the community. It's prayer time. The SS shoot their machine-guns, destroy the furniture, desecrate the sacred scrolls of the Torah, tear up the prayer books and seize all the assistants regardless of age or condition: the old men, the infirm, the rabbi, children. In the Avenue de Paris, informed by some local auxiliaries, the SS arrest all Jews who pass. . . . One hundred Jewish personalities belonging to the liberal and intellectual professions and to the business community, are confined in the military prison, hostages [were shot] according to the whims of the occupier."[39]

Rauff's demands to the leaders of the Jewish Workforce Recruitment Committee were impossible to achieve. Pressed to hand a list of Jews ready for obligatory forced labor as well as other ultimatums that Rauff kept increasing, Borgel and Dr. Léon Moatti approached Admiral Estéva and the new secretary-general of the Tunisian government, Vimont, for assistance. Estéva asked Rauff for a delay, but he failed to receive it. On the other hand, Vimont at 10:00 P.M. informed the council, who did not have a list ready, that they had a twelve-hour extension to add more names. Rauff was fuming; he screamed à la Hitler, "A genoux cochons de Juifs! Tête baissée, les mains derrière le dos! (On your knees Jewish pigs! Heads down, hands behind your back!)."[40] Sabile writes, "He accused them of sabotage [being spies for the Allies], threatened them, asked for 3,000 equipped with [raincoats and shoes], shovels and picks—1,500 for the Caserne Foch and the other 1,500 for the road of Moghrane. If not the SS would take hostages and grab 10,000 more."[41]

The advice of the intermediaries was for them to resign themselves and to obey. Rauff's vindictiveness had no limits.

> La vue des Juifs agenouillée dans la boue car il n'a pas cessé de pleuvoire—tête baissée, mains au dos—n'arrête pas les vociférations hystériques du Colonel. Il brandit cette fois son revolver, profère des jurons à jet continue, d'une voix etranglée, gutural, puis il finit par annoncer aux volontaires qu'ils seront fusillés dans la journée.
>
> (The sight of the Jews kneeling in the mud because it does not stop raining—heads down, hands back—does not stop the hysterical shouts of the colonel. He brandishes his revolver this time, utters continuous cursing, in a choked, guttural voice, and finally announces to the volunteers that they will be shot that day).[42]

Rabbi David Hagège on October 4, 1944, tells of the inhumanity of the guards. An eighteen-year old man, Mazouz, who had a clubfoot and could scarcely walk, was among those taken. His friends tried to help him, but the Germans restrained them, so they had to leave him. A German soldier kicked him and shot him.[43]

A survivor of a labor camp told me in 1982 in Tel Aviv, "There was always a reason for this guy to blame us. He accused us for collaborating with the Allies and for the constant bombardment of the port and cities, for which the Germans made us pay thousands of francs. All this Rauff did to get some personal physical and financial benefit. Woe if we did not listen to him! To refuse to carry out any order was detrimental to the community." Indeed, Rauff's instructions had to be met promptly, or the punishment would be more severe. He would increase the number of compulsory workers and compel the community to pay all costs—food, clothing, and tools—impose insurmountable fines on the entire community or take hostages from among the Jewish elite to ensure that his orders were properly discharged. "Twenty Jewish political activists were arrested and deported to extermination camps in Europe, where they all died."[44] It was difficult for the members of the Jewish leadership to recruit the number of laborers demanded by the Germans. The Jewish people criticized their leaders for their arbitrary way of selecting these individuals. Different means were proposed; they even "begged the young to volunteer for the forced labor by offering each 100 francs per day. Only 100 (120 by another count) did."[45] Unable to comply with the orders, the leaders asked Vimont and Muhammad VII al Munsif Bey (Moncef Bey), referred to as "The Protector of the Jews," "to do the recruiting for them, since they couldn't do it themselves. How sad for the community to ask others to set laws against their people. . . . S. A. Moncef Bey tells them to be calm and accept their destiny."[46] As Sheryl Ochayon describes, "[i]n the face of these violent incidents, the Jewish community decided to obey the Germans' instructions."[47] By so doing the leaders hoped that the pogrom would not be carried out. Moreover, they thought that the Allies were about to liberate the country.

Benjamin Ychay, a lawyer and president of the Jewish Central Committee in Tunisia, testified in Israel: "Between 3,000 and 4,000 men from 18 to 50 [other sources state between 17 and 30 or 15 to 45] were subjected to work under painful, humiliating, and degrading tasks in the most dangerous places."[48] They were forced to work on roads, railroad projects, front lines, airfields, and harbors under difficult conditions—beatings, poor housing, inadequate food, exhaustion, maltreatment, and constant Allied bombardments. Anyone who violated a German order was executed without trial or deported by air to Auschwitz, Buchenwald, and other concentration camps in Europe.[49] The SS was planning to build a concentration camp with gas chambers near Kairouan, but it was not completed due to the lack of time. It was estimated that "2,575 of the Jews succumbed from hardship." Moreover, "the Allied victory prevented the Nazis from extending the 'Final Solution' to the Jews of Tunisia."[50]

In 1982, while in Tel Aviv, I was informed by a Jewish survivor from the camps who emigrated from Tunisia that many Jews were saved by Muslims who refused to abide by the German rules. He added, "With all the suffering, thank God the tragedy of our people was not as bad as those of our brethren in Europe."

It should be noted that Italy protected its five thousand Italian citizens in its sector by obstructing the implementation of the Vichy and German anti-Jewish laws. Serels states, "They fared much better than did their coreligionists in the German occupied areas."[51] Sarah Sussman notes, "The Jews of North Africa were relatively fortunate because their distance from German concentration camps in central and Eastern Europe permitted them to avoid the fate of their coreligionists in Europe."[52] Reuven (Roger) Cohen objects to Paul Guez's assertion that minimizes the suffering of the Jews in Tunisia when he says that "compared to the ordeals suffered by the Jewish Communities of Europe, those of the Jewish Community of Tunisia appeared insignificant."[53] Nataf explains that if "[o]ur fathers did not recount their sufferings [it is] because the sufferings of the Jews of Europe were such that they had a kind of modesty to talk about theirs."[54]

The Jews of Tunisia suffered in as many ways as those in the concentration camps in Europe, save for one major difference. There were no crematoria or piles of dead in Tunisia. Serge Klarsfeld notes, "The Jews of Tunisia have experienced anguish, ransoms, looting, suffering and dozens of deaths.

But if their situation has not been worse, they owe it to the intelligence and skill of the leaders of their community" who faced with courage the daily menaces of their brethren and the coercions of the Nazi leaders.[55] This they were able to accomplish with the support of Tunisian, French, and Muslim notables. The Jews who were gathered in labor camps gave their own testimonials about their experiences.

Gilbert Habib, then sixteen, picked up on December 9 in front of the Great Synagogue, tells, "We were forced to walk 60 kilometers in the rain, in the cold, and in the mud. At each attempt to slow down, the kicks and whips fell on us. . . . We were locked in a stable, forced to work at night. . . . We remained three days without eating." Habib continued:

> When it rained, we returned to the camp with wet clothes, and had nothing to change into. We slept on wet straw. There was no hygiene in the camp. Only a few faucets to quickly wash in the morning. Lice and scabies were commonplace. We were awake around 5 or 6 in the morning and given a hot colored water called coffee, a quarter of bread, and one or two sardines or one or two anchovies. We then went to work. We had only a half-hour break for lunch. For supper we were given soup that had the taste of boiled water rather than a soup of vegetables.
>
> The grueling work was directed and supervised by Germans who horsewhipped us for no reason, except that we were Jews. The most awful thing was the rollcalls in the middle of the night. Now and then, holding the whip, they woke us up 3 or 4 times during the night to check if everyone was there.[56]

LIBYA

After Italy took Libya from the Ottoman Empire in 1911, "[t]he Jews received official status and were an important religious-ethnic group due to their key role in the Libyan economy."[57] However, the situation deteriorated with the enactment of the Manifesto of Race (Leggi per la Difesa della razza) published on July 14, 1938, which prepared for the enactment of the racial laws in Fascist Italy in October 1938. Anti-Jewish laws were applied against the Jews by the Fascists in spite of Governor-General Italo Balbo's wishes to the contrary. "Balbo was reluctant to carry out the Racial Laws . . . because he believed that the laws would do irreparable damage to the domestic and foreign prestige."[58] The anti-Jewish laws forbade foreign Jews to settle in Italy, in Libya, or in the colonial possession of the Aegean; deprived them of their Italian citizenship; required them to leave Italy; in the case of the Libyan Jews, forbade them to change residency without a license; "banned them from jobs in the government, banking, insurance, education, entertainment industry and the practice of law"; and prohibited marriage between Aryan Italians and Jews. Jewish students were prohibited from attending institutions of higher education and high schools; property was looted or confiscated; military personnel were reduced in rank or forbidden to serve; and Jewish shops were ordered to open on Saturday.[59] "Jews who refused to open on the Sabbath were flogged in public squares or executed, as was the case of two individuals. Those who opened their stores, in order not to break the Jewish law, either put an Arab in charge or refused to benefit from the sales of that day."[60]

The Italian people were protective of the Jews in the occupied territories. Jews from other countries took refuge in Italy, and those in the concentration camps in Italy were well treated. As I recall and as reported by members of my family who had lived in Rhodes, even under the regime of Mussolini, Jewish life was not dire until September 8, 1943, when the Germans occupied Italy and its territories.

Once the Germans occupied Libya, the Jews were scattered according to their nationality: some 1,600 who held French or Tunisian citizenship (*protégés français*) were sent mainly to Tunisia, "then under Vichy administration and Nazi occupation."[61] Of the 2,000 holding British passports, approximately 1,300 were sent to detention camps across Libya and the rest shipped to Naples. Subsequently they were transferred to camps in Bologna, Castelnovo ne' Monti, Firenze, and Siena, Italy. These prisoners were treated well by the Italians. In 1943 after Italy surrendered to the Allies, the Germans took control of the camps, and in May 1944 they transferred some detainees from Italy to different European camps, mainly to Bergen-Belsen and the Innsbruck-Reichenau camp in Austria. These inmates were forced to work under appalling conditions. They had to fight the cold climate, hunger, insults, physical abuses, and the constant threat of killings by the SS.

On orders of Mussolini, 2,500 Jews from Cyrenaica were sent by truck to Giado concentration camp in Tripolitania, which was run by the Italian Fascist and anti-Semitic Marshal Ettore Bastico.[62] Conditions in the camp were insufferable. The rations were inadequate. The allowance of 150 grams of bread a day was supplemented by food purchased from Arab merchants at high prices and through receipt of food packages from the community of Tripoli. Their living quarters were overcrowded and despicable. Their labor in building roads and front lines was demanding. At least 562 internees died due to illness and bad conditions.

Most of the three thousand men from Tripolitania were sent to Sidi Azaz, an "isolated and desert-like camp located 62 miles from Tripolitania," while the rest were assigned to work in Cyrenaica. "The work began at 6:00 am and ended at 5:00 pm. They received 500 grams of bread, rice, or pasta as food . . . the Italian guards allowed the prisoners to rest on the Sabbath." Another camp

Figures 7.1. and 7.2. Pencil sketch of Libyan boy (*above left*) and Libyan girl (*above right*) by Albert Menasche in Bergen-Belsen, 1944. Courtesy of Menasche.

was Bukbuk, which had no guards or fences due to its remote location. The prisoners' duty was to pave roads from Libya to Egypt.[63]

The following testimonies of Libyan Jews in their own words convey their experiences throughout Tunisian, Libyan, and European camps. Hay Zuaretz, a survivor, testified that Fascist Italy banished thousands of Jews to concentration camps, mainly to Giado. In the camp they were divided into barracks, twenty or twenty-five families in each. "Hundreds died of starvation. It was crowded, sick with typhoid, infested with white lice. Whoever was sick at night is found dead in the morning. Every day six to eight dead, every day people died [from malnutrition]. My brother died, my very young sister died. . . . It was painful, very painful. We won't forget it: to this day I haven't forgotten. When I think about it now I start crying."[64]

Linda Tayar from Tripoli reports that on a Saturday two Germans notified them to get ready to be taken to Italy. "They took whoever they found in the street and put them on a truck. They started shouting "Raus, raus!" (Out, out). They took everybody and threw them in such a small wagon—they put 70 of us in it. One on top of the other." They were transported in a small boat. From Italy they were transferred to Bergen-Belsen. In the camp they were not separated from the men. The families "were placed in a big room

Figure 7.3. Libyan women at work, pencil sketch by Albert Menasche in Bergen-Belsen, 1944. Courtesy of Menasche.

with board beds and straw mattresses. . . . We'd go out early in the morning, they'd line us up. It was cold and had snow." They stayed there eight months. For Linda, "It seemed like a thousand years. I wasn't scared. Fear stops when you see harsh sights on a daily basis. You see people drop dead beside you. Your heart breaks, but it also becomes like a pig's heart. You know that today it's him, tomorrow it might be me. . . . No one believed we'd get out from Bergen-Belsen."[65]

Yosef Daduch, who was born in Benghazi in 1921, told how the Italian Fascists put a Star of David on the houses of the Jews in Benghazi in April 1940. The Fascists, Daduch continued, "took over the streets, assassinated, raped, all around, all they could do . . . all over Libya." Daduch told of the collection and transport of the Jews in Benghazi to the concentration camp of Jarboujr: "Every week they sent four transports with fifty individuals, that is two hundred individuals. And they took them to Jarboujr. This was a station without end. . . . They made of it a concentration camp, they closed it at 692 meters high from the level of the sea. Two thousand thirty kilometers distant from Benghazi. Some four hundred to five hundred kilometers from Tripoli. Deserted, mountains, no one was there. During the day the commander came with his *kirbaç* [whip], forced everyone to work—clean the camp, all the stones." A German officer consulted with the Italian Fascist commander of the camp: "Then the commander would take us to the mountain to build bases, platforms for the cannons, trenches." The commander forced people to work from morning until late at night. If he thought they slacked off, he used the whip. Daduch said that many people were injured, many died, and some "became half crazy." Daduch was thirteen months in the concentration camp. He recalled, "We were 3,800. Seven hundred or eight hundred died from hunger, typhus. Only three thousand were to return."[66]

Viktor Rekah, born in Tripoli in 1919, had immigrated to Palestine prior to the war and thus escaped the persecution of the Jews. He served as president of the Libyan immigrants and became very familiar with the situation in Libya during the war. He confirmed what Yosef Daduch had said, as I summarized, that "those from Benghazi suffered the most. Those from Tripoli controlled the commerce, they had a large community, thus they did not suffer as much as those in Benghazi. Is this true?" Rekah replied, "It is true. But in Tripoli, there was in Tripoli a camp called Babuk. The Germans started to deport young men and their families to the concentration camp to work on the roads, build trenches . . . all this work." This was forced labor for the German army. It started, Rekah explained, "[i]n 1942 while Rommel was still there. During the attack of Rommel against Montgomery. They had to build trenches. During this time, the people were badly treated. There was the plague, typhus in the camps. . . . There were people who could not go along any more, and they died. Until Montgomery came and conquered this part of Libya [in Benghazi]. He liberated those camps."[67]

Joseph Labi, a Libyan Jew born in Benghazi in 1928, came from a religious background. His grandfather Eliyahu Labi was a rabbi and religious court judge in Benghazi. This is Joseph Labi's story as he gave it to Yad Vashem on February 10, 2010:

> In 1941 the Italians confiscated money and property from the Jews. Then they took all the Jews [including my entire family] from Benghazi, Tobruk and Derna to Giado, a concentration camp. The Germans entered Libya in the second half of 1941. All individuals holding Allied citizenship were expelled, including many Jews. I was a British citizen, they took us to northern Italy, to a village where just women and children remained. They took all the men to a concentration camp in Florence, then to Germany, to the Bergen-Belsen concentration camp. I was completely alone. Life in the camp meant torture and starvation. People who'd arrived earlier from Romania and Poland were tired of living. They wanted to die. They went to the fence on purpose so they'd be shot. I saw a sharpshooter up high [in the guard tower] kill them. Then they threw them in a pit outside the camp. Among our people from Libya, the old people would not eat because the food wasn't

kosher. They gradually perished. I was given this Tallit [he shows a picture] in Bergen-Belsen by an Ashkenazi rabbi. He said: "Come and pray." I said, "I don't know how. I didn't have a Bar Mitzvah." So he gathered about ten men and I had my Bar Mitzvah. I was sad because there was nobody from my family to celebrate my Bar Mitzvah with me. I was 17. I grew up without parents [tears running down his face] and I was put in this camp, but I wanted to live. I constantly fought to survive.[68]

In March 1945, because of his British citizenship, Joseph Labi was released from Bergen-Belsen on a prisoner exchange deal between Great Britain and Germany. From the camp he was sent to France. He then went to Portugal: "When we reached Lisbon, we realized that hell was over for us."[69] Once he reached Benghazi, Joseph, with the assistance of the Jewish Brigade, went dressed as a soldier first to Alexandria and then was smuggled into British Mandate Palestine, where he joined the Palmach, the elite force of the Haganah army during the British Mandate, and fought for the independence of Israel. "Despite all the adversity, persecution, and deprivation, Labi married, and he and his wife Yvonne have a son and daughter, seven grandchildren, and a great-granddaughter. . . . He has managed, by many 'miracles,' to survive a childhood that was taken from him. A life, a town, a home and his family were destroyed. He is a survivor."[70]

Following is the testimony given by Labi Zion in July 25, 1968, to the Central Archives for the Disaster and Heroism of Yad-Vashem, Jerusalem (File 033167). It deals with the tribulations of a Tunisian Jew caught in the war in Tripoli, Libya, repatriated to Tunisia during the German occupation of the country, and then returned to Libya.

My name is Labi Zion, born in Tripoli on March 15, 1890. I was taken prisoner in 1940 when Italy entered the war because I had a Tunisian passport under the French government. I was sent to a concentration camp in the desert, 400 kilometers from Tripoli (Buerat-El Hasun / Bu'ayrat al Hsun), with Christian and Arab Muslim guards. In the camp were English, French and other foreigners. We were there 3 months. I must say that the treatment was kind, was good. We were generally respected by the Italian authorities. After three months in the camp, I was sent back home to Tripoli, and we stayed for two months.

As a result of military operations in Africa, I was with many other foreign citizens, and once again interned in the same concentration camp of Buerat-El Hasun. I stayed there a year. I was freed by the intervention of Bey Frebisha, a Sheik well known and a very well-respected personality who had very high connections. He was my *ex-principale* [former chief] in many jobs and he loved me. He wanted to help me. After, thanks to his personal intervention, I was released from the prison camp. I have to say that until then (I do not remember exactly) we did not suffer. During my internment, my wife and children remained at home in peace.

Later the Italians forced us to go back to Tunisia, considering us Tunisians. Giving us the order to leave, they told us that the Tunisian authorities asked for us. So we had to settle everything in Tripoli, home and the rest. I went to Tunisia, the city of Gabes, a distance of 363 kilometers. In Tunisia we were undisturbed until the arrival of the Germans from North Africa [Libya], during the campaign of Gen. Erwin Rommel. As soon as they arrived in Gabes, they immediately began to look for houses and they came also to ours. They were high officers and also fully armed soldiers. They rushed into the house and entered with great arrogance. That day it was Saturday and we were at the table, they asked us to give them the things of value, especially gold and money. We said that we did not have anything because we were refugees from Tripoli and that everything we had, mainly clothing, was in the wooden crates next to them. They opened up the boxes and were convinced that what we were saying was true. They threatened to kill us, they put a gun on my chest. Then a German officer took from my wife the earrings from her ears, which were made of gold with diamonds, and three gold rings from her fingers. They made the same requisitions from our Jewish neighbors, too. Rabbi Haim Nori (who died in Israel a year ago, 1969) brought out a strongbox. The same was done to a goldsmith called Pesach and to many others. On the same Saturday evening the Germans withdrew under the strong pressing by the English. While retreating, they ferociously destroyed all our neighborhood. Fortunately, some houses, including ours, remained intact.

After the retreat of the Germans, all our misfortunes were over. But because of all the shock experienced and the great panic and fear, I lost my memory. As soon as we could, we return to Tripoli and came to Israel in 1948. We arrive illegally on a boat in which we were 66 people, paying 13,000 Italian liras per person (we were four—my wife and the eldest daughter with a child), so the journey cost a bunch of money. The trip was hard and dangerous. We arrived in Israel just at a time when the liberation war ended with the Arabs and the British.

Both Viktor Rekah and Yosef Daduch told me about their efforts to obtain reparations for the Jews of Libya who had been in concentration camps. Each cited the reparations that the Germans paid to the Ashkenazim. One Libyan Jew said to Rekah in reference to the Polish Jews who received compensation from Germany, "Look here, we also were in concentration camps in Libya. Therefore, we too should receive compensation from Germany." Rekah told me of his efforts to obtain compensation: "Then I went to see Mr. Goldman who was the president of the World Jewish Congress." Rekah implored him for equity: just as had been done "for the Jews of Poland," he asked to be done "for the Jews of Libya." He was not successful on this attempt.[71] Daduch, however, did have success. In his capacity as secretary of the Jewish Association, Daduch wrote "to the president of the Italian Council. . . . He told me that all these persecutions came about [due] to German pressure. . . . Nothing came of it." Daduch consulted a German delegate of the United Restitution Organization who in turn "searched the libraries and archives of the German government." The German delegate "found a letter of 1941 or 1942" of the German ambassador of Tripoli who sent it to the German ambassador in Italy. He said, "We sent the Jews of Italian nationality to Jarboujr Concentration Camp." The letter also referenced the Jews of Tripolitania and the Jews of Cyrenaica. Daduch explained that "with this we made a case to Germany and they recognized, and paid for nine months of concentration and they are paying until the present the widows, old people."[72]

Thus concludes the little-known story of the Jews of North Africa and Libya during the Second World War. Sadly, there remain survivors yet to be interviewed, but they are passing. It is my hope that these Jews will no longer be invisible.

8
The Place of God in the Holocaust

The question resounds in numerous interviews: Where was God during the Holocaust? How could He watch His people die by the trainloads, millions and millions of men, women, and children burned in the furnaces? Marta Wise, a Czechoslovakian survivor, had a ready response, "People often ask, 'Where was God during the Holocaust?' My question is, 'Where was man?'"[1] Several survivors asserted, "God does not care for us, so we can rest. Now let Him choose another people. We are tired of being the chosen one. What good did it do us?" Linda Breder quipped, "There was no God in Auschwitz. There were such horrible conditions that God decided not to go there. We didn't pray because we knew that it would not help." She concluded, "Many who survived are atheists. They simply don't trust in God. It's over. God is no longer with us."[2]

I interviewed survivors about the place of God in the Holocaust and their religious beliefs during and after the Holocaust. One Sephardic survivor from Greece stated,

> Me ambezaron de ser un djudio orguyozo, respektar mi relijion, i kumplir los mandamientos. Asistí a los servisios en la keila todas las mañanas, en Shabbat, i los *Yamim Noraim*, resiti la *Shema* al despertarme i antes de irme a la kama. Mantuve el dicho, "Primero vemos la kara dil Dio i despues el de la djente." Ma, en el kampo, todo lo ke veia, todo era las sufrienas, las flamas ke no kedavan de salir del uluk, las haftunas, las matansas. Todo esto empeso una mueva aktitud en mi. El meoyo me se rodeava. A ken kulpar por esta trajedia? A los maldichos alemanes, a mis pekados, o al Senyor del Mundo? Muestros padres mos dizian ke El Kriador ayuda a su puevlo, ke El era muestra salvasion." Ma aun demandavamos, si se avia olvidado de mozotros. Donde estava?

> (I was taught to be a proud Jew, to respect my religion, and to abide by the commandments. I attended services in the synagogue every morning, on Shabbat, the High Holidays of the New Year, and the Day of Atonement, I recited the *Shema* when I woke up and before going to bed. I abide by the rule, "First we see the face of God and then that of the people." But, in the camp, all that I saw was the suffering, the flames that did not cease from emerging from the chimney, the whippings, and the killings. All of this unleashed a new attitude in me. My brain wandered: Who to blame for this tragedy? The damned Germans, my sins, or the Lord? Our parents kept telling us that the Creator helped His people, that He was our salvation. But we still kept asking if He had forgotten us. Where was He?)

A second survivor interjected: "Muchos de mozotros, kansados de la vida, abandonamos no tanto la relijion, ma al Dio por su kayades, su manko de interes en mozotros. . . . Avia otros ke mantenian sus kreensias en El, i ke rogavan" (Many among us, tired of life, abandoned not so much our religion, but rather God for his silence, His lack of interest in us. . . . There were others who maintained their beliefs in Him, who prayed). A third said, "Avia algunos ke no kreyan ni en la relijion ni en el Dio. Al rekonoser el kuerpo de alguno a ken estavan al punto de aronjar en un oyo o en el orno, resitavan Kadish por su alma" (There were some who did not believe either in religion or in God. Upon recognizing the body of someone they were about to throw in a pit or oven, they recited the Kaddish [the mourner's prayer] for his soul). When I asked Jacques Stroumsa, originally from Salonika, about the religious sentiment of the people, he answered: "Look, we were religious without knowing it. That is, all of Salonika was one big Keila [Community]. I remember that I was not religious, a fanatic. We, however, followed the Law, we observed the Sabbath, and we believed in the Torah. On the Holydays we went to the Great Synagogue. . . . My father was Professor of Bar Mitzvah. He instructed the young of the best families of Salonika." Of Auschwitz, Stroumsa said, "I can never forget the faces of my people before being shot or gassed. It was dreadful, I saw so many people die, not only *savios* [learned people], not only rabbis, not only men without sins. Why did all of this take place? The question that one kept asking, and asking, 'Where was the Almighty then? Why did He allow the Nazis to destroy so ferociously the Jewish people?' You see, the conditions in the camp were so horrible that God decided not to go there."[3] Stroumsa finally concluded, "It's over. God is no longer with us. To survive I joined the orchestra." In a video interview conducted by eSefarad, Stroumsa explained, "In Auschwitz not only I stopped believing in God but even after leaving Auschwitz, for many years, my questions to God persisted: 'Why have you allowed so many crimes?' But further I questioned, 'Where were men, the so-called humanitarians?'" Before the end of the video, he touched the tattooed number on his left arm and said, "It is true that the most important question they could [ask] me was, 'Where was God in Auschwitz?' and I ask, 'Where were men?'"[4]

While Rosemary and I were present at one of Moshe Shaul's meetings in Jerusalem in 1985, the question of the Holocaust came up. As one survivor expressed it, "No avia salida. Este era muestro destino" (There was no way out. This was our destiny). Another woman said,

> Yorimos lagrimas amargas, rogimos, admitimos muestros pekados, rekonosimos ke la negregura de los ombres fue la kavza de muestro sufrir. Ma, porke esta trajedia kayo sovre mozotros i no sovre otros? Eran eyos mas *sadikim* ke mozotros? Fue todo un yerro? De ken? Fue un esfunyo?
>
> (We cried bitter tears, we prayed, we acknowledged our sins, we recognized that the wickedness of men was the cause of our suffering. Nonetheless, why did this tragedy fall on us and not on others? Were they more pious than us? Was it all a mistake? By whom? Was it a dream?)

In response to the question, "Was it a dream?", a survivor, who had lost all his family, interjected, "No, it was true. We were there. We lived it. And no one came to help. Where were the other nations, the so-called friends? 'Was it all our fault?' you ask. Were we such evil people? Where was God when it all took place, when we agonized? Was He even aware of our existence?"

Alfred Elkoubi told me of "a particular emotional memory" from Auschwitz: "I had found, two or three years before, Elie Wiesel in Jerusalem. I approached him and said, 'Do you recognize me?' He said, 'I do not think so. I think that we met, but I cannot place you.' 'I will tell you an event that you will understand that we were in the same commando in Auschwitz. It is an event that cannot be forgotten, Mr. Wiesel. We had a common friend, a Hungarian that must have the same age as us, seventeen, eighteen years old, sixteen, fifteen years, I do recall well.'" Some people had tefillin in the camp. Alfred Elkoubi and Elie Wiesel "would wear the tefillin every morning and were sure that no one would see us." Elkoubi concluded, "And Elie Wiesel remembered that we had this friend, and we found ourselves thanks to this recollection."[5]

On June 30, 1982, in Izmir, Turkey, I asked Esther Morguez Algrante who was to blame for the tragedy of the Holocaust. I expected a direct answer from her, but I didn't get it. Algrante was a student of the Torah, a scholar of rabbinical studies, a thinker, a truth-seeker, and a descendant of pious rabbis dating back to the Iberian Peninsula. My great-uncle Yeoshua Musafir, also from

Izmir, had known her for years and prepared me for the interview: "Nothing is uncomplicated for Esther. Even her personal life is challenging," he said. Indeed, I found her to be a person torn between her devoutness for Ashem and her questions about how He had abandoned His people. After discussing several topics, she wanted to talk to me about her harsh existence: her being a widow with little means of survival; her feeling lonely with no one for comfort except an old sister; her meagre life in a depressing apartment; and her distinguished past that was no more. With sadness, she asked me to visit with her daughter Rejin, who suffered from a tragic physical disability and spent her days lying on a bed in a dark and musty room. The sight was devastating. I asked myself, "Why did she want me to experience it?" Only later did I realize that she needed to share her personal anguish with me. As expressed in our interview and in following letters, the experiences of tragedy were an intricate part of her survival. Sad as she was, she did not complain of her hardship as a mother. Her only wish was for the Lord to have given her a healthy baby. "She is mine," she proudly said, "and I will take care of her as best I can. At least she has me, and I can take care of her." Despondently, she continued, "Ansi es ke yo entiendo la dolor de estas madres ke pedrieron a sus ijos en talas situasiones desgrasiadas. Por esto nunka puedo pardonar esta Almanya. Lo ke va repozar mi korason es kuando Almanya estara enfasada de la karta jeografik del mundo" (So I understand the pain of these mothers who lost their children in such miserable conditions. That is why I can never forgive Germany. What will soothe my heart is when Germany is wiped out from the geographic chart of the world).

In a long monologue, Esther blames Israel's enemies for their cruelties, and God for not putting an end to the calamity and saving the six million victims whom He should never have condemned to death. She could not endure the slaughter of her people. She lamented still being alive when her coreligionists died a terrible death just for being born Jews. Imploring God and reminding Him of her love for Him, she received no answer, nor could she find an answer to the horrors of the Holocaust. She remained utterly exhausted and disheartened. Even though she railed against the silence of the Almighty, she could not reject Him. Rather, in a loud voice, she hallowed Him by declaring, *Baruh dayan ha-emet* (Blessed is the Judge of truth), a blessing of resignation said at a time of sadness. Thus, she humbly acknowledged her "faith in the majesty of God whose ways are not for us to know."

Noting the dichotomy in her statements, I asked Esther to further clarify them. She said, "God is a mystery that we cannot decipher. He is the protector of Israel, and He is easy to anger. He punishes us for our never-ending sins, and at the same time he is merciful and compassionate. Unfortunately, human beings are hardly conscious of what they have done, of their sinful actions, and in their despondency they, just as I have, turn against God, the Almighty, not for comfort but to blame Him for the tragedy that befell my people, and for their apprehension."

Discussing her poetry, I asked her why she limited herself mainly to the Jews of Warsaw and did not refer to the Jews of Xanti, Salonika, or Rhodes. She grounded her answer in religion, stating "that is exactly what the Germans lack." She continued:

> Mira, Monsieur Lévy. Mira. Tenemos mozoros en muestra ley ke kada puevlo ke se ulvida de su relijion no es dinyo de bivir. . . . Kuando veo a toda populasion de Izmir, i mizmo de Istambol, aniyilandose sin dinguna verguensa, alora me do kuenta ke siempre la baze de mi ministri, la baze de muestra relijion, es la relijion.
>
> (Look, Mr. Lévy. Look. We have in our Law that every nation that forgets its religion is not fit to live. . . . When I see all the people of Izmir, even from Istanbul, destroy themselves with no shame, then I realize that forever the basis of my ministry [teaching], the basis of our religion, is religion itself.)

Thus, Esther Morguez Algrante placed the blame for God's action on the sins of the people, on those who did not remain faithful to their Maker. She exclaimed, "Let me tell you, even when I am discouraged, I never stop leaning on my beloved [God]." She added, "You see, '*Maase mishma en Ars Sinai*,' verily, there is no sin in Mount Sinai." She continued, "Your question, 'Who is to be blamed,' demands a lot of thought. For better or for worse, God, from the beginning of creation, allowed men and women to choose their destiny. And you know what happened? God had faith in us, and we ignored His trust and opted for our own personal well-being, disregarding Him and His other people."

Algrante added, "However, in our hearts we know that man creates his own torment and that the Lord is just, and at the proper time He will look after us. God, too, sheds tears upon seeing His children go through so much grief." In a similar theme about God's grief, Yehuda Bauer recounts the following story: "A well-known Holocaust survivor once observed that whenever he visited the site of the Bergen-Belsen concentration camp, it rained. 'Do you know why?' he asked. 'God is weeping. He is weeping in shame for the guilt He bears for the murder of the Jewish people.'"[6] Algrante wanted to end the interview with one of her favorite anecdotes:

> Senyor Lévy, le dire una kozika mas por reir. Un dia le disho un malah del Patron del Mundo, "De ke no salvas a tu puevlo ke esta en galut," i el Dio le

respondio al malah, "De ke me keres avlar de Menahen, Lilli, Jack. Yo tengo a Avraam, Itzhak, Yako, Moshe, Aron, David, Shelomo, Sara, Rebeka, Lea, Rahel. De [ke me avlas de] Jack i de los pekadores aki en los bares, en los restorantes, en lugares ajenos onde se keren olvidar ke son djudios. Esto es lo ke aze muncha pena al Senyor del Mundo."

(Mr. Lévy, I'll tell you one more thing just to laugh. One day an angel said to the Master of the World, "Why don't you save your people who are in exile?" and God answered to the angel, "Why do you want to speak to me about Menachem, Lilli, Jack? I have Abraham, Isaac, Jacob, Moses, Aaron, David, Solomon, Sarah, Rebecca, Leah, Rachel. Why do you speak to me of Jack and of the sinners who are here in the bars, in the restaurants, and in strange places where they want to forget that they are Jews?" This is what hurts the Master of the World a great deal.)

Algrante's statements recall the question Haim Chemouel Tchimino from Kavala asked Yehuda Haim Perahia about the Chosen people and their suffering. In "A Reply," Perahia responded:

Friend, you ask me why they hounded us to death,
Are we such sinners to merit this fate?
Why did God take us to be His chosen people
And for that reason bear endless tortures and sufferings?
What you ask cannot be resolved in a few words,
Many, there are so very many, basic and convincing answers to give.
I do not possess complete and absolute competence to clarify them.
In all the workings of the universe I see the hand of Providence,
To this mighty and invisible power everything is subjected.[7]

Chelomo Mordehay Reuven (Le Rêveur Solitaire, The Solitary Dreamer) left Salonika for Palestine in 1935 when still in his teens. When I asked him to comment on the place of God, the Law, and the Covenant in the tragedy, Reuven replied that while he attended a Shoah meeting in the synagogue as a Jew and member of the Tel Aviv municipality, he raised his hands toward the heavens and asked God how "it was possible for some to survive and yet for so many others, among them rabbis, honest merchants, the best of the city, to perish?" On another occasion, again in the synagogue, he spoke of a lost Hebrew text on the Holocaust found in a bottle in Warsaw. It was written by a young *dezaparesido* (unaccounted individual/disappeared). Reuven translated it. As he told me, "This young man declared himself a believer in spite of what had taken place in the Holocaust. He told Ashem, 'I believed in you.' However, finding himself in a terrible situation, he confronted God and asked Him to 'Forgive the many more who also have lost their faith.'" Reuven admitted that "this concept was difficult to understand." I asked him, "How is it possible that such a tragedy be allowed?" Reuven simply answered, "There are small animals who [see more] than man or hear noises far beyond what man [can hear]. Man is much more limited and cannot conceive such things. I can only explain that the universe was created by a Divine force, and the human spirit cannot conceive why such a crime was allowed. This is the only answer that I can give, I do not have any other."

In the summer of 1982, during my visit to Israel, I spent four weeks interviewing Sephardic survivors of the Holocaust, exchanging ideas with scholars at Bar Ilan University in Ramat Gan and at the Hebrew University in Jerusalem. I also conducted research and spoke with scholars at Yad Vashem, the World Holocaust Remembrance Center, in Jerusalem. The result was so devastating that I had to seek the counsel of a Sephardic rabbi in Bat Yam. I asked him, "How can a benevolent God be so full of anger, so destructive of His people? Indeed, in the Torah, He offers hope, blessings, forgiveness, mercy, and life; yet in the same Bible, He warns of dire consequences if the people do not follow His commandments. Being all-knowing, He was aware that his people would not be perfect."[8] The rabbi did not answer. Frustrated, I continued, "Sir, please tell me, if God can forgive Hosea's wife Gomer, a harlot, an adulteress, an unfaithful wife, if He grieves over her actions and yet redeems her and returns her to her husband, why did He not extend the love He showed for Gomer to the victims of the Holocaust? Rabbi, Gomer was accused of specific sins; what were the inmates of the Holocaust accused of? Of their own transgressions or those of their people?" To my impassioned query, the rabbi at last replied:

> El Todo Poderoso es yeno de ravya, ataka, destruye, es selozo kuando mos aleshamos de El. Al mizmo tiempo es rahman i tiene sentiminetos por su puevlo. Dinguno save las maneras del Dio. Porke mos eskojo komo su puevlo? Komo prometio, aun kon los pekados del puevlo de Israel, El siempre topa una manera de perdonarlos. Aunke El los kastiga, El no los destruye; este es el mirakolo. Es una union ke el mizmo Dio no puede romper. Lo entiendes? El Dio no puede egzistir sin Israel igual ke mozotros no podemos sin El. El tiene menester de la nasion, Su nasion, i mozotros de El. No ay manera para ke el rompa la ketuba. Mira, dainda estamos bivos por miles de anyos.
>
> (The Almighty is full of rage, attacks, destroys, and is jealous when we stray away from Him. At the same time, he is merciful and has feelings for his people. No one knows of God's deeds. Why did He choose us as His people?

As He promised, regardless of Israel's sins, He always finds a way to forgive them. Even though He punishes them, He does not destroy them; this is the miracle. It is a union that He cannot break. Do you understand? God cannot exist without Israel, just as we cannot without Him. He has need of the nation, His nation, and we of Him. There is no way for Him to break the Covenant. Look, we are still in existence for thousands of years.)

Noticing that I still had questions, the rabbi continued in English, "As I already said, God chose the Israelites not to destroy them totally but to give them a chance to redeem themselves as was the case of Gomer when she realized that she went astray. Thus, it is then, when the people will realize that they, too, went astray, that He will forgive them and *restore* the nation, a remnant, to greatness until the end of times. I repeat, He does not want to destroy Israel. He cannot *annul* the Law that He *voluntarily* enacted. The biblical and rabbinical commentaries have stressed that the *Covenant* is not only crucial for the Jews but also for the Creator (my emphasis)."

While I appreciated the words of this kindhearted rabbi, they did not answer my questions or ease my relentless angst. I kept asking myself, as did many of the survivors I interviewed, "How many Inquisitions and Holocausts can we endure? How many allegations of blood libel must we be blamed for? How many will fall to the autos-da-fe such as in the Spanish Inquisition or into the furnaces and ditches in Hitler's killing camps? How many times will Ashem inflict such terrible punishment on His Chosen?" As Pope Benedict XVI asked in a trembling voice when he visited Auschwitz in May 28, 2006, "Why, Lord, did you remain silent? How could you tolerate all this?" I couldn't forget the tragedy and all the suffering of my people, those who brutally died and those who survived physically but not emotionally. Their feeling of helplessness haunts them every day of their lives. As Raoul Menasche told me on June 3, 1982, "Somos komo los kodreros dispersados en los kampos sin chuban" (We are like the scattered lambs in the fields without a shepherd).[9]

I continued my search. In response to my question, "Is the Covenant still valid today considering the state of affairs in the world and especially regarding the Jews and the Holocaust?" Isaac Missistrani, one of the leaders of the Turkish Jewish Community in Bat Yam, Israel, tried to provide an answer in our interview during the summer of 1985. His response was not much different than the rabbi's. He, too, placed the blame on the people.

No fuimos obedientes, mos aleshimos de El, abandonimos sus mandamientos, olvidimos el Shabat. Ma el Senyor del Mundo deve aver savido de muestros djemidos i rogos. Ken save porke no responde a muestras orasiones Porke desho ke tanta maldad kayera sovre sus ijos? El es piadozo i siempe esta

> konsiente de mozotros. Save bien ke no ay otro puevlo ke dezea en oras de pas o adversidad, alegria o apreto, libertad o kautiverio, el retorno a Sion i al santo Yerushalayim. Ke otro puevlo lo bendize mizmo en oras de tristeza? Desbarasarse de mozotros no profita ni a El ni a mozotros. Ken roga noche i dia la yegada del Mashiah? Ken sino mozotros protejamos su Torah. Aun kon todo el mal ke mos aharva, tenemos de menester de Ashem. Ansi es ke devemos esperar por el dia de la *rehmision*. Tenemos ke tener esperansa, no ay otro remedio.
>
> (We were not obedient; we went astray from Him. We abandoned His Commandments. We forgot the Sabbath. However, the Almighty must have known of our wailing and prayers. Who knows why He did not react to our prayers? Why did He allow so much evil to befall His children? The Lord is merciful and always has been conscious of us. He is well aware that there are no other people who yearn in peacetime or adversity, happiness or anxiety, freedom or captivity, their return to Zion and holy Jerusalem. What other people bless Him even in moments of grief? Getting rid of us helps neither Him nor us. Who prays night and day for the coming of the Messiah? Who, if not us, safeguards His Torah? Still, with all the cruelty that strikes us, we need Him. So, we must wait for the day of redemption, we must have hope, there is no other solution.)

I replied, "But the wait has been long, and there is no end to the suffering."

Rosemary and I delivered a lecture to a Sephardic group in Herzelia, Israel, in May 1990. Most of those in attendance expressed their faith in God. As one survivor opined, "He does punish His people when they sin, but He also redeems them in *oras de apreto* (in dire hours). He punishes us, but in His immense love, He does not destroy us. I have seen many miracles in Auschwitz. By chance I was sent to work to the kitchen when there was a selection, many were taken to the crematorium, and I survived." The son of a Holocaust survivor, who lost most of his family to the flames, did not agree. Sadly, he remarked:

> Esperar en mirakolos no amejoro la situasion del djudio. Porke el Dio no tuvo piadad de los inosentes ijikos ke murieron komo ovejas? Donde estava el Dio guadrado? No sentia los djemidos de su puevlo? No veia las lagrimas amargas de las madres korer komo rios? No vido djente inosente biva un segundo, pasar por las kamernas de gas, i un segundo despues konvertida en seniza?
>
> (Waiting for miracles did not improve the situation of the Jew. Why didn't God pity the innocent children who died like sheep? Where was God hid-

> ing? Did He not hear the laments of His people? Didn't He see the bitter tears of the mothers run like rivers? Didn't He see innocent people alive one minute, pass through the gas chambers, and a second later be turned into ash?)

Then, sarcastically, he added,

> Mira lo ke paso. Il Dio mando a Eliyahu en una karosa de fuego i en vez de salvar a su puevlo, tomo a todos los djudios—viejos, djovenes, ijikos, ombres, mujeres, rezien nasidos, *ani*, rikos—i los yevo a todos no a Gan Eden sino a los kampos de matansa. No diskrimino de uno a otro, i todos mozotros lo pagimos.
>
> (Look what happened, the Lord sent Elijah in a chariot of fire, and instead of saving his people, He took all the Jews—old, young, children, men, women, even infants, poor, rich—and took them not to Heaven but to the death camps. He did not discriminate one from another, and all of us paid for it.)

On September 14, 2011, I wrote to the Reverend Dr. Marc D. Angel, whom I have known for several decades as a fellow scholar and friend. He is the founder and director of the Institute of Jewish Ideas and Ideals, and rabbi emeritus of Congregation Shearith Israel—The Spanish and Portuguese Synagogue in New York. I asked him about the view of survivors of the Holocaust toward God, His granting free will to the people, and His role in the tragedy. On September 15, 2011, Rabbi Angel graciously responded:

> Shalom Isaac,
>
> You raise age-old questions. Indeed, the biblical book of Job deals with the issue of human suffering, and God's actions/non-actions.
>
> My general feeling is that we need to focus on humanity, rather than on God. The Holocaust was caused directly and exclusively by Nazis and their collaborators—and a world that was apathetic to the suffering of Jews and others. Yes, God redeemed the ancient Israelites from Egypt. . . . Since those times, it has been extremely rare for us—or any other people—to witness overtly miraculous salvation in times of duress. Maimonides quoted the Talmudic teaching that "the world operates according to its own pattern," *i.e.*, don't count on miracles.

Rabbi Angel then referred to all the horrible tragedies, from the destruction of the First Temple through the oppression, indignities, and cruelties against the Jews in Christian and Muslim countries, even up to the present time. He continued:

Through all those sufferings, Jews also wished that God would have performed miracles to save them. But these miracles did not happen, or at least did not happen in an overt way.

When I consider all these barbarities against Jews, including the barbarities of the Holocaust, my faith in God is not challenged—since faith does not assume that God will intervene to save me every time I have a problem. However, my faith in humanity is severely tested. How is it possible for human beings to act like beasts? How is it possible for "civilized" people to participate in or condone heinous crimes against fellow human beings? Is it possible to save humanity from its own evil propensities?

The great wonder is that in spite of centuries of oppressions, the Jewish people as a whole have retained not only faith in God—but faith in humanity. That is the amazing and profound mystery of the Jewish people. In spite of everything, we believe in God and we believe in humanity.

In August 2013 I wrote to Yehuda Hatsvi, who was born in Salonika in 1932 and moved with his parents to Palestine in 1934. Hatsvi is widely known among the Sephardim as a scholar, editor, translator, and frequent commentator in the online *Ladinkomunita*. I asked him about the place of God in the Holocaust. He replied:

Dear Professor Levy,

In fact, your question is exactly the same as my own, I cannot tell you why the Master of the Universe who promised to protect His people from all suffering and evil, didn't keep his promise. Our sages say, "We do not know the affairs of God."

After the victory of the Six Day War (1967) no Jew in Israel had the opportunity to declare that this victory was a miracle for God's sake in favor of his people. All the streets in Israel were festooned with flags and placards bearing the message: "Kol aKavod leZAHAL" (All Honor for the IDF / All Glory for the Israel Defense Forces). What I want to say is that many of the people (at least in Israel) no longer expect that God would fulfill His promises.

The Shoah was a colossal catastrophe, which no human pen can fully express. But the Shoah was not the only disaster that happened to our people. The calamities of our people by the hand of Assyria, Babylonia, and Rome were no less a terrible and fatal wound.

Making a conscious link between the Holocaust and the persecution of the Jews in Spain, Hatsvi praises those Jews from the Iberian Peninsula who remained faithful to their religion. Forced by the Edict of Expulsion (March 31, 1492) to choose either exile to unknown lands or conversion to Catholicism, a good portion rejected conversion.

As Hatsvi said, "We do have the right to pass judgment on God." He questions the Lord, "How many times must we appeal for help on the basis of all the tragedies that have struck the Jews, and other countless sacrifices that they have endured?" He, however, concludes by warning the Jews, "It is now time for us to amend our ways and truly be the shining light of all nations."

In his article "God, Where Are You?" Rabbi Nathan Lopes Cardozo questions and challenges God for the suffering of His children in the camps.[10] Cardozo gives voice to "the most faithful devotees that were speaking to God and praising Him." He continues, "[I]t is extremely difficult to believe that You are actually living among us." He reproaches God for not stopping "any of these butchers," but rather allowing them "to savagely snuff out the lives of His people." Still, declaring his belief in God, Cardozo realizes that the "Jews are the greatest miracle of all. We have outlived all our enemies—the Egyptians, Greeks, Romans and many others." He adds, "God's grandeur of all creation is too powerful" to be denied.[11]

While some have accused Cardozo of heresy because he questions God, he is not unlike those much greater than he—Habakkuk, Job, and King David. He feels the privilege of being a Jew who is encouraged to ask questions and pose arguments. Cardozo refers to Jeremiah (12:1–2), the great prophet, who declared: "You will win, O, Lord, if I make a claim against You. Yet, I shall present charges against You. Why does the way of the wicked prosper? Why are the workers of treachery at ease? You have planted them, and they have taken root. They spread, they even bear fruit. You are ever-present in their mouth."[12]

Rabbi David Weiss Halivni, a survivor of Auschwitz and renowned Talmudic scholar, has "wrestled with God's relationship to the Holocaust." He criticizes those who draw a direct link between the Holocaust and the sins of the Jewish people. Citing Jewish scriptures, Halivni queries, "*Do we attribute the Shoah to sin?*" Halivni concludes, "*It is written in the Torah, a second time in the Prophets, a third time in the Writings, and a fourth time in the words of our sages, that the Shoah was not the consequence of sin*" (his emphasis). Halivni concludes, "We must not blame such a catastrophe on the sins of the victims."[13] He then turns to Jeremiah 30:10, where the Lord God promises Jacob, i.e., the land of Israel, that He will save and bring its faithless children who broke the Covenant back to their land, but in Jeremiah 30:11 and 46:26, God says, "I am with you and though I will completely destroy all the nations among which I scatter you, I will not completely destroy you. I will discipline you but only in due measure; I will not let you go entirely unpunished." Halivni then refers to Rabbi David Kimhi (known as RaDak of Narbonne, France, 1160–1232) about God's promise to Jacob, His servant, to punish the people "only in just measure as much as we can suffer according to our capacities." RaDak interpreted this as follows: "I will chastise you, God promises, in proportion to what you can tolerate, not in proportion to my anger and fury, and not in proportion to your evil deeds."[14] Regardless of God's promises and admonishments, the inmates in the death camps could not tolerate any Nazi actions from the time they were stuffed into the horrendous trains. Why, then, did God wait so long after the death of six million of His Chosen and millions of other prisoners to bring the suffering to an end? Couldn't He see the flames fed by the murdered innocents spewed day and night as ashes through the chimneys?[15]

Itzhak Ben Rubi, during our several interviews in 1968 at his house in Tel Aviv, told me, "I was quite aware of the arguments between the people and God ever since biblical times. I often wonder how the Jews felt humiliated and crushed throughout the centuries, especially under the Inquisition and the Nazis. No one came to their defense. Even Ashem overlooked their miseries in spite of His promises to safeguard them, in spite of His promises to Adam, Noah, Abraham, and David." Then Ben Rubi concluded with a statement that brings to mind Jeremiah 3:5: "Will He remain angry forever? Will He keep it to eternity?" Knowing Ben Rubi, I suggest that he believed in an open conversation with God, and although He may be silent or absent, He is conscious of the suffering of his children.

The Jewish poets of Latin America remembered the tragedy that befell their brothers and sisters in the death camps. Solomon Lipp, referring to Argentinian José Rabinovich, states that the poet "evokes the horrid memories of this century's catastrophe . . . and in his desperation he argues with God—an old Jewish tradition. Seized by a moment of madness from which there is no return," he insulted Him:

El Dios mio estaba drogado.	My God was drugged.
Yo le gritaba,	I screamed at him,
lo insultaba,	I insulted Him.
Y Dios dormia.	And God slept.[16]

Lipp refers to León Pérez, also an Argentinian who made his home in Israel, as an individual whose "anguish and desperation extend outward to include all who suffer from the horrors of man's inhumanity to man." Pérez, in a mordant accusation, "calls out to God in anguish and bitterness: How could it all have happened? Where was He? Six millions dead!"

> Dios eterno: dicen que poco a poco
> te estés volviendo viejo, te estés poniendo sordo.
> Tal vez estés enfermo, o preocupado, o triste.
> Tal vez no seas feliz con todo lo que hiciste . . .
> Nos hemos agotado de haber llorado tanto.
>
> (Eternal God: they say that little by little
> you're getting old, you're getting deaf.
> Maybe you're sick, or worried, or sad.
> Maybe you're not happy with everything you did . . .
> We are exhausted from having cried so much.)[17]

In desperation Pérez, in his poem "El pacto roto" (The Broken Pact), cries out to his people, "No lo olvidéis, / abandonad a Dios, / que ha sido el cómplice de todo" (Do not forget / abandon God / who has been the accomplice of everything).

Shaul Chazan, a Salonikan survivor of Birkenau, recalled the transports arriving: "Then the Germans slaughtered those people—almost 3,000 that arrived on this transport—not one by one, but by the thousands. Even at that early phase, I asked myself, 'Where are God's promises?' They threw the gas in and murdered them all!" Chazan recalled hearing people pray, "'Shema Yisrael.' There wasn't much to say, not much more than 'Shema Yisrael.'"[18]

The survivors had a stream of questions, "Where was God? Where was man? Where were the nations? We cried, pleaded, why did He not listen? Where were the much-needed wonders and miracles?" Unfortunately, not in the camps. The questions resound; answers elude. Shaul Chazan admits, "Today [after the liberation] I ask myself in amazement what happened there and I try to find answers." Perhaps he has not found the answer, but he has found a miracle, "I believe in God, but not like religious people who've never experienced a thing. The miracle of my survival proved the existence of a supreme force that controls the world."[19] Even in the worst moments, in the height of suffering in Auschwitz, Henry Levy declared, "The Sephardim always hoped for a miracle and accepted the omnipotence of Hashem (God). . . . We recognized that there is no life without Him." Quoting a *nono* (grandfather/old man), who had survived the tragedy, "Where there is darkness, He will bring light. Where there is despair, He will always bring hope. . . . Our God helped us to live by our faith."[20]

Alfred Elkoubi told me about the concerns with the religious calendar during "those days in Auschwitz . . . we asked when Rosh Ashana fell, when fell Yom Kippur, how we would fast when we already were in a deplorable state, and I will tell you that I have precise memory about me and my friends [and how] we fasted." He continued, "I have also a recollection that, in all my days in Auschwitz, I had a strong feeling about religion since the war forced us to forget the kashrut, forget attending the synagogue. But at Auschwitz this religious feeling was stronger, and we got closer to religion."[21]

Notes

Introduction

1. For an account of my time in Rhodes, the journey to Tangier, and ultimately to the United States, see Zumwalt, "Stories, Food, and Place."

2. Sevillias, *Athens-Auschwitz*, 19. *Threpsini* is a natural sweetener or jam made from raisins, used in bread and pastries. It can also be eaten with a spoon.

3. Kerem, "New Finds on Greek Jewish Heroism."

4. Rodrigue, *Sephardim and the Holocaust.*

5. "Testimony and History."

6. Lévy, *And the World Stood Silent*, 19–20.

7. Kremer, *Holocaust Literature*, xxiv. For more details on the language, see xxi–xxviii.

8. Kremer, *Holocaust Literature*, xxiv.

Chapter 1

1. I interviewed Violette Fintz in Brussels in July 23, 1984.

2. The second provision of the September 1 Grand Council meeting—September 7, RDL. n. 1381—called for the expulsion from Italy and its possessions of any Jew who came after January 1, 1919.

3. Franco, *Jewish Martyrs of Rhodes and Cos.*

4. The family name before leaving Rhodes was spelled "Levi."

5. This is motif D1620, "Statues or images that act as if alive," in Thompson, *Motif Index of Folk Literature.*

6. M. Matsas, *Illusion of Safety*, 336.

7. M. Matsas, *Illusion of Safety*, 119.

8. Menascé, *Gli ebrei a Rodi*, 281.

9. Menascé, *Gli ebrei a Rodi*, 285.

10. Fintz, "From Rhodes Island," 286.

11. We interviewed Evangelos [Vagelis] Moustakas on August 21, 1984. Moustakas is one the best-known artists in Greece. His sculpture of Alexander the Great in the boardwalk of Salonika is considered one his most famous works.

12. "Short History of the Jews of Greece."

13. "Massacre of the Greeks of Phocaea."

14. "Short History of the Jews of Greece."
15. Schwartz, Review of Naar, *Jewish Salonica.*
16. M. Matsas, "Two Greek-Jewish Holocausts."
17. Arditti, "Saloniki."
18. Leon Cohen, interview in Givatayim, Israel, in June 1985.
19. *Nea Genea* (Νέα Γενεά, New Generation), May 15, 1943.
20. Matarasso, *La Communauté Juive de Thessalonique sous l'occupation allemande*, 59.
21. "Anti-Jewish Atrocities in Occupied Greece," p. 9, *Jewish Chronicle*. This testimony titled "Reports on Jewish Situation: The Situation of the Jews in Greece," appears in the *World Jewish Congress: Advisory Council on European Jewish Affairs*, New York, February 1944.
22. This paragraph is a composite of two works. It contains direct quotes from both texts; some sections I paraphrased. The manuscript from Dr. Isaac Aaron Matarasso was translated from French to English by Lévy. Text one is taken from the "Deuzième enquete" (Second Investigation), pages 59–61, of Dr. I. A Matarasso, *La Communauté Juive de Thessalonique sous l'occupation allemande*, 125–235. The second work is also by Dr. Isaac Aaron Matarasso, "And Yet Not All of Them Died."
23. Daniel Bennahmias in Fromer, *Holocaust Odyssey*, 4–5.
24. Menasche, *Birkenau (Auschwitz II)*, 15–16, 17.
25. Bourla, *Chimera*, 18.
26. Bourla, *Chimera*, 19.
27. Leon R. Cohen, "We Were Dehumanized," 308.
28. Hecht, "Jewish Traveler: Corfu."
29. Constantinidis, "Greek Island That Hid Its Jews from the Nazis."
30. Kokkinidis, "How Brave Greek Islanders Saved a Jewish Family."
31. According to Constantinidis, "The bishop and the mayor had informed the leader of the Jewish community, Moses Ganis, of the German plans, prompting a massive operation to hide the island's Jews in villages, farms and the homes of Christians" ("Greek Island That Hid Its Jews from the Nazis").
32. Ikonomopoulos, "Remembering the Jews of Corfu."
33. Fromer, *Holocaust Odyssey of Daniel Bennahmias*, xix, quoting from Nyiszli, *Auschwitz: A Doctor's Eyewitness Account.*
34. Fromer, *Holocaust Odyssey of Daniel Bennahmias*, xix.
35. Ikonomopoulos, "Remembering the Jews of Corfu."
36. Ikonomopoulos, "Remembering the Jews of Corfu."
37. Sam Angel, a survivor, interviewed in Atlanta, Georgia, on March 15, 1982.
38. *Danai* is also rendered *Danae* and *Tanais.*
39. M. Matsas, *Illusion of Safety*, 155.
40. See M. Matsas, *Illusion of Safety*, 55–56, quoting Thrasyboulos Spandikadis, *Chronika*, June 1988, 8.
41. Sgourakis, "Destruction of the Jews of Crete." See M. Matsas, *Illusion of Safety*, 156–57.
42. Shlomo Carmiel, in M. Matsas, *Illusion of Safety*, 156.
43. Jennie Tarabulus, *I Never Knew Them.*

44. Fleming, *Greece—A Jewish History*, 210.
45. Vassilev, "Rescue of Bulgaria's Jews."
46. "Bulgaria."
47. Vassilev, "Rescue of Bulgaria's Jews."
48. "Fate of the Bulgarian Jews."
49. "Bulgaria Virtual Jewish History Tour."
50. "Fate of the Bulgarian Jews."
51. "Fate of the Bulgarian Jews."
52. Wiernek, *Year in Treblinka*, ch. 9, np.
53. Interview with Sami Menahen Ben-nun at the Association of Bulgarians in Tel Aviv in 1990.
54. Some changes have been made to clarify the original message.
55. Except for a few minor changes for ease of comprehension, the quotations are verbatim.
56. Interview of Leon Reuven Cohen in Givatayim, Israel, on June 17, 1982.
57. Peretz, "Siniza i fumo" (Ash and smoke), 168–69. This poem and a second one, "Echados adientro el fuego" (Cast into the fire) appeared in *Aki Yerushalayim* 21, year 6 (April 1984): 25–27. It is reproduced by permission of Avner Peretz and Moshe Shaul, the editor of the series. Translated into English by Isaac Jack Lévy.
58. René Molho, "Personal Interview", 1981, 168.
59. Menasche, *Birkenau (Auschwitz II)*, 21–22.
60. Menasche, *Birkenau (Auschwitz II)*, 22.
61. Menasche, *Birkenau (Auschwitz II)*, 22–23.
62. Leon Reuven Cohen interview, 1982.
63. Menasche, *Birkenau (Auschwitz II)*, 22.
64. Menasche, *Birkenau (Auschwitz II)*, 22.
65. Menasche, *Birkenau (Auschwitz II)*, 23.
66. Menasche, *Birkenau (Auschwitz II)*, 105.
67. Bourla, *Chimera*, 49–50.

Chapter 2

1. Borowski, *This Way for the Gas*, 35. Borowski was a non-Jew who was deported from Warsaw by the Nazis, first to Auschwitz and then to Dachau.
2. Kounio, *Liter of Soup*, 10–11.
3. I interviewed Ben Stern in Columbia, South Carolina, on March 2, 1982.
4. Stella Levi, *Amigos Sepharadi*, 3.
5. Plank, *Mother of the Wire Fence*, 26.
6. Menasche, *Birkenau (Auschwitz II)*, 71.
7. Greif, *We Wept without Tears*, 60–61.
8. The interview took place in 1989 in Ashdod, Israel, at the home of Izahar Avzaradel, also from Rhodes. The meeting covered several topics—the traditions of the home, the long and painful voyage to the death camps, culinary home remedies, etc. Izahar performed the ritual of *prekante* against the evil eye. Rosemary filmed most of the interview.

9. Greif, *We Wept without Tears*, 61.

10. Venezia, *Inside the Gas Chambers*, 108.

11. Heink, "Latest Effort to Combat 'Denial.'" Heink comments on Dr. Moshe Zimmermann's essay "Massenmord durch Giftgas in der Wahrnehmung der Überlebenden" (How Survivors Perceive the Mass Murder by Poisonous Gas).

12. Halivini writes that Nyiszli was from Viseul, de Sus (her hometown), and that he had a grudge against its Jewish people. In the camp Nyiszli, a pathologist, volunteered to assist the heinous Dr. Mengele in Auschwitz and worked closely with the members of the Sonderkommando. Although some reviewers praised him for his book, there are those such as Bruno Bettelheim, the writer of the foreword for Nyiszli's book *Auschwitz: Doctor's Eyewitness Account*, who do not. Nyiszli's own words attest to his constant praise for his own work, and for "his concern for mere survival," rather than emulation for the members of the Sonderkommando, who sadly performed their horrifying duties knowing all along that they too would not escape the furnaces. Nyiszli's life was spared due to his collaboration with Mengele.

13. Bülow, "Dr. Miklos Nyiszli, an Eyewitness."

14. Banu, "10 Wicked Women."

15. Menasche, *Birkenau* (*Auschwitz II*), 34. For more details see pages 31–39.

16. I interviewed Sam (Samuel) Profeta in Salonika on June 21, 1982. Sam was highly respected for his dedication to helping the young, who referred to him as "Uncle Sam." He was a good athlete. Life in the camp was the worst, yet he believed that one had to be patient, have courage, and try to survive. As will be covered later, Sam underwent several medical experiments.

17. Henry Levy, "Jews of Salonica and the Holocaust," 234.

18. Langbein, *People in Auschwitz*, 79. Langbein is quoting Benedict Kautsky.

19. Bourla, *Chimera*, 56.

20. Bowman, "Introduction," xxii.

21. Rahmani, *Rhodes, un pan de notre mémoire*, 90.

22. Shimony, "Review: Resisting the Father's Narrative," 104, 95. Shimony (95) quotes from Aini's autobiographical novel, *The Rose of Lebanon*, in which she describes the neighborhood in which she lived in Tel Aviv: "Small-time craftsmen in rented shops, and small-scale merchants who lived above their source of livelihood, or a few steps away from it, went to sleep with this reality of poverty to wake up in the mornings as alien residents, of the sort one should keep away from. Under an ever changing sky hung the grime of their daily, despairing toil, and no one was promised a thing. They had the wrong ethnic origin, the door opening political party membership card had the wrong name on it, the word Holocaust was uttered in the wrong language, and their skin color blended in with that of the natives" (Aini, 227).

23. In endnote 3, 111, Shimony states that the narrator's father, like all the Greek Jews in Israel, felt excluded from the established Holocaust narratives. The story of the Greek Jews, as well as those of all Sephardic Jews who perished and suffered in the death camps, was not told to the nation (Israel). Lea Aini's father, especially on Holocaust Remembrance Day, "yearns for visibility, for recognition

from the State that they were there, too, they had perished more than anyone." In the 1910s and early 1920s, in Rivington Street of Manhattan, New York, the new Sephardic immigrants were also assumed not to be Jewish, because they looked different and did not speak Yiddish.

24. Langbein, *People in Auschwitz*, 95.

25. Ouziel, "Remembering the Holocaust."

26. I interviewed Shabetai Hanuka in Tel Aviv, Israel, on June 28, 1990. Yakov Cohen, son of a survivor, painted Daniel Marcos shot with a green tomato in his hand.

27. Henry Levy, "Jews of Salonica," 232.

28. Eliezer Sotto, interviewed by SB (Sandra Berman) in 1987. Esther and Hubert Taylor History Collection. Courtesy of the Breman Jewish Heritage Museum of Atlanta, Georgia.

29. Eliezer (Eli) Sotto, interview, 2001. As unbelievable as Sotto's story seems, the eating of coal in dire circumstances was confirmed by the Associated Press (*USA Today*, 2007): "The Chinese miners eat coal, drank urine while trapped" (Beijing, AP). Two brothers who tunneled out of a collapsed mine were forced to eat coal and drink urine during the nearly six-day ordeal . . . illegal mine in Beijing Fangshan district. Another such incident was reported by Calum MacLeod (Wednesday, August 30, 2000) in the *Independent*: "Four Chinese miners trapped deep underground by a landslide showed remarkable endurance by surviving for 13 days on a diet of coal and leaves."

30. Judith Sternberg-Newman in Langbein, *People in Auschwitz*, 97.

31. See Langbein, *People in Auschwitz*, 68.

32. Menasche, *Birkenau* (*Auschwitz II*), 127.

33. See "Mass Cannibalism at Nazi Camp Told: Doctor [Fritz Leo] Testifies [on September 28] about Captives Eating Flesh," in Lauenburg, Germany, *Pittsburgh Press*, September 28, 1945, p. 10.

34. Venezia, *Inside the Gas Chambers*, 124.

35. See "Cannibalism in Prison Camp," *Guardian* (Thursday, April 19, 1945).

36. *Pikkuach nefesh* is the principle to save a life; it overrides all the Commandments in the Torah, save for those against murder, adultery, and idolatry (Birnbaum, *Encyclopedia of Jewish Concepts*, 512).

37. Kounio (*Liter of Soup*, 53) reports that it was difficult to clean himself for lack of water; however, if he was not clean, his punishment would have been twenty-five blows to the back. Ironically, he adds that the Germans required all the inmates to take a bath once a week; they gave them no towels to dry themselves, claiming that the air would evaporate the water from their bodies.

38. I interviewed Sam Angel on March 15, 1982, in Atlanta, Georgia.

39. Bourla, *Chimera*, 78.

40. Rees, *Auschwitz: A New History*, 173. See chapter 4 (165–217) dealing with corruption in Auschwitz.

41. Rees, *Auschwitz: A New History*, 173 (ellipses and brackets in original).

42. Rees, *Auschwitz: A New History*, 173.

43. I interviewed Leon Reuven Cohen in Givatayim, Israel, in July 1985.
44. Halivni, "Birkenau Revolt," 138.
45. Rees, *Auschwitz: A New History*, 173.
46. Halivni, "Birkenau Revolt," 138.
47. Nyiszli, *Auschwitz: A Doctor's Eyewitness Account*, 122.
48. Hagouel, "History of the Jews of Salonika," 26.
49. Menasche, *Birkenau (Auschwitz II)*, 55–56.
50. Shields, "Sonderkommando."
51. Menasche, *Birkenau (Auschwitz II)*, 55–56.
52. Langbein, *People in Auschwitz*, 193–94.
53. Greif, *We Wept without Tears*, 57.
54. Joroff, "Dark and Perverse."
55. Jacob Robinson in Greif, *We Wept without Tears*, 57. See also Robinson, *And the Crooked Shall Be Made Straight*, 109 and 200. Greif paraphrases Salmen [Zalman] Lewental, in *Diary*, as saying, "The first *Sonderkommando* groups were composed of the most modest and outstanding people. However, they were unable to survive and were soon killed. Everyone who remained in the *Sonderkommando* was of the less estimable type, people of lesser quality who came from the lower classes, in the negative sense of the term." See Greif, *We Wept without Tears*, 50. According to my interviewees, not all of the modest and outstanding people were exterminated: many survived the tragedy.
56. Venezia, *Inside the Gas Chambers*, 67.
57. Chazan, "Life Didn't Matter Anymore," 278.
58. Chazan, "Life Didn't Matter Anymore," 270.
59. Chazan, "Life Didn't Matter Anymore," 266.
60. See *Nizkor Project, The Trial of Adolf Eichmann.*
61. Bourla, *Chimera*, 49–50.
62. Young, Review of *Amidst a Nightmare of Crime.*
63. Gabai, "I'll Get Out of Here!," 191.
64. Greif, *We Wept without Tears*, 15.
65. I interviewed Leon Cohen in Givatayim, Israel, on June 17, 1982.
66. Venezia, *Inside the Gas Chambers*, 129.
67. I interviewed Leon Cohen in Givatayim, Israel, in June 1984.
68. Venezia, *Inside the Gas Chambers*, 154–55.
69. Czech, *Kalendarium*. This chronicle contains the daily events that took place from 1939 to 1945 in Auschwitz-Birkenau. See also Czech, *Auschwitz Chronicle 1939–1945*; Langbein, *People in Auschwitz*, 138.
70. M. Matsas, *Illusion of Safety*, 241.
71. Fromer, *Holocaust Odyssey*, xvii.
72. Molho and Nehama, *In Memoriam: Hommage*, 282. For the most part, I paraphrased these accounts.
73. Venezia, *Inside the Gas Chambers*, 97.
74. I interviewed Ben Stern in Columbia, South Carolina, on March 2, 1982.
75. Langbein, *People in Auschwitz*, 194.

Chapter 3

1. Chare and Williams, *Matters of Testimony*, ix.

2. Nahmia, *Cry for Tomorrow*, 81–82.

3. Menasche, *Birkenau (Auschwitz II)*, 39.

4. Menasche, *Birkenau (Auschwitz II)*, 40.

5. Greif, *We Wept without Tears*, 360n59.

6. Pezzetti, "Shoah, Auschwitz," 159, 170ff.

7. Menasche, *Birkenau (Auschwitz II)*, 43.

8. Menasche, *Birkenau (Auschwitz II)*, 44.

9. See Memorial and Museum Auschwitz-Birkenau, Former German Nazi Concentration and Extermination Camp, "The Construction of the Camp."

10. Bunker 2 was reactivated for the "Hungarian Jews Action" and finally demolished. Crematory IV was set on fire by its Sonderkommando during the uprising on October 7, 1944, and thereafter was no longer operational. Crematories II and III were blown up by the SS on January 20, 1945. Crematory V was blown up as the last one January 26, 1945, just before the liberation of Auschwitz. Also see Greif, *We Wept without Tears*, 133–39, for Shlomo and Abraham Dragon's description of the cottages and the duties that they were forced to perform.

11. Nahmia, *Cry for Tomorrow*, 62.

12. Yassini, *Memorial Book of the Ciechanow.*

13. Kolko, "Ciechanow Jews," 41.

14. Kolko, "Ciechanow Jews," 41–42.

15. Kolko, "Ciechanow Jews," 41–42.

16. Kolko, "Ciechanow Jews," 41–42.

17. Zabludowicz, "My Experiences in World War II."

18. Zabludowicz, "My Experiences in World War II."

19. Ackerfeld, "Rosa Robota: Her Life," 402.

20. "Couriers of the Jewish Underground."

21. "Auschwitz Concentration Camp."

22. Heilman, "Anna Heilman—Part I."

23. Heilman, "Anna Heilman—Part II."

24. "Couriers of the Jewish Underground."

25. Heilman, "Anna Heilman—Part I."

26. "Couriers of the Jewish Underground."

27. "Couriers of the Jewish Underground."

28. "Auschwitz-Birkenau Uprising."

29. Heilman, "Anna Heilman—Part I."

30. *Revolt of the Greek Jews.*

31. Abraham and Shlomo Dragon, "Together—in Despair and in Hope," 168.

32. Abraham and Shlomo Dragon, "Together—in Despair and in Hope," 169.

33. Fromer, *Holocaust Odyssey*, 99, 78–79 note 25, my paraphrase. Author's emphasis.

34. "Prisoner Revolt at Auschwitz-Birkenau."

35. Kounio, *Liter of Soup*, 71.

36. Mallenbaum, "On Holocaust Day We Forget."

37. Eliezer Eisenschmidt, "Thanks to One Polish Family," 253.

38. Heffler, "Part III—Rebellion: Active and Passive Resistance."

39. Two revolts took place in July and September, prior to the revolt of October 7, 1944. Two members of the Greek Army officers (Errera and Josef Baruch) were arrested after they returned from the Albanian front. Errera had part in the planning before he was murdered, and Baruch in the planning and in heading the revolt of October 7, 1944, with a Russian Jewish officer (*Revolt of the Greek Jews*).

40. I interviewed Jacko Maestro by telephone from my home in Dahlonega, Georgia (USA), on February 25, 2013.

41. Kerem, "New Finds on Greek."

42. Kounio-Amariglio, *From Thessaloniki*, 90.

43. Nahmia, *Cry for Tomorrow*, 85.

44. Nahmia, *Cry for Tomorrow*, 85.

45. Nahmia, *Cry for Tomorrow*, 68.

46. Bolkosky interview with Salvatore and Lili Katan. Verbatim.

47. This entry is a composite of several sources. Copyright 2009 by Chris Webb.

48. Langbein, *People in Auschwitz*, 201–2.

49. Eisenschmidt, "Thanks to One Polish Family," 245.

50. Eisenschmidt, "Thanks to One Polish Family," 234.

51. Eisenschmidt, "Thanks to One Polish Family," 248.

52. According to Errikos Sevillias, *Athens-Auschwitz*, 39–40, "[t]he ash was not always disposed of in the Vistula River. At times it was used to make macadam or pressed into small blocks of fertilizer in which segments of bones could be found." Often they used ash to clean the ovens. The bones were beaten into dust. Macadam, made of broken crushed stone bound with tar or bitumen and ash, was used to surface roads. Kounio (page 19) writes concerning the body fat, "When the bodies in the ovens were burned, the fats they produced were drained off through pipes into a large pit behind the furnace. The fat was put into barrels and taken away in trucks." Sevillias adds that the "fats drained from the crematoria were either used to stoke the crematoria [or pits] or to make soap." Leon Cohen shares my interviewee's opinion, "[E]scape or rebellion was becoming an obsession for us Greeks. We decided not to give up. How? When? We had no idea but we were determined to wait for the right opportunity" (Leon Cohen, *From Greece to Birkenau*, 77).

53. Eisenschmidt, "Thanks to One Polish Family," 251.

54. Several surviving witnesses gave accounts of Errera's bravery. These included Errikos Sevillias, Shlomo Venezia, Leon Cohen, Marcel Nadjari, Dr. Miklos Nyiszli, Alter Fajnzylberg, Henryk Mandelbaum, Albert Menasche, and Daniel Bennahmias.

55. The participants that accompanied Errera vary according to the informant: Bowman (1986) says that they were "three or four Jews"; Igor Bartosik states only "Errera and his Greek friend"; Eisenschmidt twice mentions "two Greek Jews and three Polish Jews"; and Shlomo Venezia mentions "a small squad of Greek Jews."

56. Molho, *In Memoriam*, 1973, 282–83.

57. Jean Cohen, "Rebellion of Greeks in Auschwitz."

58. Molho, *In Memoriam*, 1973, 282–83.

59. Venezia, *Inside the Gas Chambers*, 92. In order to give another view of Errera's story, I am including the following ideas that I put together by combining Kounio's, S. Venezia's, and Molho's reports (see 282–83 in Molho, 41–42 in Kounio, and 90–92 in S. Venezia). There are some discrepancies in the stories. Venezia writes that Errera was a member of the Greek navy and that only Hugo Baruch went along to the River Sola, while Kounio states that Errera was in the Greek army [navy] and that three prisoners went along with him to the Vistula River. Molho names the three Greek prisoners that went along with Errera. Venezia's story diverges somewhat from what I was able to find. For Errera the decision to escape was done prior to the arrival of the trucks to the bank of the Vistula River. Quoting Hugo Venezia (not a relative), Shlomo said that "Errera had a plan he had to knock down the guard who'd come to open the door of the truck for them. . . . When the truck stopped . . . [and the guard approached] to tell them to get out . . . Errera knocked him out with a great blow of his spade." Meanwhile, Hugo had to go and take the driver by surprise. Hearing the noise, the guard came out holding a pistol. Hugo, a young man barely eighteen years old, "stood there paralyzed, frozen stiff with fear when faced with the driver pointing his pistol" (S. Venezia, *Inside the Gas Chambers*, 94). Errera jumped into the river and started swimming. The driver then fired, and Errera was hit in the thigh [not the head] (Venezia, *Inside the Gas Chambers*, 90–92).

60. Menasche, *Birkenau (Auschwitz II)*, 91.

61. Cohen, *From Greece to Birkenau*, 77.

62. Sevillias, *Athens-Auschwitz*, 42.

63. Bowman, "Jews in Wartime Greece," 54.

64. Eisenschmidt, "Thanks to One Polish Family," 253.

65. Eisenschmidt, "Thanks to One Polish Family," 253.

66. Eisenschmidt, "Thanks to One Polish Family," 253.

67. Eisenschmidt, "Thanks to One Polish Family," 254.

68. Eisenschmidt, "Thanks to One Polish Family," 254.

69. "Sonderkommando Revolt: Auschwitz-Birkenau, 7 October 1944."

70. "Sonderkommando Revolt: Auschwitz-Birkenau, 7 October 1944."

71. Bartosik, "Sonderkommando: Interview."

72. Mallenbaum, "On Holocaust Day We Forget."

73. The original title of the DVD documentary is *Greeks in Auschwitz-Bikenau* (Tomai). The "Additional Info" reiterates that "on 7 October 1944, over 60 Greek Jews, led by *Josef Baruch* [my emphasis] an officer in the Greek army from Ioannina, participated in an uprising in Birkenau which succeeded in killing several SS men and blowing up crematorium IV."

74. Photini Tomai [Phōteinē Kōnstantopoulou], *Greeks in Auschwitz-Birkenau.*

75. Bowman, "Introduction: The Greeks in Auschwitz," xxv.

76. Greif, "Sonderkommando in Auschwitz-Birkenau," 43.

77. Greif, "Sonderkommando in Auschwitz-Birkenau," 43.

78. Bowman, "Introduction: The Greeks in Auschwitz," xxiv.

79. Langbein, *People in Auschwitz*, 201. In the section "Extra" of this book, Langbein "was classified as a non-Jewish political prisoner, he was assigned as clerk to the chief SS physician of the extermination camp complex, which gave him access to documents, conversations, and actions. . . . [He was also] a member of the Auschwitz resistance."

80. Langbein, *People in Auschwitz*, 3–4, quoting Frankl. Langbein writes, "Victor Emil Frankl [is] an Austrian neurologist and psychiatrist and Holocaust survivor."

81. Fromer, *Holocaust Odyssey*, 72.

82. Bowman, *Agony of Greek Jews*, 8.

83. Fromer, *Holocaust Odyssey*, 74.

84. Kounio, *Liter of Soup*, 66–67.

85. Kounio, *Liter of Soup*, 67 (my emphasis).

86. Kounio, *Liter of Soup*, 68.

87. Kounio, *Liter of Soup*, 69.

88. Kounio, *Liter of Soup*, 70. Kounio gives a partial list of the survivors: Hugo B. Venezia, Andre Nachama Kapon, Ioakov Broudo, Dani Marc Nachmias, Alberto Tzachon, the Selomo brothers, and Mois Venezia. He also names Alberto Errera, who was murdered before the uprising, and Isaac Venezia and Daniel Bennahmias, who survived.

89. Menasche, *Bierkeanu (Auschwitz II)*, 92–93.

90. Menasche, *Bierkeanu* (*Auschwitz II*), 93 (my emphasis).

91. See "Revolt of the Greek Jews." Also see Fromer, *Holocaust Odyssey*, 66, endnote 6; this term is clarified: "The Sephardim used the word *ntou* (pronounced 'du'), which means 'movement,' 'attack,' or 'revolt.' It is a slang term." The Greek word given by the lady to Piotr Setkiewicz is "*ντου*."

92. Molho, *In Memoriam, Sho'at Yehude Yavan: 1941–1944.*

93. Bowman, *Agony of Greek Jews*, 53n28.

94. I interviewed Shabetai Hanuka on June 28, 1990, in Tel Aviv, Israel. Hanuka informed me that Shaul Senor was a well-educated individual. In Warsaw he ran the clothing section, and whenever possible he provided some clothes to his friends. Senor was allowed to go to town accompanied by Germans. In Warsaw he met a Polish Christian woman and became good friends. She helped him a great deal. They decided with the help of a guard to run away on a certain day. "Unfortunately, on that day the guard was changed. Senor was hit in the leg and taken to the hospital, where they took care of him. On a Sunday, the Germans called the *appel* and hanged him in front of all the camp. His brother, Isaac, fainted and two companions held him up for several hours, thus protecting him from the Germans. The hanging took place on Sunday when no one worked." The hanging was "a theatrical spectacle" for the Germans.

95. Kerem, "New Finds on Greek Jewish Heroism."

96. Kerem, "New Finds on Greek Jewish Heroism."

97. Venezia, *Inside the Gas Chambers*, 129.

98. On February 25, 2013, Yitzchak Kerem mailed me the following report: Kerem and Eduardo Retyk, "Maestro Jacko." See *Shoa* in *Enciclopedia del Holocaustoi*, 339. Jacko could not escape the Death March. He spent time in Mauthausen and Melk, where he was subjected to hard labor.

99. I interviewed Shabetai Hanuka in Tel Aviv, Israel, on June 28, 1990.

100. M. Matsas, *Illusion of Safety*, 251.

101. I interviewed Elie Cohen in Tel Aviv on June 14, 1982.

102. Zalman Gradowski's "writings describing the gruesome details of Auschwitz death camp were found buried near the crematorium, and now published by H. Chaim Wolnerman." See Israel Gutman in the "Sonderkommando Revolt, Auschwitz-Birkenau."

103. Several other known records were taken in secret out of the "Gypsy camp Auschwitz" offices and were buried in July of 1944 by three Poles, Tadeusz Joachimowski, Ireneusz Pietrzyk, and Porębski. The contents of this material were published in 1993.

104. Gabai, "I'll Get Out of Here!," 193.

105. Nahmia, *Cry for Tomorrow*, 128.

106. M. Matsas, *Illusion of Safety*, 264.

107. Berry Nahmia, arrested by the Germans, was the sole survivor of her family. She was a beautiful eighteen-year-old.

108. "Sonderkommando Photographs."

109. Halivni, "Birkenau Revolt," 130.

110. "Alberto Errera." Some individuals claim that Errera was born in Larissa. Heinz Kounio states that he was born in Salonika, married a woman from Larissa, and in March 1944 was deported from that city.

111. Bowman, *Agony of Greek Jews*, 95, and Venezia, *Inside the Gas Chambers*, 113–14.

112. Menasche, *Birkenau (Auschwitz II)*, 91, 92.

113. Langbein, *People in Auschwitz*, 201.

114. Cohen, "Rebellion of Greeks in Auschwitz."

115. Mietek Morawa, a twenty-year-old Pole. The Germans trusted him and kept transferring him from one job to another. His main task was to fix the bicycles of the SS. He was a bigoted anti-Semite. He was assigned to a *Kapo* and worked in Crematoria I and II. Filip Muller later claimed, "When the Jews were being shot, he [Mietek] . . . held a victim's head—with pleasure." And "Tadeusz Joachimowski believes that young Mietek became so brutalized on the Sonderkommando because he saw nothing that could have aroused compassion in him." See Langbein, *People in Auschwitz*, 198.

116. Cohen, "Rebellion of Greeks in Auschwitz."

117. Langbein, *People in Auschwitz*, 201.

118. Cohen, *From Greece to Birkenau*, 82.

119. Nahmia, *Cry for Tomorrow*, 86.

120. Aini, "No Other Jews like Them." The prisoner L. Werbel states, "In this battle some 300 armed prisoners gave their lives. Among them was Z. Gradowski

from Suwalki." He could very well have been there and died; however, no mention was made of any Sephardi leaders and Sonderkommandos who also gave their lives. See Bowman, "Jews in Wartime Greece," 60n27; and Kabeli, "Resistance of the Greek Jews."

121. Kounio-Amariglio, *From Thessaloniki to Auschwitz*, 114–15.

122. Nadjari in Nahmia, *Cry for Tomorrow*, 87.

123. "Auschwitz II Birkenau Sonderkommando Testimony Clips."

124. Nadjari in Nahmia, *Cry for Tomorrow*, 87.

125. Cohen, *From Greece to Birkenau*, 81.

126. Jean Cohen, "The Rebellion of Greeks in Auschwitz, October 7, 1944." The article is in Greek; it was freely translated into English for me. I took the liberty of improving the language. Jean Cohen, the son of the Salonikan survivor Leon Reuven Cohen, told me about this episode of the Holocaust.

127. Cohen, *From Greece to Birkenau*, 82.

128. Nahmia, *Cry for Tomorrow*, 86.

129. "Sonderkommando Revolt: Auschwitz-Birkenau" quotes Filip Muller also placing Scharfuhrer Busch, Unterscharfuher Gorges, and several SS men and guards in the yard in front of Crematorium IV [German numbering]. Berry Nahmia states that the selection took place at Crematorium III [new numbering].

130. Venezia, "Jewish Survivor."

131. Venezia, "Jewish Survivor."

132. Cohen, *From Greece to Birkenau*, 83.

133. Damian Mac Con Uladh, "Remembering the Greek Jews." The author writes that the revolt rose in Crematorium IV and that the flames rising over the building [were] the signal for Crematorium II to go into action. It was also believed that a Greek army officer from Ioannina led the Greek Jews during the revolt.

134. Cohen, *From Greece to Birkenau*, 84–85.

135. Cohen, *From Greece to Birkenau*, 84–85, 87.

136. Cohen, *From Greece to Birkenau*, 88.

137. Cohen, *From Greece to Birkenau*, 88.

138. Fromer, *Holocaust Odyssey*, 70.

139. Venezia, "Jewish Survivor."

140. Fromer, *Holocaust Odyssey*, 70–71.

141. Chazan, "Life Didn't Matter Anymore," 280.

142. Chazan, "Life Didn't Matter Anymore," 280.

143. Mayes, "Auschwitz Revolt."

144. "Rosa Robota: Heroine of Auschwitz."

145. Fromer, *Holocaust Odyssey*, 71–72.

146. Bowman, "Jews in Wartime Greece," 54.

147. Venezia, "Jewish Survivor."

148. Menasche, *Birkenau (Auschwitz II)*, 94.

149. Bourla, *Chimera*, 102.

150. Kounio, *Liter of Soup*, 79.

Chapter 4

1. Tyson. "Holocaust on Trial."

2. "Nazi Medical Experiments."

3. Langbein, *People in Auschwitz*, 104.

4. Kounio-Amariglio, *From Thessaloniki to Auschwitz and Back*, 88.

5. Kounio-Amariglio, *From Thessaloniki to Auschwitz and Back*, 88–89.

6. "Salonika, Greece."

7. Bowman, ed., "Fourth Investigation: Medical Experiments," 205.

8. Bowman, ed., "Fourth Investigation: Medical Experiments," 209.

9. Bowman, ed., "Fourth Investigation: Medical Experiments," 211.

10. I interviewed this individual in Tel Aviv in July 1990; she did not wish to have her name used.

11. "Aribert Heim." See also Laura Moser, "Chasing Dr. Aribert Heim, the 'Butcher of Mauthsausen.'"

12. Aini, "No Other Jews like Them."

13. Langbein, *People in Auschwitz*, 85.

14. Aini, "No Other Jews like Them."

15. For a more detailed account of the atrocities, see Hedgepeth and Saidel, *Sexual Violence*.

16. Menasche, *Birkenau (Auschwitz II)*, 43–45.

17. See Lagnado and Dekel, *Children of the Flames*.

18. Lopez, "Mazaltov Behar Mordoch."

19. I interviewed Aliza and Ovadia Baruch in Tel Aviv on June 16, 1982.

20. "Story of Ovadia Baruch."

21. Bolkosky, "Interview with Salvatore and Lili Katan."

22. "Alexander Katan."

23. "History's Judgment: SS Dr. Eduard Krebsbach."

24. "Alexander Katan." In 2000 the filmmaker Hedda van Gennep made a film, *Dood Spoor*, that deals with Alfons Katan's mission to remove the photos.

25. See Santa Puche, *Libro de los testimonios*, 149–50, paraphrased.

26. Asher Varon was interviewed by Yad Vashem. I am grateful to Yad Vashem for sending me a copy of the tape in June 1981. Unfortunately, the recording is flawed.

27. Similar comments were reported by inmates who worked in the crematoria and from nurses who were assigned to work in the *revier* (the infirmary in Block 10).

Chapter 5

1. Toth, "Why We Fight."

2. Hazan, *Un día más de vida*, 119.

3. I interviewed Alfred Elkoubi in Paris, July 15, 1984.

4. Hazan, *Un día más de vida*, 120.

5. Hazan, *Un día más de vida*, 121.

6. "Death Marches."

7. "Auschwitz Concentration Camp."

8. Modiano was interviewed several times while he was lecturing in schools and large groups. Following are two films narrating the story of the Holocaust: "La vita ad Auschwitz e dopo" (Life in Auschwitz and after), February 21 2013, Cinema Diana-Ispica (RG); *Per questo ho vissuto: Sami Modiano racconta Auschwitz* (For this I have lived—Sami Modiano tells about Auschwitz), 4 parts. By Instituto G. Curcio-Ispica-RG.

9. Fromer, *Holocaust Odyssey*, 83–84.

10. Venezia, *Inside the Gas Chambers*, 126.

11. Nahon, *Birkenau*, 109, 112, 114.

12. Nahon, *Birkenau*, 113–14, 115.

13. Nahmia, *Cry for Tomorrow*, 123. See also Russo, "Trezoros: The Lost Jews of Kastoria."

14. Nahmia, *Cry for Tomorrow*, 124, 126.

15. Retsov was also known as Rastov or Rostock.

16. Nahmia, *Cry for Tomorrow*, 126, 127, 128.

17. Nahmia, *Cry for Tomorrow*, 153.

18. Nahmia, *Cry for Tomorrow*, 175.

19. Nahmia, *Cry for Tomorrow*, 177.

20. Nahmia, *Cry for Tomorrow*, 179.

21. Lewkowicz, *Jewish Community of Salonika*, 213.

22. Lewkowicz, *Jewish Community of Salonika*, 216.

23. Lewkowicz, *Jewish Community of Salonika*, 215–16.

24. Molho, "Testimonio III," 154.

25. Venezia, *Inside the Gas Chambers*, 127.

26. Varon, "Testimonio IX," 223–24.

27. Varon, "Testimonio IX," 222–25.

28. Varon, "Testimonio IX," 206.

29. Coné, "Testimonio VII," 204–6.

30. Coné, "Testimonio VII," 208.

31. Violette Fintz was interviewed by Yad Vashem in June 1981. In 1982 I received a copy of the interview. See Fintz, "Testimonio IV." I also interviewed Violette in Brussels on July 23, 1984, and I've been in contact with her for many years by telephone and mail.

32. Venezia, *Inside the Gas Chamber*, 127.

33. Kerem, "New Finds on Greek Jewish Heroism," n51.

34. Henry Levy, "Jews of Salonica and the Holocaust," 236.

35. Henry Levy, "Jews of Salonica and the Holocaust," 236, 240.

36. See n94 of Chapter 3 for the account of Isaac Senor's older brother Shaul.

37. Henry Levy, "Jews of Salonica and the Holocaust," 241.

38. Henry Levy, "Jews of Salonica and the Holocaust," 243.

39. Renner, "For Holocaust Survivor."

40. Henry Levy, "Jews of Salonica and the Holocaust," 245.

41. Sotto was interviewed on September 16, 2001, by Sara Ghitis. Transcript ID: OHC 10677, 19 pages. I am appreciative to the museum for providing me a copy of the interview.

42. Eliezer Sotto, "Interviewed by Sara Ghitis," 7.

43. Eliezer Sotto, "Interviewed by Sara Ghitis," 8.

44. Eliezer Sotto, "Interviewed by Sara Ghitis," 9 (verbatim).

45. Eliezer Sotto, "Interviewed by Sara Ghitis," 9 (verbatim).

46. Eliezer Sotto, "Interviewed by Sara Ghitis," 10 (verbatim).

47. Eliezer Sotto, "Interviewed by Sara Ghitis," 10 (verbatim).

48. Eliezer Sotto, "Interviewed by Sara Ghitis," 18 (verbatim).

49. Eliezer Sotto, "Interviewed by Sara Ghitis," 19 (verbatim).

50. Eliezer Sotto, "Interviewed by Sara Ghitis," 19 (verbatim).

51. "Obituary: Eliezer 'Eli' Sotto," 2017.

Chapter 6

1. The "guevos haminados" (hard-boiled eggs) are popular among the Sephardim. See Nehama, *Dictionaire du Judéo-Espagnol*, 234. They are served daily, especially as a *meze*, an aperitif, along with *raki*, made of twice-distilled grapes and aniseed.

2. Romano, *Jevreji Jugoslavije 1941–1945*, 575.

3. Romano, *Jevreji Jugoslavije 1941–1945*, 575.

4. Sarner, *Rescue in Albania*, 46.

5. Shirley Cloyes DioGuardi sent me a copy of the remarks she made at the United Nations International Holocaust Remembrance Day on January 27, 2014, titled, "The Albanian Rescue of European Jewry."

6. Sarner, *Rescue in Albania*, 1.

7. Sarner, *Rescue in Albania*, 3.

8. Perez, "Our Conscience Is Clean," 25–26.

9. See Mojzes, *Balkan Genocides*, 93.

10. Friedenreich, "Jewish Community of Yugoslavia."

11. Friedenreich, "Jewish Community of Yugoslavia."

12. Romano, *Jevreji Jugoslavije 1941–1945*, 590. For the participation of the Jews who joined the partisans, see 582–90.

13. Matkovski, *History of the Jews in Macedonia*, 109.

14. Matkovski, *History of the Jews in Macedonia*, 97, 98.

15. Matkovski, *History of the Jews in Macedonia*, chapter VII, 108–27, deals with the concentration of Jews in camps and their liquidation.

16. Matkovski, *History of the Jews in Macedonia*, 134.

17. Sarner, *Rescue in Albania*, 6.

18. Sarner, *Rescue in Albania*, 43.

19. Sarner, *Rescue in Albania*, 46.

20. Cara and Margjeka, "Kanun of Leke Dukagjini," 179–80. Cara and Margjeka quote Edith Durham, *High Albania* (New York University Press, 1998) and Leonard Fox, trans., *The Code of Lekë Dukagjini/Kanuni i Lekë Dukagjinit* (Gjonlekaj, 1989).

21. "Righteous."

22. Gershman, "Jews Saved by Albanians." The Kanun preceded the Koran. Some theories claim that it dates back to the Bronze Age; others speculate that it derives from ancient Illyrian tribal laws, or from Indo-European prehistoric eras.

23. Sarner, *Rescue in Albania*, 62.

24. Sarner, *Rescue in Albania*, 59.

25. Sarner, *Rescue in Albania*, 59.

26. Sarner, *Rescue in Albania*, 59.

27. For a comprehensive study of the *Pentcho* incident, see Alcalay, *Persistence of Hope*, 165–70.

28. Shachar, *Lost Worlds of Rhodes*, 159.

29. For information on the camp, see Alcalay, *Persistence of Hope*, 162–77.

30. Carbonara, "Woman Visits Camp Where She Was Born."

31. Giuffrida, "Ferramonti Was Not a Death Camp."

32. Carbonara, "Woman Visits Camp Where She Was Born."

33. Alcalay, *Persistence of Hope*, 174.

34. Pugliese, "Ferramonti di Tarsia."

35. "Riccardo Pacifici."

36. International Sephardic Leadership Council (ISLC), 3. According to the ISLC, this statement was prepared by Prof. Edith Shaked and compiled from Jacques Sabile, *Les Juifs de Tunisie sous Vichy et l'Occupation* (Paris: Edition du Centre de Documentation Juive Contemporaine, 1954).

37. ISLC, 3.

38. Patterson, *Genealogy of Evil*, 114.

39. Sells, "Fabricating Palestinian Responsibility."

40. ISLC, 5.

41. Gensicke, "From Jerusalem to Nazi Berlin." The author shows how Amin al-Husseini used murder, terrorism, intrigue, extortion, and the abuse of religion to obtain his goals. His broadcasts to Muslims in North Africa during World War II were appeals for martyrdom in order to help the Germans, as that would guarantee Paradise. After the war he continued to act in precisely the same manner. His greed for wealth, hunger for power, despotism, ruthlessness, and intransigence were all factors that brought disaster upon his people and have, unfortunately, set a standard that remains in Palestinian politics today.

42. For a comprehensive study on the Mufti of Jerusalem, see Sells, "Holocaust Abuse." Sells asserts, "Because the story of the development of this narrative [on the mufti] has not been fully told and because the use to which it is being employed bears upon the core ethic of Holocaust historiography, I trace it here with as much precision as possible" (727).

43. Sells, "Fabricating Palestinian Responsibility."

44. Sells, "Holocaust Abuse," 728, quoting Wisliceny. For more detail, see footnote 6. Wisliceny later signed the Steiner affidavit and attested "that with some minor exceptions, it accurately reflected what he told Steiner during the war." See *Andre Steiner Interview.*

45. ISLC, 9.

46. Lebel, *Mufti of Jerusalem.*

47. Sells, "Holocaust Abuse," 746.

48. Eichmann did meet with the mufti several times, for example, when he accompanied the mufti when he visited incognito the gas chambers at Auschwitz. See Sells, "Holocaust Abuse," 727–28, quoting Wisliceny. They also met in January 1942 in Eichmann's *Kartenzimmer* (map room) in Berlin, when Eichmann laid out for the mufti the plans for the destruction of European Jewry, a fact "dismissed by most serious historians" (Sells, "Holocaust Abuse, 733).

49. Achcar, *Arabs and the Holocaust*, 157.

50. ISLC, 10.

51. ISLC, 11.

52. ISLC, 12.

53. Vermaat, "Dutch Holocaust Survivor."

54. Vermaat, "Dutch Holocaust Survivor."

55. Sells, "Holocaust Abuse," 728. Sells's comments were taken from Wiesenthal's 1947 *Grossmufti-Grossagent der Ache: Tatsachenbericht*, 37, and Wiesenthal's 1990 *Justice, Not Vengeance.*

56. Segev, "Courting Hitler," July 17, 2014, np.

57. Jacobson, "Inconvenient History."

58. Rubin and Schwanitz, "From Station Z to Jerusalem," in *Nazis, Islamists, and the Making of the Modern Middle East*, 2.

59. Gensicke, "From Jerusalem to Nazi Berlin."

60. Batia, "The Turban and the Swastika, Amin Al-Husseini and the Nazis," video by Heinrich Billstein.

61. "Amin al-Hussein—Tell the Children the Truth, Part II."

62. After World War II, Arthur Pier (Asher Ben-Natan) first hunted for Adolf Eichmann and then became an Israeli diplomat and future director-general of the Israeli Ministry of Defense. In the 1950s he signed the Luxembourg Agreement "by then-Chancellor Konrad Adenauer and then-Israeli Foreign Minister Moshe Sharret, [in which] Bonn committed itself to pay 3.5 billion German marks in compensation to the Jewish victims" ("Asher Ben-Natan, Obituary").

63. Sells quoting Pier, in "Fabricating Palestinian Responsibility." In a feature-length theatrical documentary titled *Killing Kasztner: The Jew Who Dealt with the Nazis*, Cohen and Ross search for the truth. Kasztner, in a deal with Adolf Eichmann, was able to ransom 1,600 Hungarian Jews. Once in Israel, Kasztner was accused of and condemned for treason. The Supreme Court overruled the verdict. However, a member of a Jewish rightwing association assassinated him in Tel Aviv. Kasztner was known as the Jewish Schindler.

64. Gabai, "I'll Get out of Here!," 205.

65. Chazan, "Life Didn't Matter Anymore," 277. Gideon Greif states, "The Mufti mentioned here is not the Mufti of Jerusalem, Hajj Amin al-Husseini, but his nephew Mussa Abdallah al-Husseini who visited Auschwitz in 1944 accompanied by a German called Grobe. In 1951, Abdallah was responsible for the assassination

of King Abdullah of Jordan. He was hanged in Amman [on September 6, 1951]" (374n18).

66. Zatezalo, "Jadovno: Complex of Ustasha Camps." It is based on Ćulibrk's edited work *The Jadovno, Slana and Metajnai.*

67. Lukajić, *Friars and Ustashas Are Slaughtering*, 625–39. Lukajić explains why it was difficult to blame Croatia for its actions: "The trial of the Jasenovac death camp commander Dinko Šakić was staged for the Western media with the intention of NOT revealing the true story of Jasenovac. The Western, NATO powers were to convey the opposite—to whitewash the genocide the Catholic Croat Nazis committed on the Serbian, Jewish and Gypsy population. The revamped Nazi Croatia was about to be invited into the NATO club of 'democratic nations.'"

68. Bisset, "Croatia Should Apologize for World War II Genocide."

69. Manhattan, *Vatican's Holocaust*, 48.

70. Paris, *Genocide in Satellite Croatia*, 233.

71. "Catholic Church's Holocaust in Croatia."

72. Gasic, "My Spanish Bosnian Life."

73. Gasic, "My Spanish Bosnian Life."

74. Ateljević, "Jasenovac: System of Croatian-Ustasha Camps of Genocide," 48.

75. Gasic, "My Spanish Bosnian Life."

76. Gasic, "My Spanish Bosnian Life."

77. Sells, "Holocaust Abuse," 746.

78. "Jasenovac was a system of Ustasha death camps established on territory occupied by Nazi Germany's military forces, but no Nazi German executioner took part in the crimes of genocide and holocaust. Crimes of genocide in the Independent State of Croatia were perpetrated by Croatian Ustasha, Pavelić's 300 members, and especially the domobrani (Domobranstvo) (Croatian home guard)" (Ateljević, "Jasenovac: System of Croatian-Ustasha Camps of Genocide 1941–1945," 44).

79. See "Ustaše—The Fascists That Made the Nazis Look like Boy Scouts."

80. Lukajić, *Friars and Ustashas Are Slaughtering*, 287–90. This story is based on the testimony given by Radomir Glamočanin, a Jasenovac survivor.

81. "Serbs' Darkest Hour."

82. "Serbs' Darkest Hour."

83. Löwenthal and Kovac, *Crimes of Occupants*, 11.

84. Löwenthal and Kovac, *Crimes of Occupants*, 14.

85. Paris, *Genocide in Satellite Croatia*, 152.

86. Labudovic, "Where Jewish History Has a Name."

87. Labudovic, "Where Jewish History Has a Name."

88. Labudovic, "Where Jewish History Has a Name."

89. Labudovic, "Where Jewish History Has a Name."

90. Ateljević, "Jasenovac: System of Croatian-Ustasha Camps of Genocide," 31.

91. Zatezalo, "Jadnovo: Complex of Ustascha," 40–44.

92. "Fascist Croatia, Independent State of Croatia."

93. Ivanović, *Book by Jasenovac Survivor.*

94. Löwenthal and Kovac, *Crimes of Occupants*, 17.

95. Lituchy, "What Was Jasenovac?"
96. "Brutal Second World War: The Ustashis."
97. Seabrook, "Anten Pavelić: The Butcher of the Balkans."
98. Burgwyin, "General Roatta's War against the Partisans in Yugoslavia," 314–29.
99. "General Edmund Glaise von Horstenau."
100. "General Edmund Glaise von Horstenau."
101. For my remarks dealing with Italian and German reports on the attitude of the Ustasha, see "General Edmund Glaise von Horstenau."
102. "Brutal Second World War: The Ustashis."
103. "General Edmund Glaise von Horstenau."
104. Milosević, *Jasenovac—the Cruelest Death Camp of All Times* (1983).

Chapter 7

1. Sabban, "Customs of Libyan Jews," 87.
2. Ochayon, "Jews of Algeria, Morocco and Tunisia."
3. Serels, "Moroccan Jews on the Road to Auschwitz," 107–13.
4. Elias, "Why North African Jews Are Missing from the Holocaust Narrative."
5. Miller, "Sephardim and Holocaust Historiography," 226. See Abitbol's *Jews of North Africa during the Second World War.*
6. Hurowitz, "You Must Remember This: Sultan Mohammed V Protected the Jews of Casablanca." Also see Jean-Paul Fhima, "Morocco's Forgotten Labour Camps."
7. Hurowitz, "How the Sultan of Morocco Saved His Jewish Subjects."
8. Ochayon, "Jews of Algeria, Morocco and Tunisia."
9. "Morocco during World War II."
10. Boum, "Eyewitness Dejlfa: Daily Life in a Saharan Vichy Labor Camp," 154.
11. "Morocco during World War II."
12. There is not a fixed number of labor camp sites for Jews in North Africa. In the case of Morocco, the number varies from fourteen to thirty.
13. Fhima, "Morocco's Forgotten Labour Camps."
14. Rohr, *Antisemitism and Opportunism*, 125–26.
15. In 1965 the Algerian Jews were granted the right of individual naturalization.
16. "Crémieux Decree."
17. Souames, "Home, for Algeria's Jews, Is Elsewhere."
18. Ochayon, "Jews of Algeria, Morocco and Tunisia."
19. See Arendt, "Why the Crémieux Decree Was Abrogated."
20. In "The Jews of Algeria, Morocco, and Tunisia," Ochayon writes that the Jewish community established its own Jewish education system in Algiers, Oran, and Constantine. "By the start of the 1942 school year, 20,000 Jewish children were accommodated by these schools, 70 elementary schools and 5 secondary." The program was a success; unfortunately, the Vichy authorities caused the collapse of this system, as they did in December of 1941 by suppressing the university program that had lasted a few months.
21. Ochayon, "Jews of Algeria, Morocco and Tunisia."

22. "The Jews Who Helped Americans Free Algeria from the Nazis."

23. See "Report on the Present General Situation of Jews in Algeria." See Sophie B. Roberts, *Citizenship and Antisemitism in French Colonial Algeria.*

24. Jacob, "Summary of and Reflections on Certain Documents." A copy of a five-page typewritten manuscript was given to me by a member of the Tel Aviv Archives department.

25. "Collection of Reports and Documents," 31.

26. "Collection of Reports and Documents," 33.

27. "Report on the Present General Situation of Jews in Algeria."

28. Jacob, "Summary of and Reflections on Certain Documents," 4–9.

29. Schroeter, "Between Metropole and French North Africa," 19.

30. "Collection of Reports and Documents," 11.

31. Jerenberg, "Germany Finally Recognizes Algerian Jews."

32. Reuven (Roger) Cohen, "Réflexions sur le Judenrat de Tunis."

33. Stein and Boum, "Labor and Internment Camps in North Africa."

34. Sabile, "Les Juifs sous l'occupation," 13.

35. Borgel, *Ėtoile jaune et croix gammée*," 25ff.

36. Sabile, "Les Juifs sous l'occupation," December 1948, 13.

37. Serels, "Non-European Holocaust," 133. For the detailed duties assigned to the committee and the constant German demands for monies and workers, see 133–46. As the Allies were advancing, the Germans became harsher and more demanding.

38. Ochayon, "Jews of Algeria, Morocco and Tunisia."

39. Nataf, "Cérémonie du 70e anniversaire," March 11–12, 2012.

40. Sabile, "Les Juifs sous l'occupation," January 1949, 10.

41. Sabile, "Les Juifs sous l'occupation," December 1948, 14.

42. Sabile, "Les Juifs sous l'occupation," January 1949, 10.

43. Sabile, "Les Juifs sous l'occupation," January 1949, 12. This killing was confirmed by Sidi Fredj. One of my informants said that Mazouz was the first victim that was shot.

44. "North Africa and the Middle East."

45. Sabile, "Les Juifs sous l'occupation," December 1948, 14.

46. Sabile, "Les Juifs sous l'occupation," December 1948, 15.

47. Ochayon, "Jews of Algeria, Morocco, and Tunisia."

48. Ychay testimony. Ychay continued serving his community in Israel when he relocated to Jerusalem. I am grateful to Yad Vashem for availing me of several testimonies.

49. Holland, "Neglected Story of the Holocaust in North Africa."

50. Holland, "Neglected Story of the Holocaust in North Africa." Also see Attal and Sitbon, "Jewish Community of Tunis."

51. Serels, "Non-European Holocaust," 140.

52. Sarah Sussman, "Judeus na África do Norte" (Jews in North Africa). Translated from Portuguese.

53. Reuven (Roger) Cohen, "Réflexions sur le Judenrat de Tunis."

54. Nataf, "Cérémonie du 70e anniversaire."

55. Nataf, "Cérémonie du 70e anniversaire."

56. Nataf, Cérémonie du 70e anniversaire."

57. "Holocaust in Italian Libya."

58. Maurice Roumani, "Aspects of the Holocaust in Libya," 125.

59. See "Italy and the Holocaust: Italian Racial Laws."

60. Maurice Roumani, "Aspects of the Holocaust in Libya," 125.

61. Judith Roumani, "Benghazi—Bergen-Belsen," 226.

62. Meghnagi, "Libyan Jews between Memory and History," 246. See also Maurice Roumani, "Aspects of the Holocaust in Libya," 126.

63. Passages on Libya are paraphrased from Maurice Roumani, "Aspects of the Holocaust in Libya," and "The Jews of Libya," by Ochayon.

64. Zuaretz, "Holocaust Survivor Testimonies: Libya."

65. Tayar, "Holocaust Survivor Testimonies: Libya."

66. I conducted the interview with Yosef Daduch in Holon, Israel, on June 6, 1982. We spoke Italian.

67. I conducted the interview with Victor Rekah in French in Tel Aviv on June 10, 1983.

68. For the account of Joseph Labi's son, see Labi, "Tribute to Old Man and the Sea."

69. "Forgotten 'Nakba.'"

70. "Forgotten 'Nakba.'"

71. Vicktor Rekah, June 10, 1983.

72. Yosef Daduch, June 6, 1982.

Chapter 8

1. Wise, "Personal Testimony by Holocaust Survivor Marta Wise."

2. Rees, *Auschwitz: A New History*, 298.

3. I interviewed Stroumsa in Jerusalem on July 29, 1985.

4. Stroumsa (Strumzah), *Violinist in Auschwitz.*

5. I interviewed Alfred Elkoubi in Paris on July 15, 1984.

6. Bauer, *They Chose Life*, 59.

7. Isaac J. Lévy, *And the World Stood Silent*, 1989, 119.

8. This statement refers to Joshua 24:19–20. Joshua declares to the heads and representatives of the people, "You are not able to serve the Lord; for He is a holy God; He is a jealous God; He will not forgive your transgressions or your sins."

9. I interviewed Raoul Menasche on June 3, 1982, in Petah Tikva, Israel, and in Tel Aviv on June 7, 1982.

10. Nathan Lopes Cardozo is a prolific writer, renowned philosopher, scholar, and sought-after lecturer. He is the founder and dean of the David Cardozo Academy and the Bet Midrash of Avraham Avinu in Jerusalem.

11. Cardozo, "God, Where Are You?"

12. Cardozo, "God, Where Are You?"

13. David Weiss Halivni, *Breaking the Tablets*, 17.

14. David Weiss Halivni, *Breaking the Tablets*, 19.

15. David Weiss Halivni, *Breaking the Tablets*, 40–41.
16. Lipp, "Israel and the Holocaust," 542.
17. Lipp, "Israel and the Holocaust," 542.
18. Chazan, "Life Didn't Matter Anymore," 266.
19. Chazan, "Life Didn't Matter Anymore," 284.
20. Henry Levy, "Jews of Salonica," 234–35.
21. I interviewed Alfred Elkoubi in Paris on July 15, 1984.

Bibliography

Abitbol, Michel. *Jews of North Africa during the Second World War*. Translated by Catherine Tihanyi Zentelis. Detroit: Wayne State University Press, 1989.

Achar, Gilbert. *The Arabs and the Holocaust: The Arab-Israeli War of Narratives*. New York: Henry Holt, 2009.

Ackerfeld, Lance. "Rosa Robota: Her Life, Struggle against the Germans and Her Death as a Martyr," 401–6. Yizkor Book Project Manager, Lance Ackerfeld. July 2, 2003. www.jewishgen.org/Yizkor/Ciechanow/cie398.html, accessed July 15, 2016.

Aini, Lea (Leah). "No Other Jews like them." *Haaretz*, August 12, 2010. https://www.haaretz.com/life/books/1.5099256, accessed October 10, 2016.

———. *Vered Halevanon* (Rose of Lebanon). Or Yehuda: Kinneret, Zmora-Bitan, 2008.

———. "The Violence of the Survivors." Translated by Hannah Komy Ofir. *Ben Gurion University Review*, no. 3 (2013). https://in.bgu.ac.il/en/heksherim/Pages/2013.aspx, accessed July 15, 2019.

"Alberto Errera." https://en.wikipedia.org/wiki/Alberto_Errera, accessed May 23, 2014.

Alcalay, Albert. *The Persistence of Hope: A True Story*. Newark: University of Delaware, 2007.

"Alexander Katan." https://.org/wiki/alexander_katan, accessed June 13, 2016.

Algrante, Morgues Esther. *9 Eylül: Poesias*. Istanbul: Baski Kaykar, 1975.

"Amin al-Hussein—Tell the Children the Truth, Part II." In From the Muslim Brotherhood to the Third Reich, Amin Al-Husseini / Adolf Hitler Connection, 1933–2002. http://www.tellthechildrenthetruth.com/amin_en.html, accessed December 5, 2016.

Andre Steiner Interview. Claude Lanzmann Shoah Collection. Spielberg Film and Video Archive, USHMM. Story Number: RG-60.5010, 1979. https://collections.ushmm.org/search/catalog/irn1003919, accessed July 17, 2017.

"Anna Heilman." https://en.wikipedia.org/wiki/Anna_Heilman, accessed June 10, 2019.

"Anti-Jewish Atrocities in Occupied Greece: The Greek People React Vigorously against the German Plan to Exterminate the Greek Jews." *Jewish Chronicle* 4, no. 9 (December 3, 1943).

Arditti, Alfred. "Saloniki." Yad Vashem 292–21-א (03/917), 2/4/58.

Arendt, Hanna. "Why the Crémieux Decree Was Abrogated." AJC Archives. www.ajcarchives.org/AJC_DATA/Files/CR11.PDF, accessed February 16, 2018.

"Aribert Heim." https://en.wikipedia.org/wiki/Aribert_Heim, accessed March 18, 2013.

"Asher Ben-Natan, Obituary." *Telegraph*. July 13, 2014. https://www.telegraph.co.uk/news/obituaries/10964480/Asher-Ben-Natan-obituary.html, accessed June 9, 2019.

Ateljević, Žana, ed. *Jasenovac: System of Croatian-Ustasha Camps of Genocide 1941–1945*. Banja Luka, Donja Gradina, May 8–10, 2000. Translated by Tatjana Ateljević and Sanja Pejović. Banja Luka: Second International Conference Jasenovac, 2001.

Attal, Robert, and Claude Sitbon. "The Jewish Community of Tunis." Originally published in *From Carthage to Jerusalem—The Jewish Community of Tunis* (exhibition catalogue). Tel Aviv: Beit Hatfutsot, 1986. https://dbs.bh.org.il/place/tunisia?gclid=EAIaIQobChMI7avb6rmA2QIVF4rICh2KoQSbEAAYASAAEgLdSPD_BwE\, accessed January 30, 2018.

"Auschwitz-Birkenau: The Revolt at Auschwitz-Birkenau (October 7, 1944)." Jewish Virtual Library American-Israeli Cooperative Enterprise. https://www.jewishvirtuallibrary.org/jsource/Holocaust/aurevolt.html, accessed May 27, 2016.

"Auschwitz-Birkenau Uprising." http://www.mixbook.com/photo-books/education/auschwitz-birkenau-uprising-4573638, accessed August 24, 2016.

"Auschwitz II Birkenau Sonderkommando Testimony Clips." YouTube video. USC Shoah Foundation. January 23, 2009. https://www.youtube.com/watch?v=5SoTJ9cv028, accessed November 22, 2017.

"Auschwitz Concentration Camp." nd. https://www.sources.com/SSR/Docs/SSRW-Auschwitz_Concentration_Camp.htm, accessed September 8, 2016.

"Balkan Wars and the Jews." *American Jewish Year Book* 15 (October 2, 1913 to September 20, 1914 / 5674): 188–206.

Banu, Sufia. "10 Wicked Women in Nazi Concentration Camps—WondersList." http://www.wonderslist.com/10-wicked-women-nazi-concentration-camps, accessed March 22, 2017.

Bartosik, Igor. "Sonderkommando: Interview with Auschwitz Historian Igor Bartosik." http://www.auschwitzstudygroup.com/articles/345-sonderkommando-interview-with-auschwitz-historian-igor-bartosik, accessed July 14, 2016.

Bar-Zohar, Michael. *Beyond Hitler's Grasp: The Heroic Rescue of Bulgaria's Jews*. Avon, MA: Adams Media, 1998.

Batia, Chaya. "The Turban and the Swastika, Amin Al-Husseini and the Nazis." YouTube video. By Heinrich Billstein, August 8, 2012. www.youtube.com/watch?v=1CIgw_jHxjs, accessed June 19, 2014.

Bauer, Yehuda. *They Chose Life: Jewish Resistance in the Holocaust*. Foreword by

Bertram H. Gold. New York: American Jewish Committee, Institute of Human Relations, 1973.

Ben, Joseph., ed. "Jewish Leadership in Greece during the Holocaust." In *Proceedings of the Third Yad Vashem International Historical Conference, April 4–7, 1977*, 335–52. Jerusalem: Yad Vashem, 1979.

Benbassa, Esther, and Aron Rodrigue. *Sephardi Jewry: A History of the Judeo-Spanish Community, 14th–20th Centuries.* Berkeley: University of California Press, 2000.

Ben-Rubi, B. Itzahk (Isaac). *El sekreto del Mudo.* Tel Aviv: Lidor, 1953.

———. *Locos kon seriedad: Pieza en tres actos.* Spanish version by Ester de G. Camhi. Mexico City, 1958. Originally published in Tel Aviv in 1951 or 1952 in Judeo-Spanish.

Berlin, Gail. "The Kanada Commando as a Force for Resistance in Auschwitz: Redefining Heroism." *Proteus* 12, no. 2 (1995): 32–36.

"Biography of the Auschwitz Sonderkommando." http://www.sonderkommando.info/index.php/sonderkommandos/les-differents-sonderkommandos/bios-des-individus, accessed September 24, 2016.

Birnbaum, Philip. *Encyclopedia of Jewish Concepts.* New York: Hebrew Publishing Company, 1991.

Bisset, James. "Croatia Should Apologize for World War II Genocide before Joining the EU." October 12, 2014. http://www.catholicarrogance.org/CroatianHolocaust.html, accessed August 14, 2016.

Bolkosky, Sidney. "Interview with Salvatore and Lili Katan." August 18, 1981. Mardigian Library, University of Michigan, Dearborn.

Borgel, Robert. *Ėtoile jaune et croix gammée: Récit d'une servitude.* Tunis: Editions Artypo, 1944.

Borowski, Tadeusz. *This Way for the Gas, Ladies and Gentlemen.* Translated by Barbara Veddor. Introduction by Jan Knott. New York: Penguin Books, 1967.

Boum, Aomar. "Eyewitness Dejlfa: Daily Life in a Saharan Vichy Labor Camp." In *The Holocaust and North Africa*, edited by Aomar Boum and Sarah Abrevaya Stein, 149–67. Stanford, CA: Stanford University Press. 2019.

Boum, Aomar, and Sarah Abrevaya Stein, eds. *The Holocaust and North Africa.* Stanford, CA: Stanford University Press, 2019.

Bourla, Isaac. *Chimera: A Period of Madness.* The Sephardi and Greek Holocaust Library III. New York: Sephardi House and Bloch, 2007.

Bowman, Steven. *The Agony of Greek Jews, 1940–1945.* Stanford, CA: Stanford University Press, 2009.

———. "Could the Dodecanesi Jews Have Been Saved?" *Newsletter of the Jewish Museum of Greece* 26 (Winter 1989): 1–2.

———. "Introduction: The Greeks in Auschwitz." In Rebecca Camhi Fromer, *The Holocaust Odyssey of Daniel Bennahmias, Sonderkommando*, xi–xxv. Tuscaloosa: University of Alabama Press, 1993.

———. *Jewish Resistance in Wartime Greece.* Portland, OR: Vallentine Mitchell, 2006.

——. "Jews in Wartime Greece." *Jewish Social Studies* 48, no. 1 (1986): 46–62.

——. "Joseph Matsas and the Greek Resistance." *Journal of the Hellenic Diaspora* 17, no. 1 (1991): 49–53.

Bowman, Steven, and Isaac Benmayor, eds. *The Holocaust in Salonika: Eyewitness Accounts*, New York: Sephardic House, 2002.

——. "Fourth Investigation: Medical Experiments on Hostages." In *Holocaust in Salonika: Eyewitness Accounts*, 205–11. Translated from the Greek by Isaac Benmayor. New York: Sephardic House and Bloch, 2002.

Browning, Christopher. *Jewish Resistance in Wartime Greece*. Portland, OR: Vallentine Mitchell, 2010.

"Brutal Second World War: The Ustashis." *Pictures from History: Rare Images of War History, WW2, Nazi Germany*. [blog] https://pictureshistory.blogspot.com/2009/10/brutal-second-world-war-ustashis.html, accessed July 24, 2017.

Bulajić, Milan. *Jasenovac: The Jewish Serbian Holocaust (the Role of the Vatican) in Nazi-Ustasha Croatia (1941–1945)*. Belgrade: Fund for Genocide Research, Stručna knjiga, 2002.

"Bulgaria." United States Holocaust Memorial Museum. https://www.ushmm.org/wlc/en/article.php?ModuleId=1 0005451, accessed June 26, 2017.

"Bulgaria Virtual Jewish History Tour." Jewish Virtual Library. http://www.jewishvirtuallibrary.org/bulgaria-virtual-jewish-history-tour, accessed June 26, 2017.

Bülow, Louis. *Dr. Miklos Nyiszli, an Eyewitness from Auschwitz*. Auschwitz.dk. www.auschwitz.dk/Nyszli.htm, accessed January 24, 2019.

Burgwyin, H. James. "General Roatta's War against the Partisans in Yugoslavia: 1942." *Journal of Modern Italian Studies* 9, no. 3 (2004): 314–29. https://doi.org/10.1080/1354571042000254746, accessed April 25, 2018.

Cannibalism in Prison Camp: British Medical Officer's Visit to 'Most Horrible Place.'" *Guardian*, April 19, 1945. https://www.theguardian.com/world/1945/apr/19/secondworldwar.fromthearchive, accessed March 27, 2018.

Cara, Arben, and Mimoza Margjeka. "Kanun of Leke Dukagjini Customary Law of Northern Albania." *European Scientific Journal* 11, no. 28: 174–86. http://eujournal.org/index.php/esj/article/viewFile/6383/6134, accessed August 12, 2017.

Carbonara, Julie. "Woman Visits Camp Where She Was Born." *JC News*. October 11, 2013. https://www.thejc.com/news/world/woman-visits-italian-concentration-camp-where-she-was-born-1.49691, accessed June 7, 2019.

Cardozo, Nathan Lopes. "God, Where Are You? An Open Letter." *Crescas*. [blog] October 16, 2015. https://www.crescas.nl/blog/webcolumnlopescardozo/07zoz/God-Where-are-You-An-open-letter/, accessed September 11, 2018.

"The Catholic Church's Holocaust in Croatia." *Politic and Religion*. [blog] May 7, 2009. http://lukaserb.blogspot.com/2009/05/catholic-churchs-holocaust-in-croatia.html, accessed April 19, 2014.

Chare, Nicholas, and Dominic Williams. *Matters of Testimony: Interpreting the Scrolls of Auschwitz*. New York: Berghahn, 2017.

Chazan (Hazan), Shaul. "Life Didn't Matter Anymore, Death Was Too Close." In *We Wept without Tears: Testimonies of the Jewish Sonderkommando from Auschwitz,* edited by Gideon Greif, 257–85. New Haven: Yale University Press, 2005.

Cohen, Baruch C. "Nazi Medical Experimentation: The Ethics of Using Data from Nazi Experiments." *Journal of Halacha and Contemporary Society* 19 (1990): 103–26. http://www.jewishvirtuallibrary.org/jsource/Judaism/naziexp.html, accessed November 9, 2016.

Cohen, Elie Aron. *Human Behavior in the Concentration Camp.* New York: W. W. Norton, 1953.

Cohen, Jean. "Εξέγερση Ελλήνων στο Αουσβιτς. Η εξέγερση των. Ζόντερκομαντο!" (The Rebellion of Greeks in Auschwitz. 7 October 1944.) *Kopanaki News.* 6/2/2009. September 3, 2013. (In Greek).

Cohen, Leon Reuven. *From Greece to Birkenau: The Crematoria Workers' Uprising.* Translated from the French by Jose-Maurice Gormezano. Tel Aviv: Salonika Jewry Research Center, 1996.

———. "We Were Dehumanized: We Were Robots." In *We Wept without Tears: Testimonies of the Jewish Sonderkommando from Auschwitz,* edited by Gideon Greif, 286–309. New Haven: Yale University Press, 2005.

Cohen, Reuven (Roger). "Réflexions sur le Judenrat de Tunis pendant l'occupation nazie." (Reflections on the Judenrat of Tunis during the Nazi Occupation). July 8, 2011. https://harissa.com/news/index.php?q=article/r%C3%A9flexions-sur-le-judenrat-de-tunis-pendant-l%E2%80%99occupation-nazie-par-le-dr-reuven-roger-cohen, accessed February 20, 2018.

Collection Highlight, "Remnants and Recollections: The Experience of Sephardi Jews during the Holocaust." United States Holocaust Memorial Museum. http://www.ushmm.org/information/exhibitions/online-features/collections-highlights/sephardi-jews-during-the-holocaust, n.d., accessed June 23, 2016.

"Collection of Reports and Documents Pertaining to the Jewish Situation in French North Africa." 1943. World Jewish Congress. Tel Aviv University file A-1/129, 11, June 1, 1943.

Coné, Giuseppe. "Testimonio VII." In *Libro de los testimonios: Los Sefardíes y el Holocausto,* edited by Salvator Santa Puche, 1201–8. Palm Beach, FL: Sephardi Federation of Palm Beach County, 2003.

Constantinidis, Chaim. "The Greek Island That Hid Its Jews from the Nazis." Ekathimerini.com. September 7, 2014. http://www.ekathimerini.com/161394/article/ekathimerini/community/the-greek-island-that-hid-its-jews-from-the-nazis, accessed June 10, 2019.

Corporon, Yvette Manessis. *Something Beautiful Happened: A Story of Survival and Courage in the Face of Evil.* New York: Howard Books, 2017.

Cotkin, George. "Illuminating Evil: Hannah Arendt and Moral History." *Modern Intellectual History* 4 (3): 463–90. Cambridge: Cambridge University Press, 2007.

"Couriers of the Jewish Underground in Poland during the Holocaust: The Destruction of Crematorium Number Four." http://www.theverylongview.com/WATH/essays/courier11.htm, accessed December 15, 2016.

"Crémieux Decree." *Jewish Treats*, October 24, 2013. www.jewishtreats.org/2013/10/the-cremieux-decree.html, accessed September 16, 2017.

"Croatian Nazis—The Worst Monsters the World Had Known." YouTube video. April 5, 2013. https://www.youtube.com/watch?v=E6GmtZOyIQA, accessed September 13, 2016.

Ćulibrk, Jovan, ed. *The Jadovno, Slana and Metajna*. Translated by Nebojša Božić. Gospić-Jadovno-Pag: Association of Descendants and Supporters of Victims of Ustasha Concentration Death Camps in Gospić NDH, 1941.

Czech, Danuta. *Auschwitz Chronicle 1939–1945: From the Archives of the Auschwitz Memorial and the German Federal Archives*. New York: Henry Holt, 1997.

———. *Kalendarium der Ereignisse im Konzentrationslager Auschwitz-Birkenau 1939–1945* (Calendar of events in the concentration camp Auschwitz-Birkenau 1939–1945). Reinbek bei Hamburg : Rowohlt, 1989.

Dalven, Rachel [Rae]. *The Jews of Ioannina, Greece*. Philadelphia: Cadmus Press, 1990.

Dawidowicz, Lucy S. *The War against the Jews, 1933–1945*. New York: Bantam, 1986.

"Death Marches (Holocaust)." United States Holocaust Memorial Museum. http://encyclopedia.ushmm.org.content/en/article/death-marches, accessed May 31, 2017.

De Sola Pool, David, ed. and trans. *Prayers for the Day of Atonement*. 9th ed. New York: Union of Sephardic Congregations, 1998.

———. *Prayers for the New Year*. 3rd printing. New York: Union of Sephardic Congregations, 1954.

Didi-Huberman, Georges. *Images in Spite of All: Four Photographs from Auschwitz*. Translated by Shane B. Lillis. Chicago: University of Chicago Press, 2008.

DioGuardi, Shirley Cloyes. "Jewish Survival in Albania & Ethics of 'Besa.'" http://www.kosovaisrael.org/2011/07/jewish-survival-in-albania-the-ethics-of-'besa'/, accessed March 1, 2016.

Dragon, Abraham, and Shlomo Dragon. "Together—in Despair and in Hope." In *We Wept without Tears: Testimonies of the Jewish Sonderkommando from Auschwitz*, edited by Gideon Greif, 122–80. New Haven: Yale University Press, 2005.

Eisenschmidt, Eliezer. "Thanks to One Polish Family." In *We Wept without Tears: Testimonies of the Jewish Sonderkommando from Auschwitz*, edited by Gideon Greif, 215–56. New Haven: Yale University Press, 2005.

Elias, Eness. "Why North African Jews Are Missing from the Holocaust Narrative." *Haaretz*, June 22, 2018. https://www.haaretz.com/israel-news/.premium-wEliezer hy—north-african-jews-are-missing-from-the-holocaust-narrative-1.5629410, accessed June 22, 2018.

"Eliezer (Eli) Sotto." Interviewed by Sara Ghitis. Taylor Family Fund, the William Breman Jewish Heritage Museum, Atlanta, Georgia, September 16, 2001.

"Encyclopedia Judaica: Death Marches." From testimony of Eva Gestl Burns, Gratz College Holocaust Oral History Archive, 2008. http://www.jewishvirtuallibrary.org/death-marches, accessed May 31, 2017.

"Fascist Croatia, Independent State of Croatia (NDH): The Most Murderous of the

Nazi Puppet States." http://espressostalinist.com/genocide/fascist-croatia, accessed July 21, 2017.

"The Fate of the Bulgarian Jews." Holocaust Education & Archive Research Team. http://www.holocaustresearchproject.org/nazioccupation/bulgarianjews.html, accessed June 26, 2017.

Feig, Konnilyn G. *Hitler's Death Camps: The Sanity of Madness*. New York: Holmes and Meier, 1981.

"Ferramonti di Tarsia." *Shoah Resource*. Yad Vashem. https://www.yadvashem.org/odot_pdf/Microsoft%20Word%20-%205847.pdf, accessed June 4, 2019.

Fhima, Jean-Paul. "Morocco's Forgotten Labour Camps." *Times of Israel*. [blog] February 4, 2015. http://blogs.timesofisrael.com/moroccos-forgotten-labour-camps/, accessed March 8, 2018.

Fintz, Violette Mayo. "From Rhodes Island to Auschwitz." In *Sacred Memory: Recollections of the Holocaust by Survivors Living in Cape Town*, edited by Gwynne Schrire, 144–49. Cape Town: Holocaust Memorial Council, 1995.

———. "Testimonio IV." In *Libro de los testimonios: Los Sefardíes y el Holocausto*, edited by Salvador Santa Puche, 1:157–70. Palm Beach, FL: Sephardi Federation of Palm Beach County, 2003.

Fleming, Katherine Elizabeth. *Greece: A Jewish History*. Princeton: Princeton University Press, 2008.

"The Forgotten 'Nakba.'" Real Jsreets, May 22, 2016. http://www.israellycool.com/2016/05/22/the-forgotten-nakba, accessed July 22, 2017.

Franco, Hizkia M. *The Jewish Martyrs of Rhodes and Cos*. Translated from the original French by Joseph Franco. Los Angeles: Rhodes Jewish Foundation of Los Angeles, 2009.

———. *Les martyrs juifs de Rhodes et de Cos*. Elizabethville, Belgian Congo: Imprimeries et Paperteries Belgo-Congolaises, "Imbelco," 1952.

Friedenreich, Harriet Pass. "The Jewish Community of Yugoslavia." In *The Balkan Jewish Communities: Yugoslavia, Bulgaria, Greece and Turkey*, edited by Daniel J. Elazar, 12–58. Lanham, MD: University Press of America, 1984.

———. "Yugoslavia." Jewish Women's Archive. jwa.org/encyclopedia/article/Yugoslavia, accessed March 13, 2016.

Fromer, Rebecca Camhi. *The Holocaust Odyssey of Daniel Bennahmias, Sonderkommando*. Introduction by Steven B. Bowman. Tuscaloosa: University of Alabama Press, 1993.

———. *The House by the Sea: A Portrait of the Holocaust in Greece*. San Francisco: Mercury House, 1997.

Gabai, Ya'akov. "I'll Get Out of Here!" In *We Wept without Tears: Testimonies of the Jewish Sonderkommando from Auschwitz*, edited by Gideon Greif, 181–214. New Haven: Yale University Press, 2005.

Gabbai, Dario. "Dario Gabbai Remembers the Sonderkommado Uprising." YouTube video. January 14, 2015. https://www.youtube.com/watch?v=19hLniDfxkE, accessed 8/16/2016.

Gaon, Solomon, and M. Mitchell Serels, eds. *Del Fuego: Sephardim and the Holocaust*. Brooklyn, NY: Empire Press, 1987.

——. *Del Fuego: Sephardim and the Holocaust.* New York: Sepher-Hermon Press, 1995.

Gasic, Hana Montiljo. "My Spanish Bosnian Life: The Story of Hana Montiljo Gasic." *Centropa Cinema: Digital Storytelling and 20th Century Jewish Memory.* November 7, 2017. https://www.centropa.org/centropa-cinema/hana-gasic-my-spanish-bosnian-life, accessed June 9, 2019.

"General Edmund Glaise von Horstenau." *De-Construct E-Zine.* July 20, 2006. https://oslobodjenje.wordpress.com/2006/07/20/general-edmund-glaise-von-horstenau/, accessed June 10, 2019.

Gensicke, Klaus. "From Jerusalem to Nazi Berlin—The Mufti of Jerusalem and Hitler Partnership." Publication of Middle East Review of International Affairs. www.readperiodicals.com/201407/3394318201.html#ixzz3xutlvYoZ, accessed October 17, 2016.

Gershman, Norman. "Jews Saved by Albanians." YouTube video. Nov. 13, 2009. https://www.youtube.com/watch?v=2QXVjAc-aIQ, accessed August 17, 2017.

Giuffrida, Angela. "Ferramonti Was Not a Death Camp." Narrated by Judith Itzhak. October 7, 2013. www.thelocal.it/20131007/ferramonti-was-not-a-death-camp, accessed March 15, 2016.

Goldstein, Slavko. "Final Solution to the 'Jewish Question' in Yugoslavia." In *Jews in Yugoslavia*, edited by Sante Sorič, 111–17. Zagreb: Muzejski Prostor, 1989.

Greif, Gideon, ed. "The Sonderkommando in Auschwitz-Birkenau: Portrait and Self-Image," 43. In *We Wept without Tears: Testimonies of the Jewish Sonderkommando from Auschwitz.* New Haven, CT: Yale University Press, and the Sue and Leonard Miller Center for Contemporary Judaic Studies. University of Miami, 2005.

——. *We Wept without Tears: Testimonies of the Jewish Sonderkommando from Auschwitz.* New Haven: Yale University Press, and the Sue and Leonard Miller Center for Contemporary Judaic Studies, University of Miami, 2005.

Gutman, Israel, and Michael Berenbaum, eds. *Anatomy of the Auschwitz Death Camp.* Bloomington: Indiana University Press, 1998.

Hagouel, Paul Isaac. "The History of the Jews of Salonika and the Holocaust: An Exposé." *Sephardic Horizons* 3, no. 1 (2013): 1–43.

Halivni, David Weiss. *Breaking the Tablets: Jewish Theology after the Shoah.* Edited and introduction by Peter Ochs. Lanham, MD: Rowman and Littlefield, 2007.

Halivni, Tzipora Hager. "The Birkenau Revolt: Poles Prevent a Timely Insurrection." *Jewish Social Studies* 41, no. 2 (Spring 1979): 123–54.

Hazan, Martín. *Un día más de vida, Rodas-Auschwitz-Buenos Aires: La odisea de David Galante.* Buenos Aires: Ediciones Lumiere, 2007.

Hecht, Esther. "The Jewish Traveler: Corfu." *Hadassah Magazine*, February/March 2012. www.hadassahmagazine.org/2012/02/28/jewish-traveler-corfu, accessed April 4, 2019.

Hedgepeth, Sonja M. C., and Rochelle G. Saidel, eds. *Sexual Violence against Jewish Women during the Holocaust.* Waltham, MA: Brandeis University Press, 2010.

Heffler, Max G. "Part III—Rebellion: Active and Passive Resistance." Radom,

Poland, Yizkor Book Project. JewishGen. www.jewishgen.org/yizkor/radom /rade077.html.

Heilman, Anna. "Anna Heilman—Part I." Women of Valor: Partisans and Resistance Fighters. Interviewer Bonnie Gurewitsch, October 14, 1985. http://www .theverylongview.com/WATH/valor/anna1.htm, accessed September 28, 2016.

———. "Anna Heilman—Part II." Women of Valor: Partisans and Resistance Fighters. Interviewer Bonnie Gurewitsch. October 14, 1985. http://www.theverylongview .com/WATH/valor/anna2.htm, accessed September 28, 2016.

"History's Judgment: SS Dr. Eduard Krebsbach." www.company7.com/bosendorfer /mauthausen/krebsbachtestimony.html, accessed January 17, 2017.

Holland, Adam. "The Neglected Story of the Holocaust in North Africa." *JTA Roundup of Tunisian Jews Remembered.* [blog] December 12, 2009. http:// adamholland.blogspot.com/2009/12/neglected-story-of-holocaust-in-north.html, accessed May 19, 2019.

"The Holocaust in Italian Libya." http://military.wikia.com/wiki/TheHolocaustinItalianLibya, accessed February 27, 2018.

Hurowitz, Richard. "How the Sultan of Morocco Saved His Jewish Subjects during World War II." *Mosaic*, April 26, 2017. https://mosaicmagazine.com/picks /2017/04/how-the-sultan-of-morocco-saved-his-jewish-subjects-during-world -war-ii/, accessed January 30, 2018.

———. "You Must Remember This: Sultan Mohammed V Protected the Jews of Casablanca." *Los Angeles Times*, April 25, 2017. https://www.latimes.com/opinion /op-ed/la-oe-hurowitz-moroccan-king-mohammed-v-20170425-story.html, accessed June 9, 2019.

Ikonomopoulos, Marcia Haddad. "Remembering the Jews of Corfu." August 14, 2011. http://sefarad.org/lm/046/12.html, accessed April 3, 2019.

———. "The Story behind the Statistics: Variables Affecting the Tremendous Losses of Greek Jewry during the Holocaust." *Journal of the Hellenic Diaspora* 32, nos. 1–2 (2006): 90–109.

International Sephardic Leadership Council (ISLC). *Background of the Nazi Activities in North Africa and the Middle East during the Era of the Holocaust, including An Overview of the Arab World Leader: Amin Al-Hussein, the Grand Mufti of Jerusalem and His Connection with the Third Reich.* New York, April 2006.

"Italy and the Holocaust: Italian Racial Laws." http://www.italyandtheholocaust.org /italian-racial-laws.aspx, accessed June 12, 2017.

Ivanović, Ilija. *Witness to Jasenovac's Hell.* Edited by Wanda Schindley. Translated by Aleksandar Lazić. Mt. Pleasant, TX: Dallas, 2002.

Jacob, Paul. "Summary of and Reflections on Certain Documents." *World Jewish Congress: Advisory Council on European Jewish Affairs*, 4–9. June 1, 1943.

Jacobson, William A. "An Inconvenient History: The Grand Mufti, Hitler and the 'Knife Intifada.'" October 21, 2015. http://legalinsurrection.com/2015/10 /an-inconvenient-history-the-grand-mufti-hitler-and-the-knife-intifada, accessed October 17, 2016.

Jerenberg, Batya. "Germany Finally Recognizes Algerian Jews Who Survived Holocaust." *World Israel News*, February 5, 2018. https://worldisraelnews.com/germany-finally-recognizes-algerian-jews-survived-holocaust/, accessed February 18, 2018.

"The Jews Who Helped the Americans Free Algeria from the Nazis." Beit Hatfutsot—The Museum of the Jewish People and Ushi Derman. January 14, 2018. https://www.haaretz.com/middle-east-news/MAGAZINE-the-jews-who-helped-the-u-s-free-algeria-from-the-nazis-1.5730698, accessed March 17, 2018.

Joroff, David. "Dark and Perverse." *Jerusalem Post*. March 12, 1983, np.

Kabeli, Isaac. 1953. "The Resistance of the Greek Jews." *YIVO Annual of the Social Studies* 8 (1953): 281–88.

Katan, Salvatore, and Lili Katan. "New Interview: Salvatore and Lili Katan." August 18, 1981. Voice/Vision Holocaust Survivor Oral History Archive. http://holocaust.umd.umich.edu/interviews.php#katan, accessed April 17, 2016.

Kerem, Itzak. "New Finds on Greek Jewish Heroism in the Holocaust." *Sephardic Horizons*, Spring 2012. http://www.sephardichorizons.org/Volume2/Issue2/kerem.html#ednl, accessed November 20, 2012.

———. "Rescue of Sephardic Jews by Muslims in the Holocaust." *Journal of Sefardic Studies, Hebrew University of Jerusalem*, no. 2 (2014): 39–76.

———. "Sephardic and Oriental Oral Testimonies: The Importance for Holocaust Commemoration and Memory." In *Remembering for the Future—The Holocaust in an Age of Genocide*, edited by John K. Roth and Elizabeth Maxwell, 142–49. New York: Palgrave Macmillan, 2001.

Kerem, Itzak, and Eduardo Retyk. "Maestro, Jako." *Shoa, Enciclopedia del Holocausto*. Jerusalem: Yad Vashem and E.D.Z. Nativ Ediciones, 2000.

Kokkinidis, Tasos. "How Brave Greek Islanders Saved a Jewish Family during the Holocaust." April 3, 2019. https://greece.greekreporter.com/2019/04/03/how-brave-greek-islanders-saved-a-jewish-family-during-the-holocaust/, accessed April 5, 2019.

Kolko, Moshe. "Ciechanow Jews in the Uprising in Auschwitz." Yzkor Book Project Manager, Lance Ackerfeld. July 2, 2003. http://www.jewishgen.org/yizkor/ciechanow/cie370.html, accessed August 16, 2016.

Kounio, Heinz Salvator. *A Liter of Soup and Sixty Grams of Bread: The Diary of Prisoner Number 109565*. Adapted and translated by Marcia Haddad Ikonomopoulos. New York: Bloch, 2003.

Kounio-Amariglio, Erika. *From Thessaloniki to Auschwitz and Back: Memories of a Survivor from Thessaloniki*. Translated into English by Theresa Sundt (née Amariglio). Portland, OR: Vallentine Mitchell, 2000. Reprinted 2002.

Kremer, Lilian S, ed. *Holocaust Literature: An Encyclopedia of Writers and Their Work*. 2 vols. New York: Routledge, 2003.

Labi, Maurice. "Tribute to Old Man and the Sea." https://notesfromgalilee.wordpress.com/?app-download=nokia, accessed March 1, 2018.

Labudovic, Ida. "Where Jewish History Has a Name, a Face, a Story." Interview of Cadik Danon in Belgrade, Serbia, 2001. www.centropa.org/biography/cadik-danon, accessed May 26, 2019.

Lagnado, Lucette Matalon, and Sheila Cohn Dekel. *Children of the Flames: Dr. Josef*

Mengele and the Untold Story of the Twins of Auschwitz. New York: Penguin Group, 1992.

Langbein, Hermann. *People in Auschwitz*. Translated by Harry Zohn. Foreword by Henry Friedlander. Chapel Hill: University of North Carolina Press, 2004.

Lebel, Jennie. *The Mufti of Jerusalem: Haj-Amin el-Husseini and National-Socialism*. Belgrade: Cigoya (Cigoja) Stampa, 2007.

Levi, Primo. *The Drowned and the Saved*. New York: Summit Books, 1988.

———. *If This Is a Man*. Translated from the Italian by Stuart Woolf. New York: Orion Press, 1959.

Levi, Stella. *Los Amigos Sepharadi, an Association for the Study and Preservation of Sephardi Culture*. Berkeley, CA. September 1987.

———. "Primo Levi at the United Nations: Stella Levi's Opening Remarks." May 6, 2016. http://primolevicenter.org/printed-matter/stella-levis-opening-remarks/, accessed July 21, 2016.

Levy, Henry. "The Jews of Salonica and the Holocaust: A Personal Memoir." In *Del Fuego: Sephardim and the Holocaust*, edited by Haham Dr. Solomon Gaon and Dr. M. Mitchell Serels, 213–46. New York: Sepher Hermon Press, 1995.

Lévy, Isaac J. *And the World Stood Silent: Sephardic Poetry of the Holocaust*. Translated with commentaries. Urbana: University of Illinois Press, 1989.

———. *And the World Stood Silent*. 2nd ed. Urbana: University of Illinois Press, 2002.

———. "Holocaust Poetry: The Forgotten Sephardim." *Sephardic Scholar*, ser. 4 (1979–1982): 111–24.

———. *Jewish Rhodes: A Lost Culture*. Berkeley, CA: Judah L. Magnes Museum, 1989.

———. Review of "United States Holocaust Memorial Museum. In Spanish and Portuguese." *Hispania* 94 (2011): 771–72.

———. "The Yearning for the Promised Land in Sephardic Literature and Folklore." In *Jewish Culture and the Hispanic World: Essays in Memory of Joseph H. Silverman*, edited by Samuel J. Armistead and Mishael M. Caspi, 303–19. Newark, DE: Juan de la Cuesta, 2001.

———. "Yehuda Haim Perahia: A Poet from Salonika." *Romance Quarterly* 35, no. 1 (1988): 81–88.

Levy, Rebecca Amato. 1987. *I Remember Rhodes*. (In English and Judeo-Spanish). New York: Sepher-Hermon Press for Sephardic House at Congregation Shearith Israel, 1987.

Lewkowicz, Bea. *The Jewish Community of Salonika: History, Memory, Identity*. London: Vallentine Mitchell, 2006.

Lipp, Solomon. "Israel and the Holocaust in Contemporary Spanish-American Poetry." *Hispania* 64 (1982): 536–43.

Lituchy, Barry. "What Was Jasenovac?" *Jasenovac Research Institute, written by JRI Research Director Barry Lituchy*, 8–9, (c) 2000.

Lopez, Esteban Gonzalez. "Mazaltov Behar Mordoch, a Survivor of Nazi Medical Experiments." *El País*, August 27, 2012.

Löwenthal, Zdenko, and Teodor Kovac, tech. eds. *The Crimes of Occupants and*

Their Collaborators against the Jews in Yugoslavia. Belgrade: Federation of Jewish Communities of the Federative People's Republic of Yugoslavia, 1957.

Lukajić, Lazar. *Friars and Ustashas Are Slaughtering* (Fatri i unstaše kolju). Translated by Peter Makara. Edited by Wanda Schindley. Belgrade: Fund for Genocide Research, 2005.

Mac Con Uladh, Damian. "Remembering the Greek Jews who Participated in the Auschwitz Revolt 70 years Ago." EnetEnglish. October 8, 2014. http://www.enetenglish.gr/?i=news.en.economy&id=2065, accessed November 28, 2019.

Mallenbaum, Allan E. "On Holocaust Day We Forget—Róza Robota and the Holocaust Resistance." *The Jewish Magazine*, 2005. http://www.jewishmag.com/90mag/rosarobata/rosarobata.htm, accessed July 21, 2016.

Manhattan, Avro. *The Vatican's Holocaust: The Sensational Account of the Most Horrifying Religious Massacre of the 20th Century*. Springfield, MO: Ozark Books, 1986.

Mashbaum, Yael Weinstock. "It Happened Here Too: Sephardic Jews in Yugoslavia, Bulgaria, and Greece." Yad Vashem. https://www.yadvashem.org/articles/general/sephardic, accessed March 27, 2019.

"Massacre of the Greeks of Phocaea, 12–13 June 1914." *Hellenic News*, June 13, 2016. https://hellenicnews.com/massacre-greeks-phocaea-12-13-june-1914/, accessed March 31, 2019.

Matarasso, I[saac] A[aron]. "And Yet Not All of Them Died." *The Holocaust in Salonika: Eyewitness Accounts*, 1948, edited with an introduction by Steven Bowman, 125–235. Translated from the Greek and Judeo-Spanish with an intro. and notes by Isaac Benmayor. New York: Sephardic House, 2002.

———. *La Communauté Juive de Thessalonique sous l'occupation allemande (9 Avril 1940—30 Octobre 1944), recit d'un temoin*. Thessaloniki, January 1946. Manuscript number Ms. 538, Archives of the Alliance Israëlite Universelle, Paris.

Matkovski, Alexzandar. *A History of the Jews in Macedonia*. Skopje: Macedonian Review Editions, 1982.

Matsas, Joseph. "The Participation of the Greek Jews in the National Resistance, 1940–1944." *Journal of the Hellenic Diaspora* 17, no. 1 (1991): 55–68.

Matsas, Michael. *The Illusion of Safety: The Story of Greek Jews during the Second World War*. New York: Pella, 1997.

———. "The Two Greek-Jewish Holocausts 1821 and 1943–1944." Sephardic Center, Forest Hills, New York, on April 15, 2007. http://theopavilids.com/reprints/matsas3YHLecture.htm, accessed May 26, 2019.

Mayes, Hunter. "Auschwitz Revolt." April 27, 2015. https://prezi.com/71pr0g3o3x41/auschwitz-revolt/, accessed October 11, 2017.

Meghnagi, David. "Libyan Jews between Memory and History." In *Jewish Libya: Memory & Identity in Text & Image*, edited by Jacques Roumani, David Meghnagi, and Judith Roumani, 244–80. Syracuse: Syracuse University Press, 2018.

Memorial and Museum Auschwitz-Birkenau, Former German Nazi Concentration and Extermination Camp. "The Construction of the Camp." http://auschwitz.org/en/history/auschwitz-ii/the-construction-of-the-camp/, accessed June 4, 2019.

Menascé, Esther Fintz. *Gli ebrei a Rodi*: Storia di un'antica communità annientat di nazisti. Milano: Edizioni Angelo Guerini e Associati, 1992.

———. *A History of Jewish Rhodes*. Los Angeles: Rhodes Jewish Historical Foundation, 2014.

Menasche, Albert. *Birkenau (Auschwitz II): Memoirs of an Eye-Witness, How 72,000 Greek Jews Perished*. New York: Albert Martin, 1947.

Miller, Susan Gilson. "Sephardim and Holocaust Historiography." In *The Holocaust and North Africa*, edited by Aomar Boum and Sarah Abrevaya Stein, 221–28. Stanford, CA: Stanford University Press. 2019.

Milosević, Vojislav, dir. *Jasenovac—The Cruelest Death Camp of All Times* (1983). Croatian director Lordan Zafranović. Film in six parts.

Modiano, Sami. *Per questo ho vissuto: La mia vita ad Auschwitz-Birkenau e altri esili* (For that I lived: My life in Auschwitz-Birkenau and other exiles). Edited by Marcello Pezzetti and Umberto Gentiloni Silveri. Milan: Rizzoli, 2013.

———. "Sami Modiano: La mia vita ad Auschwitz." YouTube video. January 27, 2015. https://www.youtube.com/watch?v=wCJ5oHkFX4U, accessed April 2, 2016.

Mojzes, Paul. *Balkan Genocides: Holocaust and Ethnic Cleansing in the 20th Century*. Lanham, MD: Rowman and Littlefield, 2011.

Molho, Michael, and Joseph Nehama. *In memoriam: Hommage aux victims juives des Nazis en Grèce*. 2nd édition revue et augmentée par Joseph Nehama. Thessaloniki: Hellinismos Tou Exoterikou (Hellenism Abroad), 1973.

———. *In Memoriam, Sho'at Yehude Yavan: 1941–1944*. Vertag: Jerusalem, Yad Va-Shem. 1965. (In Hebrew)

Molho, René. "Testimonio III." In *Libro de los testimonios: Los Sefardíes y el Holocausto*, edited by Salvator Santa Puche. l: 135–55. Palm Beach, FL: Sephardi Federation of Palm Beach County, 2003.

Molho, René Mario. "Personal Interview." Yad Vashem. 1981.

Molho, René, and Rebecca Camhi Fromer. *They Say Diamonds Don't Burn: The Holocaust Experiences of René Molho of Salonika, Greece*. Berkeley, CA: Judah L. Magnes Museum, 1994.

"Morocco during World War II." *Cultural Studies*. [blog] http://culturestudies4all.blogspot.com/2014/12/morocco-during-world-war-ii.html, accessed March 10, 2018.

Moser, Laura. "Chasing Dr. Aribert Heim, the 'Butcher of Mauthsausen.'" http://forward.com/culture/196466/chasing-dr-aribert-heim-the-butcher-of-mauthausen/#ixzz4AoFxVkbZ, accessed March 18, 2013.

Museum of the Jewish People at Beit Hatfutsot and Ushi Derman. "The Jews Who Helped the Americans Free Algeria from the Nazis." *Haaretz*. January 14, 2018. https://www.haaretz.com/middle-east-news/MAGAZINE-the-jews-who-helped-the-u-s-free-algeria-from-the-nazis-1.5730698, accessed June 9, 2019.

"The Muslim King Who Saved Jews." *Accidental Talmudist*. [blog] January 7, 2016. https://www.accidentaltalmudist.org/heroes-blog/2016/12/7/the-muslim-king-who-saved-jews, accessed June 9, 2019.

Naar, Devin E. *Jewish Salonica: Between the Ottoman Empire and Modern Greece*. Redwood City, CA: Stanford University Press, 2016.

Nadjari, Marcel. *Chronicle [Khroniko] 1941–1945*. Thessalonik: Etz Ha Haim. (In Greek), 1991.

——. *Χρονικό 1941–1945* [*Chronicle 1991–1945*], Ιδρυμα Ετσ—Αχα'ι'μ, Thessaloniki. 1991.

Nahmia, Berry. *A Cry for Tomorrow 76859*. Translated from Modern Greek by David R. Weinberg. Jacksonville, FL: Bloch, 2011.

Nahon, Marco. *Birkenau, the Camp of Death*. Translated from the French by Jacqueline Havaux Bowers. Edited and introduction by Steven Bowman. Tuscaloosa: University of Alabama Press, 1989.

Nataf, Claude. Speech on "Cérémonie du 70e anniversaire de la rafle des Juifs de Tunisie au Mémorial de la Shoah," March 11–12, 2012. https://harissa.com/news/article/cérémonie-du-70e-anniversaire-de-la-rafle-des-juifs-de-tunisie-au-mémorial-de-la-shoah-disco?page=4, accessed February 12, 2018.

"Nazi Medical Experiments." Holocaust Encyclopedia, United States Holocaust Museum. https://encyclopedia.ushmm.org/content/en/article/nazi-medical-experiments, accessed June 5, 2019.

Nehama, Joseph. *Dictionnaire du Judéo-Espagnol*. Madrid: Consejo Superior de Investigaciones Cientificas, Instituto Benito Arias Montano, 1977.

Newman, Judith Sternberg. *In the Hell of Auschwitz: The Wartime Memories of Judith Sternberg Newman*. New York: Exposition Press, 1978.

The Nizkor Project. The Trial of Adolf Eichmann. Session 23, Part 2 of 5. Nizkor. http://www.nizkor.org/hweb/people/e/eichmann-adolf/transcripts/Sessions/Session-023-02.html, accessed June 4, 2019.

"North Africa and the Middle East." Yad Vashem. http://www.yadvashem.org/holocaust/about/outbreak-of-ww2-anti-jewish-policy/north-africa-and-middle-east.html#narrativeinfo, accessed February 28, 2018.

Notrica Jerusalmi, Sarah. 2003. "Testimonio VIII." In *Libro de los testimonios: Los sefardíes y el Holocausto*, edited by Salvador Santa Puche, 1:209–18. Palm Beach, FL: Sephardi Federation of Palm Beach County, 2003.

Novitch, Miriam. "Jewish Partisans in Yugoslavia." In *Extermination and Resistance: Historical Records and Source Material*, edited by Zvi Szner, 1:180–82. Haifa: Ghetto Fighters' House, 1958.

Nyiszli, Miklos. *Auschwitz: A Doctor's Eyewitness Account*. Translated by Tibère Kremer and Richard Seaves. Foreword by Bruno Bettelheim. New York: Arcade. 2011.

"Obituary: Eliezer 'Eli' Sotto." *Atlanta Jewish Times*, April 17, 2017. http://atlantajewishtimes.timesofisrael.com/obituary-eliezer-eli-sotto/, accessed April 21, 2017.

Ochayon, Sheryl. "The Jews of Algeria, Morocco and Tunisia." Yad Vashem. https://www.yadvashem.org/articles/general/the-jews-of-algeria-morocco-and-tunisia.html, accessed January 30, 2018.

——. "The Jews of Libya." Yad Vashem. https://www.yadvashem.org/articles/general/the-jews-of-libya.html, accessed January 29, 2018.

Olère, David, and Alexander Olère. *Witness: Images of Auschwitz*. N. Richland Hills, TX: West Wind Press, 1998.

Ouziel, Bella. "Remembering the Holocaust: 'I Don't Know Why We Didn't Die.'"

eSefarad.com, Noticias del Mundo Sefaradi, May 7, 2011. https://esefarad.com/?p=22922, accessed June 10, 2019.

Paris, Edmond. *Genocide in Satellite Croatia, 1941–1945: A Record of Racial and Religious Persecutions and Massacres*. Translated by Lois Perkins. Chicago: American Institute for Balkan Affairs, 2011.

Patterson, David. *A Genealogy of Evil: Anti-Semitism from Nazism to Islamic Jihad*. Cambridge: Cambridge University Press, 2011.

Peretz, Avner. "Siniza i fumo" (Ash and Smoke). In *And the World Stood Silent: Sephardic Poetry of the Holocaust*, edited and translated by Isaac Jack Lévy, 168–69. Urbana: University of Illinois Press, 2000.

Perez, Daniel. "Our Conscience Is Clean: Albanian Elites and the Memory of the Holocaust in Postsocialist Albania." In *Bringing the Dark Past to Light: The Reception of the Holocaust in Postcommunist Europe*, edited by John-Paul Himka and Joanna Beata Michlic, 25–58. Lincoln: University of Nebraska Press, 2013.

Pezzetti, Marcello. "The Shoah, Auschwitz, and the Sonderkommando." Historical notes in *Inside the Gas Chambers: Eight Months in the Sonderkommando of Auschwitz* by Shlomo Venezia. Edited by Jean Mouttapa, 159–88. Translated by Andrew Brown. Cambridge: Polity Press, 2011.

Phayer, Michael. *The Catholic Church and the Holocaust, 1930–1965*. Bloomington: Indiana University Press, 2000.

Plank, Karl A. *Mother of the Wire Fence: Inside and Outside the Holocaust*. Louisville: Westminster John Knox Press, 1994.

Plaut, Joshua Eli. *Greek Jewry in the Twentieth Century, 1913–1983: Patterns of Jewish Survival in the Greek Provinces before and after the Holocaust*. Madison, NJ: Fairleigh Dickinson University Press, 1996.

"Prisoner Revolt at Auschwitz-Birkenau." United States Holocaust Memorial Museum. https://www.ushmm.org/learn/timeline-of-events/1942–1945/auschwitz-revolt, accessed September 27, 2017.

"Provisional Gas Chambers Bunker 1 and Bunker 2 in Birkenau." In "The Seven Gas Chambers at Auschwitz." http://www.deathcamps.org/gas_chambers/gas_chambers_auschwitz.html, accessed September 13, 1916.

Pugliese, Stanislao G. "Ferramonti di Tarsia: Calabria's Forgotten Internment Camp." http://dev.niaf.org/publications/ambassador/20...9-Ferramonti Tarsia.pdf, accessed March 15, 2016.

Rahmani, Moïse. *Rhodes, un pan de notre mémoire*. Paris: Editions Romillat, 2000.

Rees, Laurence. *Auschwitz: A New History*. New York: MJF Books, 2005.

———. *Un grito en el silencio, la poesía sobre el Holocaust en lengua sefardí: Estudio y antología*. Barcelona: Tirocino, 2008.

———. *How Mankind Committed the Ultimate Infamy at Auschwitz*. New York: MJF Books, 2005.

"Remnants and Recollections Highlighting the Experience of Sephardi Jews during the Holocaust." United States Holocaust Memorial Museum. http://www.ushmm.org/information/exhibitions/online-features/collections-highlights/sephardi-jews-during-the-holocaust, p. 4, n.d., accessed May 12, 2015.

Renner, Gerald. "For Holocaust Survivor, a Special Day of Prayer, Holocaust Survivor Gets Details of Brother's Death." *Hartford Courant*, September 17, 1991. http://articles.courant.com/1991-09-17/news/00002115701sephardic-jews-jewish-new-year-sepharduc-congregation, accessed June 28, 2018.

"Report: Jerusalem's Grand Mufti Planned Construction of 'Auschwitz-like' Crematorium in Israel." *Algemeiner*, October 27, 2015. https://www.algemeiner.com/2015/10/27/report-jerusalems-grand-mufti-planned-construction-of-crematorium-in-israel/, accessed May 12, 2016.

"Report on the Present General Situation of Jews in Algeria, presented to the Advisory Council on European Jewish Affairs, World Jewish Congress." June 1, 1943, CDJC XC-7.

"Reports on Jewish Situation: The Situation of the Jews in Greece." In World Jewish Congress: Advisory Council on European Jewish Affairs, New York, 1944.

"Revolt at Auschwitz-Birkenau." Jewish Virtual Library. www.jewishvirtuallibrary.org/jsource/Holocaust/aurevolt.html, accessed August 1, 2016.

Revolt of the Greek Jews. Script by Nikos Pilavios, from the book by Photini Tomai. https://vimeo.com/5207246/, accessed September 16, 2017.

"Riccardo Pacifici." December 16, 2017. https://en.wikipedia.org/wiki/Riccardo-Pacifici, accessed June 28, 2018.

"The Righteous." *Sunday Morning*. CBS News. November 8, 2009. https://www.cbsnews.com/news/the-righteous/, accessed May 28, 2019.

Roberts, Sophie B. *Citizenship and Antisemitism in French Colonial Algeria, 1870–1962*. Cambridge: Cambridge University Press, 2017.

Robinson, Jacob. *And the Crooked Shall Be Made Straight: The Eichmann Trial, the Jewish Catastrophe, and Hannah Arendt's Narrative*. New York: Macmillan, 1965.

Rodrigue, Aron. *Sephardim and the Holocaust*. Washington, DC: United States Holocaust Memorial Museum, Center for Advanced Holocaust Studies, 2005.

Rohr, Isabelle. *Antisemitism and Opportunism*. Great Britain: Sussex Academic Press, 2007.

Romano, Jaša. *Jevreji Jugoslavije 1941–1945, Žrtve Genoćida i Učesnici NOR* (Jews of Yugoslavia 1941–1945, Victims of Genocide and Freedom Fighters). Belgrade: Federation of Jewish Communities in Yugoslavia. 1980. (Text in Serbo-Croatian with summary in English)

"Rosa Robota: Heroine of Auschwitz." http://www.theverylongview.com/WATH/special, accessed October 11, 2017.

Ross, Gaylon, dir. *Killing Kasztner: The Jew Who Dealt with the Nazis*. GR Films, 2008.

Roumani, Jacques, David Meghnagi, and Judith Roumani, eds. *Jewish Libya: Memory & Identity in Text & Image*. Syracuse, NY: Syracuse University Press, 2018.

Roumani, Judith. "Benghazi—Bergen-Belsen in the Context of North African Jewish Literature of the Holocaust." In *Jewish Libya: Memory & Identity in Text & Image*, 226–43. Edited by Jacques Roumani, David Meghnagi, and Judith Roumani. Syracuse, NY: Syracuse University Press, 2018.

Roumani, Maurice M. "Aspects of the Holocaust in Libya." In *Del fuego: Sephardim and the Holocaust*, 123–28. Edited by Salomon Gaon and M. Mitchell Serels. New York: Sephermon Press. 1995.

Roumani-Denn, Vivienne. "Life Interrupted: Interviews with Jews of Libyan Origin." In *Jewish Libya: Memory & Identity in Text & Image*, 185–202, edited by Jacques Roumani, David Meghnagi, and Judith Roumani. Syracuse: Syracuse University Press. 2018.

Rubin, Barry, and Wolfgang G. Schwanitz. "From Station Z to Jerusalem." In *Nazis, Islamists, and the Making of the Modern Middle East*, 1–10. New Haven: Yale University Press, 2014.

Russo, Lawrence, dir. *Trezoros: The Lost Jews of Kastoria*. Codirector, Larry Confino. Vision Entertainment Productions. English, Greek, and Hebrew (English subtitles). https://www.thenationalherald.com/196444/trezoros-the-lost-jews-of-kastoria-airing-on-pbs/, accessed May 22, 2019.

Sabban, Yishak. "The Customs of Libyan Jews." *Sephardic Scholar* 3 (1977–78): 87–95.

Sabile, Jacques. "Les juifs sous l'occupation: Les journées tragiques." *Le monde juif* 14, 3e Année (December 1948): 13–15.

———. "Les juifs sous l'occupation: Les journées tragiques." *Le monde juif* 15, 4e Année (January 1949): 10–12.

Santa Puche, Salvador. *Libro de los testimonios: Los Sefardíes y el Holocausto*, vol. 1. Palm Beach, FL: Sephardi Federation of Palm Beach County, 2003.

Sarner, Harvey. *Rescue in Albania: One Hundred Percent of Jews in Albania Rescued from Holocaust*. Cathedral City, CA: Brunswick Press, 1997.

Schroeter, Daniel J. "Between Metropole and French North Africa." In *The Holocaust and North Africa*, 20–49, edited by Aomar Boum and Sarah Abrevaya Stein. Stanford: Stanford University Press, 2019.

Schwartz, Stephen. Review of Devin E. Naar's *Jewish Salonica: Between the Ottoman Empire and Modern Greece*. *Middle East Quarterly* 24, no. 3 (Summer 2017). http://www.islamicpluralism.org/2679/jewish-Salonika, accessed March 29, 2019.

Seabrook, Kim. "Anten Pavelic: The Butcher of the Balkans." April 12, 2015. http://www.prisonersofeternity.co.uk/ante-pavelic-the-butcher-of-the-balkans, accessed April 26, 2018.

Segev, Tom. "Courting Hitler." *New York Times*, July 17, 2014. http://www.nytimes.com/2008/09/28/books/review/Segev-t.html, accessed April 18, 2016.

Sells, Michael A. "Fabricating Palestinian Responsibility for the Nazi Genocide." *Tablet Magazine*, November 4, 2015. http://www.tabletmag.com/jewish-news-and-politics/194679/palestinian-responsibility-nazi-genocide, accessed February 14, 2016.

———. "Holocaust Abuse: The Case of Hajj Muhammad Amin al-Husayni." *Journal of Religious Ethics* 43 (December 2015): 723–59.

"The Serbs' Darkest Hour." April 24, 2007. Blago. http://www.srpskoblago.org/serbian-history/recent-history/the-serbs-chose-war/the-serbs-darkest-hour.html, accessed December 17, 2007.

Serels, Mitchell. "Moroccan Jews on the Road to Auschwitz." In *Del fuego: Sephardim and the Holocaust*, 107–12, edited by Salomon Gaon and M. Mitchell Serels. New York: Sepher-Hermon Press, 1995.

———. "The Non-European Holocaust: The Fate of Tunisian Jewry." In *Del fuego: Sephardim and the Holocaust*, 129–52, edited by Salomon Gaon and M. Mitchell Serels. New York: Sepher-Hermon Press, 1995.

Sevillias, Errikos. *Athens–Auschwitz*. Translated by Nikos Stavroulakis. Athens: Lycabettus, 1983.

Sgourakis, Nikos. "The Destruction of the Jews of Crete." *Chronika* 6. Athens: Lycabettus Press, 1990.

Shachar, Nathan. *The Lost Worlds of Rhodes: Greeks, Italians, Jews and Turks between Tradition and Modernity*. Portland: Sussex Academic Press, 2013.

Shields, Jacqueline. "The Sonderkommando." *Jewish Virtual Library*. https://www.jewishvirtuallibrary.org/jsource/Holocaust/Sonderkommando.html, accessed May 14, 2015.

Shimony, Batya. Review: Resisting the Father's Narrative: A Study of Lea Aini's *Vered ha-Levanon*." *Prooftexts* 32, no. 1 (2012): 89–114.

"A Short History of the Jews of Greece: Ancient Times to the 1940's." https://www.greecetravel.com/jewishhistory/ancient.html, accessed March 28, 2019.

Silberberg, Ya'akov. "One Day in the Crematorium Felt like a Year." In *We Wept without Tears: Testimony of the Jewish Sonderkommando from Auschwitz*, 310–34, edited by Gideon Greif. New Haven: Yale University Press, 2005.

Sinnreich, Helene. "'And It Was Something We Didn't Talk About': Rape of Jewish Women during the Holocaust." *Holocaust Studies: A Journal of Culture and History* 14, no. 2 (2008): 1–22.

"Sonderkommando Photographs." https://en.wikipedia.org/wiki/Sonderkommandophotographs, accessed August 31, 2017.

"Sonderkommando Revolt." MetaFilter. January 4, 2008. www.metafilter.com/67935, accessed September 26, 2016.

"Sonderkommando Revolt: Auschwitz-Birkenau, 7 October 1944." Chris Webb, Holocaust Education & Archive Research Team. April 30, 2009. http://www.holocaustresearchproject.org/revolt/sonderevolt.html, accessed June 15, 2016.

Souames, Farah. "Home, for Algeria's Jews, Is Elsewhere." February 27, 2015. https://www.openglobalrights.org/home-for-algerias-jews-is-elsewhere/, accessed February 17, 2018.

Sousis, Marios, and Photini Tomai. *Greeks in Auschwitz-Birkenau*. DVD documentary. Distributed by Turangalila Records. http://db.yadvashem.org/films/item.html?language=en&itemId=8161071, accessed November 18, 2015.

Stavroulakis, Nicholas. *The Jews of Greece: An Essay*. Athens: Talos Press, 1990.

Stein, Sarah Abrevaya, and Aomar Boum. "Labor and Internment Camps in North Africa." *Holocaust Encyclopedia*. United States Holocaust Memorial Museum. https://encyclopedia.ushmm.org/content/en/article/labor-and-internment-camps-in-north-africa, accessed June 9, 2019.

"The Story of Ovadia Baruch." From the film *May Your Memory Be Love*. Filmed by Yad Vashem, Holocaust Education Video Toolbox, December 31, 2013.

Stroumsa (Strumzah), Jacques (Yaakov). *Violinist in Auschwitz: From Salonica to Jerusalem, 1913–1967*. Konstanz, Germany: Hartung-Gorre, 1996.

Sussman, Sarah. "Judeus na África do Norte: Opressão e resistência." (The Jews in North Africa: Oppression and Resistance.) *Holocaust Encyclopedia, United States Holocaust Museum*. https://encyclopedia.ushmm.org/content/pt-br/article/jews-in-north-africa-oppression-and-resistance, accessed June 10, 2019.

Tarabulus, Jennie. *I Never Knew Them: An Account of the Jews from Greece*. Israel Radio broadcast. April 12, 1980.

Tayar, Linda. *Holocaust Survivor Testimonies: Libya*. YouTube video. Yad Vashem, February 10, 2010. Film in Hebrew with subtitles in English. https://www.youtube.com/watch?v=2O2v5d7Cqgo, accessed February 26, 2018.

"Testimony and History." *Database of Greek-Jewish Holocaust Survivors' Testimonies*. http://gjst.ha.uth.gr/en/testimony.php, accessed April 5, 2018.

Thompson, Stith. *Motif Index of Folk Literature*. Rev. and enl. 6 vols. Bloomington: Indiana University Press, 1955–58.

Tomai, Photini. *Greeks in Auschwitz-Birkenau*. Translated by Alexandra Apostolides and edited by Photini Tomai [Phōteinē Kōnstantopoulou] and Nicholas A. Papandreou, et al. Athens: Papazisis, 2009.

Tomai, Photini, and Thanos Veremis, eds. *Documents on the History of the Greek Jews: Records from the Historical Archives of the Ministry of Foreign Affairs*. Athens: Kontanioti, 1998.

Toth, Bryan. "Why We Fight." April 16, 2009. https://www.slideshare.net/bmtoth/why-we-fight, accessed August 8, 2011.

Tyson, Peter. "Holocaust on Trial: The Experiments." March 23. 2008. *NOVA*. http://www.pbs.org/wgbh/nova/holocaust/experiside.html, accessed November 12, 2016.

US Congress. Senate. *Resolution Commending the People of Albania* . . . S. Res. 601. 112th Congress, 2nd sess. Introduced in Senate (IS) November 27, 2012. https://www.gpo.gov/fdsys/pkg/BILLS-112sres601is/html/BILLS-112sres601is.htm, accessed March 28, 2016.

"Ustaše—The Fascists That Made the Nazis Look like Boy Scouts." June 16, 2016. https://dirkdeklein.net/2016/06/16/ustase-the-fascists-that-made-the-nazis-look-like-boyscouts, accessed July 20, 2017.

Varon, Asher. "Testimonio IX." In *Libro de los testimonios: Los Sefardíes y el Holocausto*, edited by Salvator Santa Puche, 1: 219–25. Palm Beach, FL: Sephardi Federation of Palm Beach County, 2003.

Vassilev, Rossen. "The Rescue of Bulgaria's Jews in World War II." *New Politics* 12, no. 4 (2010). http://newpol.org/content/rescue-bulgarias-jews-world-war-ii, accessed June 26, 2017.

Venezia, Morris. "Jewish Survivor Morris Venezia Testimonial." YouTube video. USC Shoah Foundation. Interviewed by Carol Stulberg on October 27, 1996. Film published on May 9, 2012. https://www.youtube.com/watch?v=P-IinMCbdJA. Also see http://youtube.live/watch/QFAtSWluTUNiZEpB/jewish-survivor-morris-venezia-testimony.html, accessed October 11, 2016.

Venezia, Shlomo. *Inside the Gas Chambers: Eight Months in the Sonderkommando of Auschwitz*. Foreword Simone Veil. Historical Notes, Marcello Pezzeti, Umberto Gentiloni, and Jean Mouttapa. Edited by Jean Mouttapa. Translated by Andrew Brown. Cambridge: Polity Press, 2011.

Vermaat, Emerson. "Dutch Holocaust Survivor—'I Saw How the Mufti of Jerusalem Paid a Visit to Auschwitz-Monowitz.'" *Pipeline News*, March 5, 2012. https://www.investigativeproject.org/3479/dutch-holocaust-survivor-i-saw-how-the-mufti, accessed December 10, 2017.

"Virtual Jewish World: Salonika, Greece." Jewish Virtual Library. https://www.jewishvirtuallibrary.org/salonika-greece-virtual-jewish-history-tour, accessed February 25, 2017.

Wiernek, Yankiel (Jankiel). *A Year in Treblinka: An Inmate Who Escaped Tells of the Day-to-Day Facts of One Year of His Torturous Experiences*. Anonymous translator. New York: American Representation of the General Jewish Workers' Union of Poland, 1945. http://www.zchor.org/treblink/wiernik.htm. November 5, 2014, accessed July 3, 2017.

Wiesel, Elie. *Memoirs: All Rivers Run to the Sea*. New York: Alfred A. Knopf, 1995.

Wiesenthal, Simon. S. *Grossmufti-Grossagent Der Ache: Tatsachenbericht*. Salzburg: Ried-Verlag, 1947.

———. *Justice, Not Vengeance*. London: Mandarin Paperback, 1990.

Wise, Marta. "Personal Testimony by Holocaust Survivor Marta Wise." YouTube video. January 27, 2016. https://www.youtube.com/watch?v=MQFHX4mYfq4, accessed January 2, 2018.

Yassini, A. Wolf, ed. *Memorial Book of the Ciechanow Jewish Community*. Tel Aviv: Association of Ciechanow and the Landsmanschaften Abroad, Arzi Printers, 1962. http://www.jewishgen.org/Yizkor/Ciechanow/cie001.html, accessed August 19, 2016.

Ychay, Benjamin. Testimony [033274]. Yad Vashem, Jerusalem, May 1, 1967.

Young, Rachel. Review of *Amidst a Nightmare of Crime: Manuscripts of the Sonderkommando*. Northwest Center for Holocaust, Genocide and Ethnocide Education, Western Washington University. https://wce.wwu.edu/nwchgee/overview-amidst-nightmare-crime, accessed June 4, 2019.

Zabludowicz, Noach. "My Experiences in World War II: The Underground Movement at the Beginning of the German Occupation." http://www.jewishgen.org/Yizkor/Ciechanow/cie322.html, accessed July 18, 2016.

Zatezalo, Duro. *The Jadnovo: Complex of Ustascha Concentration Camps in 1941*. Belgrade: Museum of Genocide Victims. http://jadovno.com/arhiva/duro-zatezalo-jadovno-complex-of-ustasha-camps-in-1941.html, accessed July 21, 2017.

Zuaretz, Hay. "Holocaust Survivor Testimonies: Libya." YouTube video. Yad

Vashem. Film in Hebrew with subtitles in English. February 10, 2010. https://www.youtube.com/watch?v=2O2v5d7Cqgo, accessed February 26, 2018.

Zumwalt, Rosemary Lévy. "Stories, Food, and Place: Following a Sephardic Family to a New Home." *Sephardic Horizons* 6, no. 1 (2016). http://www.sephardichorizons.org/Volume6/Issue1/Zumwalt.html#ednre, accessed January 13, 2017.

Index

Note: Page numbers in italics refer to the illustrations.